852CBX00048BA - 42852CBX00048BA [1 : 1]

cover

MATTE

3OOK
TCO19_MD   CONTAINS: COLOR

COLORSTD
CASE
REWORK Cory Robertson
P5-MULTI
42852CB00071B/78

852CBX00048BA - 42852CBX00048BA [1 : 1]

M

ORK PD: 10-APR-26 04:00 (FRI)   REWORK PD: 10-APR-26 04:00 (FRI)

Printed at: Sat Apr 11 04:49:33 2026 on device cbhp05priority-90

Batch 42852CB00071B

42852CBX00048BA	9780197558287	From Perception to Pleasure: The Neuroscie
CASE	7.00X10.00	364 <H> 0.8125 MATTE (1)

7 DECEMBER 1941
THE AIR FORCE STORY

Bellows AFS

Wheeler AFB

Hickam AFB

Leatrice R. Arakaki and John R. Kuborn

Pacific Air Forces
Office of History
Hickam Air Force Base, Hawaii

1991

Cataloging-in-Publication Data

Arakaki, Leatrice R.
    7 December 1941 : the Air Force story / Leatrice R. Arakaki and
  John R. Kuborn
        p. cm.
    Includes bibliographical references and index.

    1. Pearl Harbor (Hawaii), Attack on, 1941. 2. United States.
Army Air Forces--History. I. Kuborn, John R. II. Title.
III. Title: Seven December 1941.
D767.92.A75 1991
940.54'--dc20   91–38701
                                                        CIP
ISBN 978-1-83931-092-8

For Sale by the Superintendent of Documents, U.S. Government Printing Office
Washington, DC 20402-9328

FOREWORD

On 7 December 1941, the "Day of Infamy," the United States and its armed forces were plunged into the most costly war in history.

On this the 50th anniversary of the Japanese attack on Oahu, the Air Force story of 7 December is told in its entirety for the first time. Often times the heroism and anguish of airmen at Wheeler, Hickam, and Bellows have been overshadowed by the main event, the attack on Pearl Harbor itself. *7 December 1941: The Air Force Story* corrects this oversight. The Japanese attack on the airfields of Oahu was an integral part of their overall plan, and their objectives were achieved. The Hawaiian Air Force was dealt a crippling blow, despite often heroic efforts to counter the attack.

But we recovered quickly, and soon air power was to play a major role in winning the war in the Pacific theater. Today 7 December stands as an important symbol in our history. The day of infamy reminds us of the need to maintain the nation's defense at a high state of readiness. It also symbolizes the beginning of nearly four years of war in the Pacific, in a geographical area stretching from the Aleutians to Australia.

Today the men and women of the Pacific Air Forces stand guard for freedom in this vast theater. We who now proudly wear the uniform remember the brave airmen of fifty years ago. We salute those who battled bravely on that December morning in defense of our nation. This book ensures that their valor and their sacrifice will not be forgotten.

JIMMIE V. ADAMS, General, USAF
Commander in Chief
Pacific Air Forces

FOREWORD

December 7, 1941, was by any assessment a devastating day. The Hawaiian Air Force suffered a crippling blow, but the genesis of recovery and final victory over the enemy emerged in the valor of those who weathered the onslaught and fought back with everything they had.

In the 50 years since then, the attack has become a faded memory for some and to many members of the younger generation just another moment in history. It deserves better understanding and commemoration, however, for this sudden, damaging strike on our forces marked the beginning of America's involvement in a terrible global war that was massive in scope and destruction.

At Hickam Air Force Base, reminders of the attack are still visible. The tattered flag that flew over the base that fateful morning is encased and on display in the lobby of the Pacific Air Forces Headquarters building, where bullet-scarred walls serve as a constant reminder to never again be caught unprepared. Memorial tablets surrounding the base flagpole pay tribute to those who sacrificed their lives for our country.

Our predecessors, with their blood and sweat, boldly wrote a major chapter of our military history. We must never forget their story and the legacy of their experience--that the price of freedom is eternal vigilance and readiness.

WILLIAM C. VAN METER, Colonel, USAF
Commander
15th Air Base Wing

v

PREFACE

Literature on the 7 December 1941 Japanese attack that launched the United States into World War II is extensive. Japan's primary objective that day was to cripple the US Fleet anchored at Pearl Harbor, and the Navy's experience during the attack has been chronicled in detail. Control of the air over the island of Oahu was essential to the success of the attack, but documentation on Army Air Forces involvement has been sparse and often fragmented. Consequently, few people understand why the Hawaiian Air Force was so unprepared to accomplish its air defense mission or realize the extent of the damage and casualties it sustained on that "Day of Infamy."

This book is an attempt to remedy that situation, and the events and actions of the US Army Air Forces on 7 December are told in the following pages. In this writing we have attempted to answer several important questions. Why was the Imperial Japanese Navy able to devastate the Hawaiian Air Force with little to no opposition? Why was the American air arm with over 200 aircraft, including long-range bombers, six radar stations, a trained ground observer unit, and extensive antiaircraft weapons units unable to perform its primary job of protecting the fleet? Why were all available aircraft unarmed and lined up like sitting ducks on the flight line at each base? Why were the radar stations shut down at 0700 on the morning of the attack? Where was the central fighter control unit, and why was it not activated prior to the attack?

To a large extent this work is based on primary source documentation. We have included numerous anecdotes from firsthand accounts of individuals who were stationed at Hawaiian Air Force installations prior to and during the attack. They provide insight into military life during an assignment in "Paradise" which turned into a "Hell in Paradise" on 7 December 1941. We hope these tales of horror, heroism, fear, and even humor bring to life the events of that day.

Our story begins with a look at the overall position of the Hawaiian Air Force before that fateful morning—its leadership, assigned personnel and aircraft, and air defense system. Next, we examine in detail the three main airfields on Oahu—Hickam, Wheeler, and Bellows—to determine what duty was like at these installations, training activities, the condition of equipment, and morale of the men. We then go into the actual attack, first describing the overall action, then detailing what occurred at each of the major bases, concluding with a discussion of events that took place after the attack.

Throughout the book, all times given are local and in the 24-hour military style; dates are also in the military format. Statistical data has been placed in appendices following the narrative. We believe the casualty lists included there are the most comprehensive compiled to date, and they cover not only Army Air Forces members, but also civilians who were killed or wounded on the three main airfields, and other Army personnel (infantry, coast artillery, etc.) killed or wounded that day. The Army casualties were added when we discovered that many of the source documents used in compiling the lists did not specify the individuals' unit of assignment, making it impossible to identify only Army Air Forces members. Of significance is the fact that all personnel originally reported as MIA (missing in action) have since been identified as either KIA (killed in action), WIA (wounded in action), or ALW (alive and well).

We have used the term "Hawaiian Air Force" when the narrative specifically talks about Hawaiian Air Force units, and "Army Air Forces" rather than "Army Air Corps" in referring to the air arm of the US Army, which today is the separate and independent US Air Force. When the Army Air Forces (AAF) was created on 20 June 1941, the Army Air Corps was not abolished but continued as one of the three major components of the AAF, along with Headquarters AAF and the Air Force Combat Command. Personnel could have been assigned to any one of the three components and frequently changed from one to another without even realizing it. To avoid confusion we decided to consistently use Army Air Forces when discussing events occurring after 20 June 1941.

Although we endeavored to learn the full names and ranks of all personnel mentioned, we were unable to do so in a few cases where source documents provided only last names or omitted ranks. The term "Jap" is used apologetically and only in direct quotes, recognizing the derogatory connotation of that word, particularly to Americans of Japanese ancestry. Also, one of the illustrations in Chapter II may be considered by some to be sexist and offensive; however, we view it as an accurate representation of artwork in the 1940s and essential to our written narrative.

Our primary source of information for this book was the historical archives of the 15th Air Base Wing at Hickam Air Force Base. Here are located official documents, personal papers and firsthand accounts of survivors, the original handwritten records of Major Charles P. Eckhert (Hickam Field's maintenance officer at the time of the attack), photographs from official sources and private collections, correspondence with various researchers, and an assortment of reference books and other published works. The resources of the National Park Service's USS *Arizona* Memorial, including their copy of the 40-volume report of the joint congressional committee which investigated the attack, were of immeasurable assistance.

We are indebted to many people who generously shared their wealth of knowledge and resources with us. David Aiken of Irving, Texas, in particular, not only took the time to review our manuscript for technical accuracy but also provided valuable information and documents that we had believed were nonexistent. Thanks to him, we were finally able to get a complete listing of the twelve B-17 aircraft and crew members who arrived from Hamilton Field in the middle of the attack. We are also most grateful to Mr. Raymond D. Emory (Pearl Harbor Survivor) and Mr. Robert E. May (Secretary-Treasurer, 11th Bombardment Group Association) for their generosity in providing us with the results of their years of research to identify those killed in action on 7 December 1941, and for also furnishing numerous other listings of personnel who were wounded in action. A debt of gratitude is owed to Gary Hawn of the National Personnel Record Center at St Louis, Missouri, for painstakingly checking all the names on our list against the records being held at the Center. This task was particularly difficult because of a fire several years ago that destroyed all the records from this particular era. In many cases Mr. Hawn had to locate several supporting documents, such as travel orders or hospital records before he could verify a name. Special thanks to Ted Darcy of Kailua, Oahu, for providing information from his data bank of aircraft crashes and for sharing microfilm from his personal collection; Mrs Betsy Camacho, Bellows Air Force Station Public Affairs Specialist, for sharing her extensive photo and firsthand account collection with us; to Susan Ohara of the graphics section at Hickam AFB for her work on the charts and maps used in this book; TSgt Bryan Lopatic, also from the graphics section for his beautiful painting used on the cover; and to the Base Photo Lab personnel for their help with the many photographs included in this publication.

This project would not have been undertaken without the support and encouragement of Dr. Timothy R. Keck, Pacific Air Forces Command Historian. Over eighteen months ago Dr. Keck came to us with the basic idea for the book and has encouraged and assisted us ever since. Mrs Patricia M. Wilson, historian and editor on the PACAF history staff, has put in more hours and hard work than both the authors combined, editing and designing the layout for the book. Editing assistance was also provided by Mr. Bernard C. Nalty of the HQ USAF History office, several 7 December survivors and Capt Mardi Wilcox, USAF, who read the rough drafts and offered comments and corrections. We are grateful to all.

Last but not least, our sincere thanks to the many individuals who contributed personal accounts and photographs. The names of those who provided us with photographs used in this book are included in parentheses following the photo captions. Names are also given for those whose stories are used directly in the book, but to all others who provided us with the flavor of what it must have been like to be on the island of Oahu on the morning of 7 December 1941, thank you, and may God grant you a special place in heaven for being here that fateful morning.

JOHN R. KUBORN
Deputy Command Historian
Headquarters Pacific Air Forces

LEATRICE R. ARAKAKI
Historian
15th Air Base Wing

CONTENTS

ILLUSTRATIONS

CHAPTER I

HAWAIIAN AIR FORCE: BEFORE THE ATTACK

"I think we can meet with confidence all threats of enemy encroachment even that of bombardment from the air."

Lt Gen Walter C. Short, USA, during a radio speech given on May 20, 1941, to the people of the Territory of Hawaii.

On 7 December 1941, the Japanese caught the Hawaiian Air Force completely by surprise. Although diplomatic relations with Japan were at a standstill, and many people felt war was just around the corner, Hawaii maintained a business-as-usual attitude. Conversely, the Japanese understood the importance of the American Fleet stationed at Pearl Harbor and devised a plan to destroy it. To reach the fleet they would need to destroy the Hawaiian Air Force. To destroy this force they would need surprise and luck. Japan would achieve the surprise, and fate would give them the luck they required. The Hawaiian Department had the forces, leadership, and equipment to stop the attack or at least make it very expensive. But fate, in a series of decisions, events, and personalities, would step in to prevent them from ever being used. The Japanese use of air power on 7 December 1941 resulted in a decisive, if short-lived, one-sided victory—indeed from their perspective as decisive as any air battle that would be fought over the next four years.

The Commanders

To understand what happened to the Hawaiian Air Force on that fateful morning, we must try to understand the leadership that brought it to that day. At the time of the attack, the Hawaiian Department, under Lt Gen Walter C. Short, commanded all Army personnel in Hawaii. Maj Gen Frederick L. Martin reported to General Short, both as commander of the Hawaiian Air Force, activated on 1 November 1940 at Fort Shafter, and as the Hawaiian Department Air Officer. In addition, General Martin had direct access on aviation matters to Maj Gen H. H. "Hap" Arnold, chief of the Army Air Forces. The Hawaiian Air Force consisted of the 18th Bombardment Wing and the Hawaiian Air Depot at Hickam Field, the 14th Pursuit Wing at Wheeler Field, and a gunnery training facility at Bellows Field. In addition, several smaller installations were scattered throughout the island chain.* For the Navy, Adm Husband E. Kimmel was Commander in Chief, and Rear Adm P. N. L. Bellinger was Commander, Naval Base Defense Air Force.

General Martin, through the Hawaiian Air Force, was in command of Army Air Forces personnel and functions associated with aviation, while General Short

_____

*See Appendix A for a complete list of units assigned to the Hawaiian Air Force on 7 December 1941.

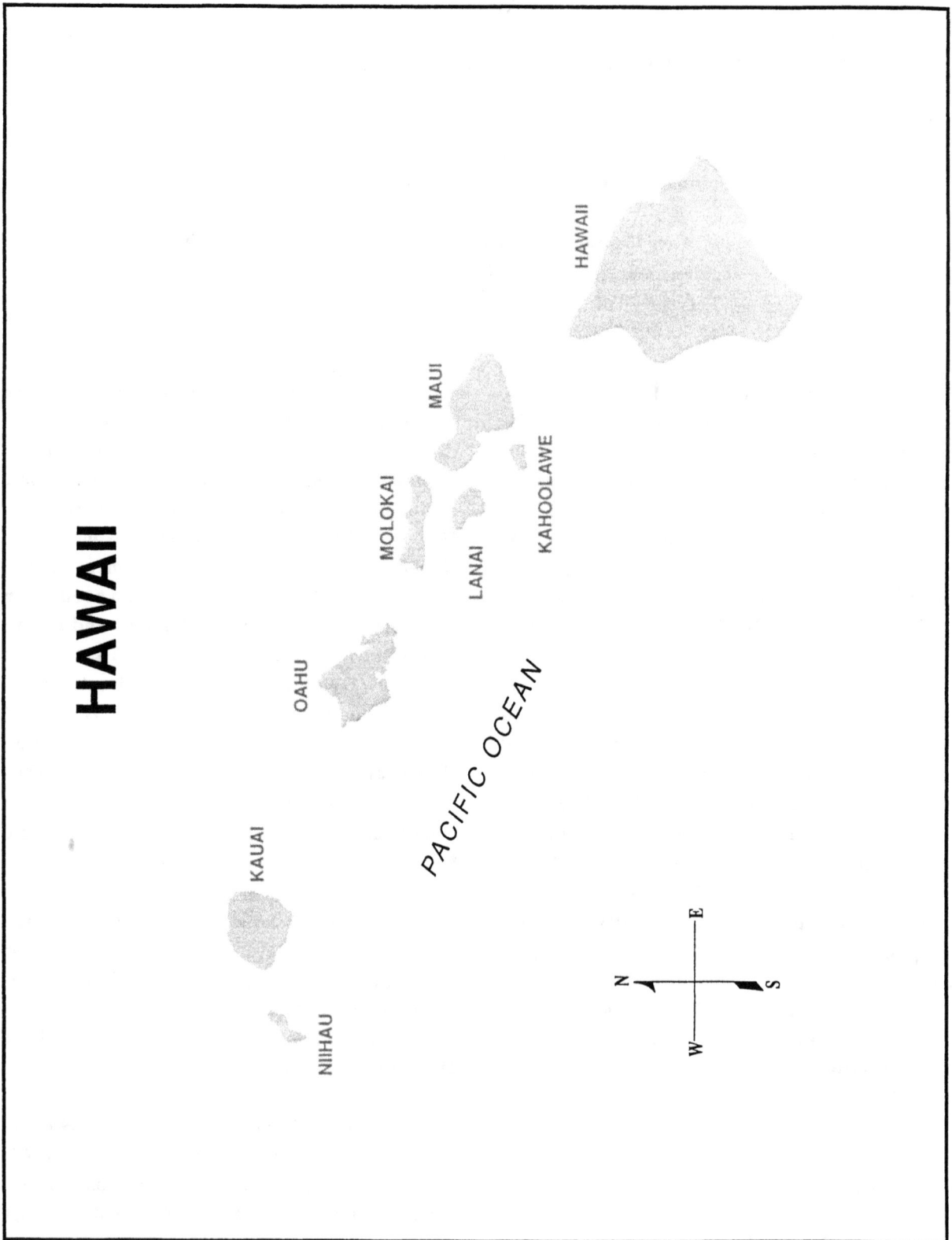

HAWAII

HAWAII

MAUI

MOLOKAI

LANAI

KAHOOLAWE

OAHU

PACIFIC OCEAN

KAUAI

NIIHAU

N
E
W
S

commanded nonaviation personnel and functions through the Hawaiian Department. Thus, although Martin controlled the airfields, he lacked control over the antiaircraft units assigned to defend them. General Martin would control the island's Air Defense Center after it became operational, but General Short controlled the radar units that supplied the center with information.

As the Hawaiian Department Commander, General Short was responsible for insuring that General Martin and the Hawaiian Air Force had the capability to accomplish their primary job, defending the Hawaiian Islands and the Navy's Pacific Fleet facilities from air attack. Training was the key to this task, and General Short was well suited for the role. Training assignments made up most of his career. At the time of the attack, he was 61 and had

worked his way up through the officer ranks by solid, dependable work. During World War I, he helped organize the First Corps automatic weapons school in France in 1917, and after the war he served as the assistant chief of staff in charge of the Third Army's training program in Germany. He attended both the School of the Line and the Army War College at Fort Leavenworth, Kansas, and later spent two years as a staff officer there. In addition to several other command assignments he worked four years in Washington DC, at the Bureau of Insular Affairs. General Short was an infantryman through and through.[1]

With a philosophy that reflected his experience, General Short demanded training in the basic infantry duties and skills for Hawaiian Air Force personnel not involved in flying. To accomplish this, the Hawaiian Department published a standing

Senior military officials at Hawaiian Department Headquarters, circa 1941. Front row (left to right): Lt Gen Walter C. Short, Commanding General, Hawaiian Department; a visiting Capt Louis Mountbatten, RN; and Adm Husband E. Kimmel, Commander in Chief, US Pacific Fleet. Top row: Maj Gen Frederick L. Martin, Commanding General, Hawaiian Air Force; and RAdm Patrick N. L. Bellinger, Commander, Naval Base Defense Air Force.

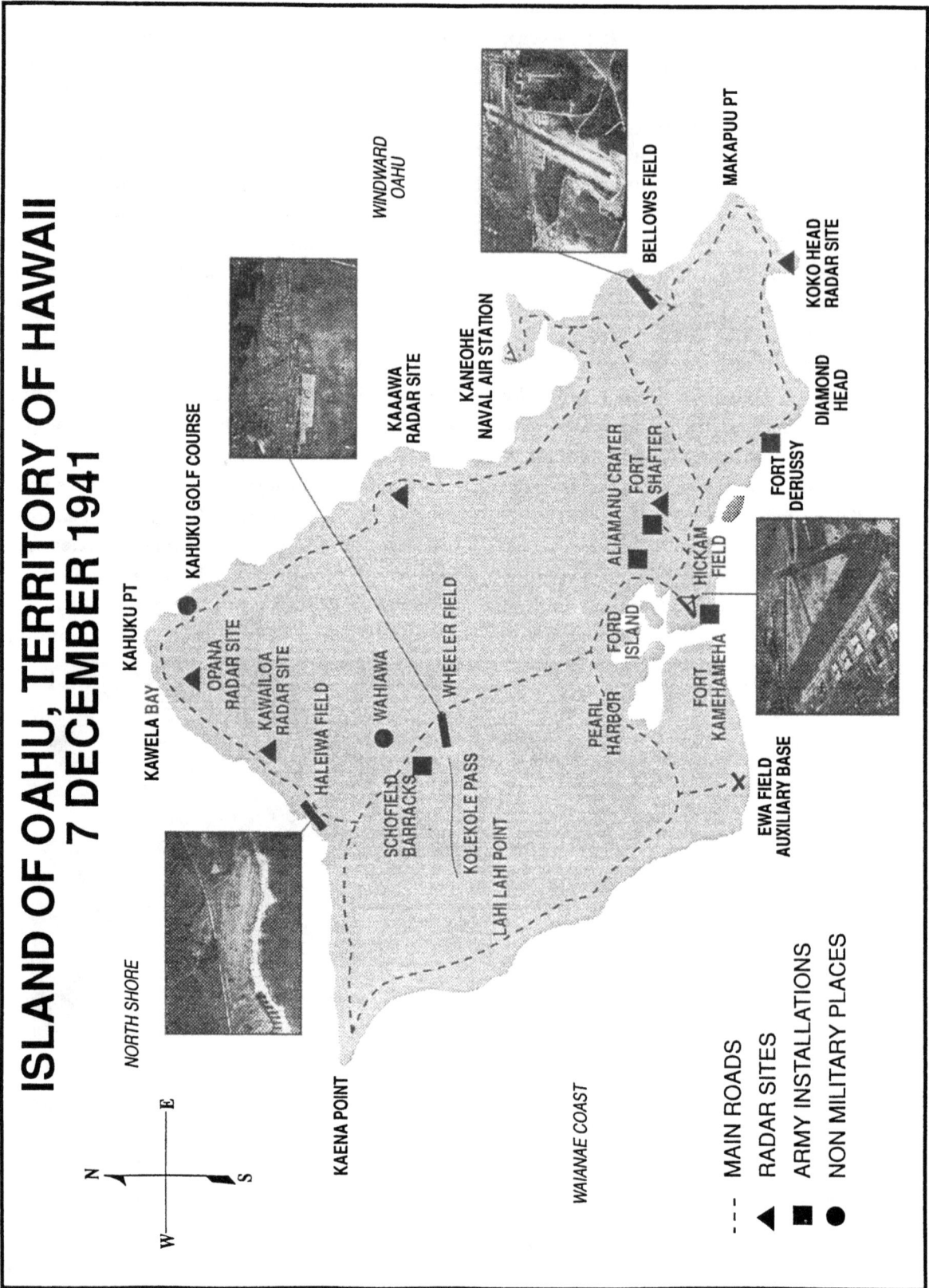

ISLAND OF OAHU, TERRITORY OF HAWAII
7 DECEMBER 1941

NORTH SHORE

WINDWARD OAHU

KAHUKU PT

KAHUKU GOLF COURSE

KAWELA BAY

OPANA RADAR SITE

KAWAILOA RADAR SITE

HALEIWA FIELD

WAHIAWA

SCHOFIELD BARRACKS

KOLEKOLE PASS

LAHI LAHI POINT

WHEELER FIELD

KAAAWA RADAR SITE

KANEOHE NAVAL AIR STATION

BELLOWS FIELD

MAKAPUU PT

KOKO HEAD RADAR SITE

DIAMOND HEAD

ALIAMANU CRATER

FORT SHAFTER

HICKAM FIELD

FORT DERUSSY

FORD ISLAND

PEARL HARBOR

FORT KAMEHAMEHA

EWA FIELD AUXILIARY BASE

KAENA POINT

WAIANAE COAST

N E S W

MAIN ROADS
RADAR SITES
ARMY INSTALLATIONS
NON MILITARY PLACES

operating procedure in July 1941 that set up a six-to-eight week schedule in basic infantry training. When Gen George C. Marshall, Chief of Staff, questioned training Army Air Forces personnel as infantrymen, General Short countered that an enemy would not attack the Hawaiian Islands until after it had destroyed American air power and with the aircraft destroyed, large numbers of Hawaiian Air Force personnel would be available for infantry duty. Furthermore, General Short felt that the Hawaiian Air Force was overstaffed and more than half, or 3,885 out of 7,229 personnel, could be used as infantry after the invasion started.* He stated that the training was necessary to give these people something to do during exercises. General Short did not believe in using the regular infantry to protect Hawaiian Air Force personnel who had nothing to do but sit around.[2]

After setting up a program to insure all personnel would be trained to defend the island against a possible invasion, General Short began an intensive effort to protect the facilities against possible sabotage from the large Japanese population living on Oahu. To this end he created three alert levels aimed at providing the most appropriate defense response based on the forms of attack he believed the island would receive. Significantly, the first level, Alert One—and the one the department would be in on 7 December—was sabotage alert. During Alert One, ammunition not needed for immediate training would be boxed and stored in central locations difficult for an enemy to reach and destroy. Thus, when the

attack began, most antiaircraft ammunition was boxed and stored far away from the actual gun locations. At Wheeler Field, maintenance personnel not only removed the machine gun ammunition from the aircraft, they removed it from the belts so it could be boxed and stored in one location. Coincidentally, the Japanese hit this central location (a hangar) during the attack and destroyed most of the ammunition stored there. Aircraft, during Alert One, would be centrally located as close together as possible for ease in guarding them. Hawaiian Air Force personnel would be used to guard not only aircraft and storage facilities on flying fields, but also warehouses and critical facilities throughout the island.

After being notified about an impending air attack against Hawaii, the Hawaiian Department would go to Alert Two. At this level, measures used in Alert One would remain in effect; in addition, personnel would activate the Air Warning Center, arm fighter aircraft and place them on alert, launch long-range reconnaissance, and arm and deploy antiaircraft units. From this intermediate level, the entire Hawaiian Department would go to Alert Three when invasion seemed imminent. At level three, the command functions would move to underground facilities and available personnel would deploy to prepared beach defenses. General Short immediately decreed Alert Three after the 7 December attack began.[3]

Maj Gen Frederick L. Martin, Commander of the Hawaiian Air Force, and leader of the air arm of the Hawaiian Department, arrived in Hawaii on 2 November 1940. He was an experienced pilot with over 2,000 hours flying time. His training included the Air Tactical School at

*This was the Hawaiian Air Force strength as of 14 October 1941; by 7 December 1941 personnel had increased to 7,460.

Langley Field, Virginia, Command and General Staff School at Fort Leavenworth, Kansas, and the Army War College. He had held several command positions including, as a brigadier general, command of the 3d Bombardment Wing at Barksdale Field, Louisiana. The Hawaiian Air Force received an experienced and well-qualified commander.

General Martin's first problem upon arrival concerned the strained relationship between the Navy and the Army in Hawaii. What had started as friendly rivalry had developed into an almost hostile environment. Aircraft from both branches buzzed and practiced low-level simulated strafing runs on each other's facilities. Only in the most essential matters did the Army and Navy cooperate, and then very reluctantly. General Short and Admiral Kimmel did have some close contact. They played golf together every other weekend, and they directed their staff members to work more closely with their counterparts. But real cooperation did not exist. General Arnold gave General Martin direct orders before leaving Washington for Hawaii to resolve this problem and increase interservice cooperation. To his credit, by 7 December, relationships between the two services had started to improve. Unfortunately, in his role as peacemaker General Martin had a tendency to place cooperation between the Army and the Navy and cooperation within the Army over Hawaiian Air Force needs. As a result, when General Short started his infantry training program, instead of insisting that Hawaiian Air Force personnel could not do both jobs, General Martin sent one protest letter and then chose to support Short and promote harmony. Again, when Short became obsessed with possible sabotage and demanded parking the aircraft close

together, Martin agreed that the sabotage danger was real and went along with him, even arguing against his own commanders who wanted to disperse the aircraft.[4]

A second problem confronting Martin was poor health. The general had a severe, chronic ulcer condition, which required surgery and would hospitalize him immediately after the attack. The need to comply with General Arnold's directive to be a peacekeeper added to his poor health. Due to the ulcer, General Martin did not drink and kept his attendance at official functions to a minimum, which tended to give the average airman an impression that the commander was a bit straight-laced and did not appreciate his men.[5]

So in the end, the Hawaiian Air Force had one general who was infantry oriented and obsessed with the possibility of sabotage and another in poor health and trying to keep everyone working together. Events were to prove this was not the best combination of commanders.

The Personnel

By 7 December 1941, the air arm of the Hawaiian Department had been built up to a total strength of 754 officers and 6,706 enlisted men. Personnel were concentrated on the island of Oahu and assigned to bomber units at Hickam Field, pursuit (fighter) units at Wheeler, the 86th Observation Squadron at Bellows, or to one of the air base groups, maintenance companies, service detachments, and other support units comprising the remainder of the Hawaiian Air Force. In addition to the three major flying installations on Oahu, there was a small training field at Haleiwa on the north shore of the island and emergency or auxiliary fields on other

HAWAIIAN AIR FORCE ORGANIZATIONAL CHART
7 DECEMBER 1941

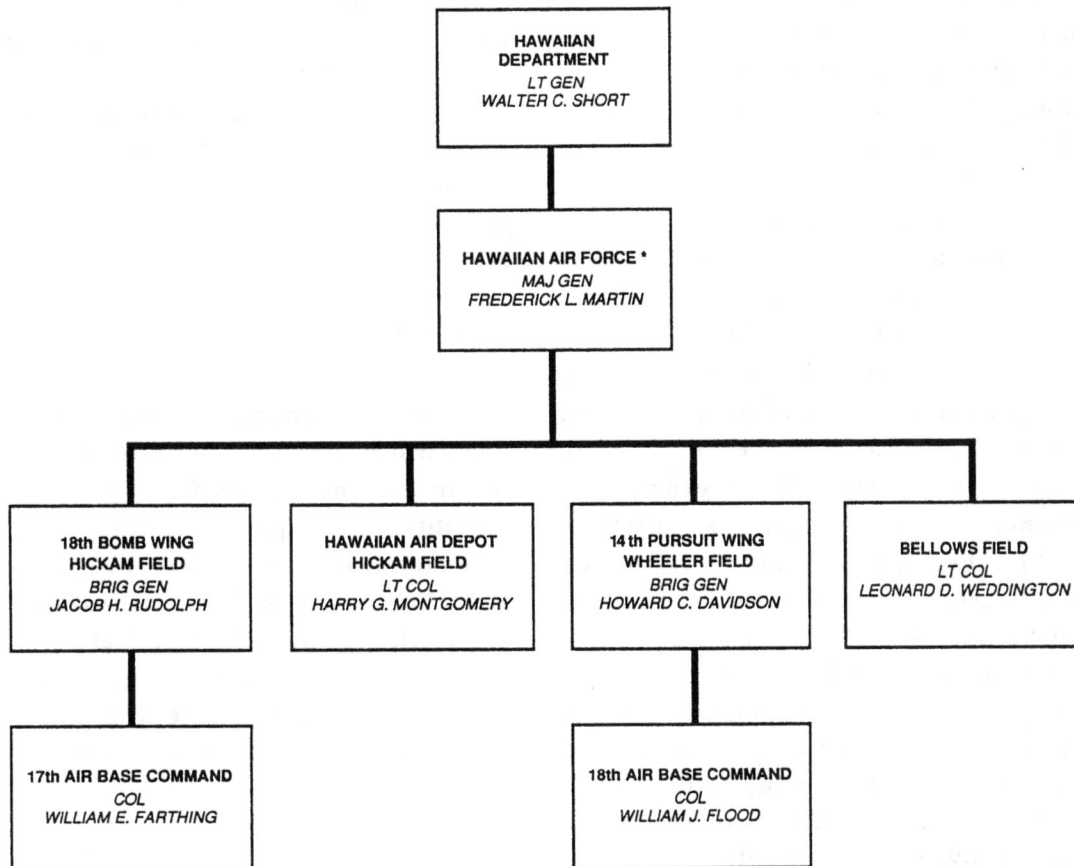

HAWAIIAN DEPARTMENT
*LT GEN
WALTER C. SHORT*

HAWAIIAN AIR FORCE *
*MAJ GEN
FREDERICK L. MARTIN*

**18th BOMB WING
HICKAM FIELD**
*BRIG GEN
JACOB H. RUDOLPH*

**HAWAIIAN AIR DEPOT
HICKAM FIELD**
*LT COL
HARRY G. MONTGOMERY*

**14th PURSUIT WING
WHEELER FIELD**
*BRIG GEN
HOWARD C. DAVIDSON*

BELLOWS FIELD
*LT COL
LEONARD D. WEDDINGTON*

17th AIR BASE COMMAND
*COL
WILLIAM E. FARTHING*

18th AIR BASE COMMAND
*COL
WILLIAM J. FLOOD*

* COMMANDING GENERAL, HAWAIIAN AIR FORCE, WAS ALSO HAWAIIAN DEPARTMENT AIR OFFICER.

islands of the Hawaiian group, including Kauai, Lanai, Hawaii, Maui, and Molokai.[6]

Personnel of the Hawaiian Air Force came from varied backgrounds. Many were Depression-era youngsters who had never ventured beyond their hometowns or states. Those fortunate enough to go on to college after graduation from high school often joined the Reserve Officers Training Corps (ROTC) program to ease their financial situation, then fulfilled their military commitment as commissioned officers. Some were selected for flight training and won their wings as army aviators. Thousands of other young men, however, faced unemployment or worked at jobs paying meager wages and had no funds to finance college educations. Enticed by posters, radio announcements, word-of-mouth, and newspaper advertisements extolling the advantages of Army life ("experience, advancement, travel, and a lifetime pension"), they dropped in at recruiting stations in great numbers to enlist. Some of those who volunteered for duty in Hawaii were not quite sure where it was located. John M. Neuhauser, of Flanagan, Illinois, for example, learned from his friend, Ned Oliver, that the US Army Air Forces recruiter was signing up men to be sent to Hawaii for training as aircraft mechanics. "Where's Hawaii?" he asked. "It's an island in the Pacific Ocean, I think," Ned said.[7]

Officers and enlisted personnel, as well as family members, sailed to Hawaii on US Army transports like the *Republic*, *Grant*, *St. Mihiel*, *Leonard Wood*, *Chateau Thierry*, *Hunter Liggett*, and *Etolin*. Those who embarked from San Francisco spent about a week on the high seas. Russell J. Tener recalled "six days of hectic ocean travel, consisting of seasickness, boredom, card playing and some KP (kitchen police)."

Others like John W. Wilson, who had enlisted in Philadelphia, spent 21 days on the Army transport that carried them from New York via the Panama Canal. When the ships rounded Diamond Head and docked at Honolulu harbor near the Aloha Tower, the new arrivals received a typical Hawaiian welcome. The Royal Hawaiian Band serenaded them as they walked down the gangplank, pretty Hawaiian girls greeted them with fragrant flower leis, and dozens of native boys jumped into the water and dove for coins tossed by the soldiers. The newest members of the Hawaiian Air Force then proceeded to one of the three major airfields on the island.[8]

The Aircraft

Both Generals Short and Martin bombarded Washington with requests for newer and more aircraft. The Air Force's inability to provide the long-range reconnaissance necessary to protect the Hawaiian Islands from a sneak attack especially worried General Martin. In early 1941, he and his Navy counterpart, Rear Admiral Bellinger, wrote the now famous Martin-Bellinger report, which not only

"HAWAIIAN PARADISE - Or the Way the Recruiting Sarge Described it!"

"Hawaiian Paradise" recruiting cartoon. (Edward J. White)

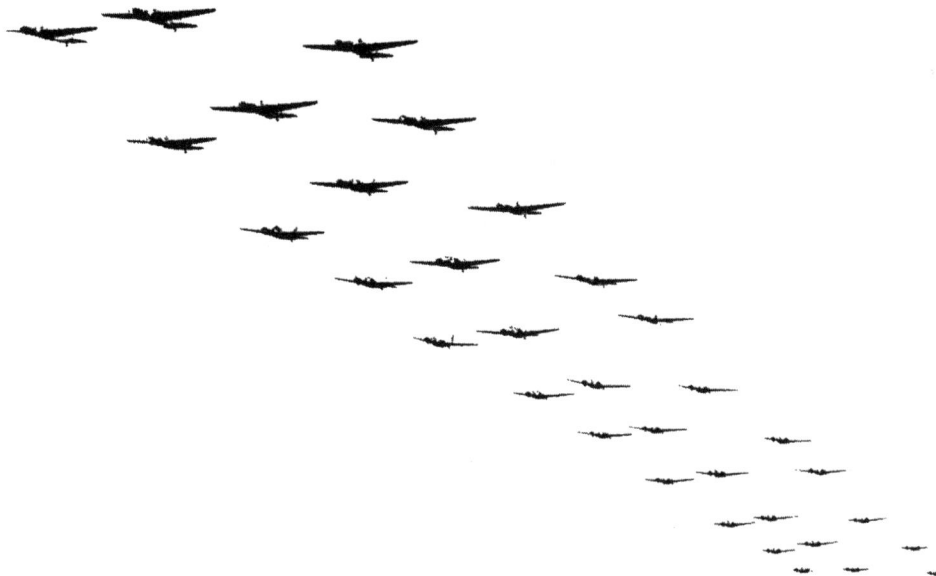

Above, B-18s in formation over Oahu, 6 April 1940. (W. Bruce Harlow). Below, B-18 at Hickam Field with winged death's head insignia of the 5th Bombardment Group on its nose.

B-17 aircraft flying over the main gate at Hickam Field, circa 1941.

detailed how a possible attack could occur, but also outlined what steps would be necessary to prevent its success. The report stated that the primary defense against a sneak attack would be long-range reconnaissance. To be effective, reconnaissance would have to be conducted in a 360-degree arc around the island and extend out at least a thousand miles. Both officers realized that with the equipment available this could not be carried out for long, so they did not recommend its implementation until war was imminent.[9]

The Hawaiian Air Force had 33 B-18 and 12 B-17D aircraft assigned, but the B-18s were old and their range was so short they would be of little value for patrol duty. As a result the Navy (which had over 60 long-range PBY Flying Boats) accepted the responsibility for long-range reconnaissance in the Hawaii area, with the Hawaiian Air Force providing short-range (20 miles out) coverage. On paper this sounded like a workable arrangement. Unfortunately Admiral Kimmel had decided that he needed the flying boats to provide long-range coverage in the areas where he planned to operate the fleet during war.* If used to patrol the Hawaiian area, he reasoned, they would deteriorate and not be available when the actual war began. In addition, there were insufficient replacement crews to keep all the aircraft manned. Admiral Kimmel then took a calculated risk, based on the belief that the nearest Japanese possessions capable of supporting a full-scale attack on Hawaii were located south

_____

*For a complete description of how Admiral Kimmel planned to use the Pacific Fleet during the war see: Samuel Eliot Morison, History of United States Naval Operations in World War II, Vol III, The Rising Sun in the Pacific 1931-April 1942, (Little, Brown and Company: Boston, 1965), pp 48-56.

P-40 formation over Oahu, 1 August 1941.
(Gene Taylor)

of the islands, and began using a minimum number of flying boats for anti-submarine patrol in that direction. So, the morning of the attack, which came from the north, the flying boats were patrolling the opposite area. The belief that an attack could only come from the south was so strong that after the attack began, the first Air Force reconnaissance aircraft to get airborne also patrolled the southern area trying to locate the enemy carriers.

A proviso in the Martin-Bellinger report called for the Navy to go to the Air Force for assistance if the Navy was unable to provide the reconnaissance coverage

necessary. The Navy never exercised this option, since it believed that an attack on Hawaii could not occur without some warning. Besides, with only 12 aircraft, Martin could lend only limited assistance.[10]

The fighter aircraft status on Oahu was somewhat better than the bomber picture. The command had 87 P-40B and 12 P-40C aircraft, with 55 in commission on 7 December. In addition, there were 39 P-36A aircraft with 20 in commission. Although Washington considered the P-36 outmoded compared to European aircraft, and even the P-40 was not considered the most modern plane, they were the best the United States had at the time. Washington had received information about the Japanese fighter, A6M2 Zero, and its superb flying qualities from Gen Claire Chennault, Commander of the Flying Tigers volunteer force in China, but senior military officials discounted this information and never sent it to the field. New fighter pilots had been arriving on the island in increasing numbers, and General Arnold had promised Martin additional aircraft as they became available. The consensus in Washington held that the fighter force defending Oahu, if somewhat small, was at least adequate for use against anything the Japanese might have. The major limiting factor for the fighters stationed in Hawaii was their short combat range, and they needed a strong ground control system to maximize their combat efficiency.[11]

The Air Defense System

The key to the Hawaiian Islands air defense was the air warning system (AWS), consisting of radar units, an air warning center, and the 14th Pursuit Wing at Wheeler. As the heart of the AWS, the air warning center contained an information

P-36 aircraft lined up at Wheeler Field.

center, fighter director, and an aircraft/antiaircraft weapon control system. The information center needed to receive data about incoming aircraft, either from long-range reconnaissance, units stationed on the outer islands, surface ship contact, or radar in order to operate. Aircraft plotters marked the flight paths on a table map where the director, with liaison officers from the bomber and fighter commands, the Navy, and civilian aviation, identified them as either friendly or unknown. If marked unknown, the director ordered fighter interceptors launched, under the aircraft controller's direction, to investigate. This was how the British operated their aircraft warning system, and in theory this was what the Hawaiian Department had in place at Fort Shafter. In actuality the system used in Hawaii bore little resemblance to the British system.[12]

The whole AWS idea was so new to the Army that no one was sure how to make it work or who should control it. The cooperation needed among various military units and government agencies was far greater than anything anybody realized at the time. Because the mobile radar systems were the first units developed for the AWS, the Army Signal Corps took initial control. After the Signal Corps had set up the system and trained the personnel, control would pass to the Air Force. Contrary to popular belief, the air warning system as used in Hawaii on 7 December 1941 was under the Army Signal Corps, not the Hawaiian Air Force.[13]

Lt Col Carroll A. Powell, Army Signal Corps, was in charge of the Hawaiian air warning system that morning. To help Powell in setting up the system and to take operational control upon its completion, Brig Gen Howard C. Davidson, 14th Pursuit Wing Commander, selected the 44th Pursuit Squadron Commander, Capt Kenneth P. Bergquist. Although Bergquist was known as a troubleshooter and had a reputation for getting the job done, the task of making the air warning system work before 7 December would prove to be too much for even his abilities.[14]

Everyone wanted to get into the act. Even the simplest job took months of coordination and frustration before it could be completed. Oahu abounded with US Government-owned locations suitable for the mobile radar units; but before a site could be used, approval had to be obtained from the National Park Service and the Department of Interior. More than once, General Short had to intervene to get the approval process moving. Cooperation within the Army was no better. Captain Bergquist placed a requisition for headsets to be used by personnel operating the control center, only to have it disapproved by the Quartermaster Corps because the latter thought the Signal Corps was the organization in charge and, therefore, authorized to request items.[15]

After completing the air warning center construction at Fort Shafter, personnel needed to be trained to operate it. The Signal Corps handled training for the personnel required to operate the radar units and those at the air warning center involved in tracking the reports on incoming aircraft. Captain Bergquist, with Capt Wilfred H. Tetley, Army Signal Corps, and Lt Cmdr William Taylor, USN, managed training of directors, controllers, and those personnel who would be temporarily assigned to the system during exercises and wartime operations. Tetley and Taylor were detached from their respective units and in no way represented the Signal Corps or the Navy during this training phase. In other words, the Signal Corps trained part of the personnel and the Hawaiian Air Force the rest, with no one in command of the complete training.[16]

During the two main exercises held with the Navy in 1941 and during several smaller exercises conducted by the center

Capt Wilfred H. Tetley (left) of the Army Signal Corps and Capt Kenneth P. Bergquist of the 14th Pursuit Wing, pictured with members of the radar site survey team, in 1941. (US Army Museum of Hawaii)

itself, either the director knew the direction of the attacking aircraft or personnel from the other branches would report for the exercise as liaisons so the incoming aircraft could be identified. On 12 November 1941, after the center was manned, the Navy launched a simulated strike from a carrier 80 miles out to sea. The radar stations easily picked up the attackers, the center quickly identified them as enemy aircraft, and within six minutes interceptor aircraft were airborne and met the attacking force 30 miles from the island.[17]

These exercises demonstrated that the Hawaiian air warning system would work if it had operational radar units, a fully staffed information center, and armed and ready-to-fly interceptor aircraft. On 7 December, the AWS met none of these requirements. The following charts show

how the system operated during the 12 November exercise and on the morning of 7 December. The solid lines between each block represent the lines of communications that were operational during each period.

The best General Davidson could do was to insure at least one pilot from the 14th Pursuit Wing was on duty every day in the air warning center to learn firsthand how the whole system operated and to offer assistance to the controller in handling pursuit aircraft. On the morning of 7 December, the system was further degraded when, although five of the six radar systems were operational and the enlisted plotters were on hand from 0400 to 0700 under Signal Corps direction, no director or aircraft controller was on duty. The only officer present was Lt Kermit Tyler, a 14th Pursuit Wing pilot. Lieutenant

THE AIR WARNING SYSTEM ON 12 NOVEMBER 1941
DURING A SIMULATED ENEMY ATTACK

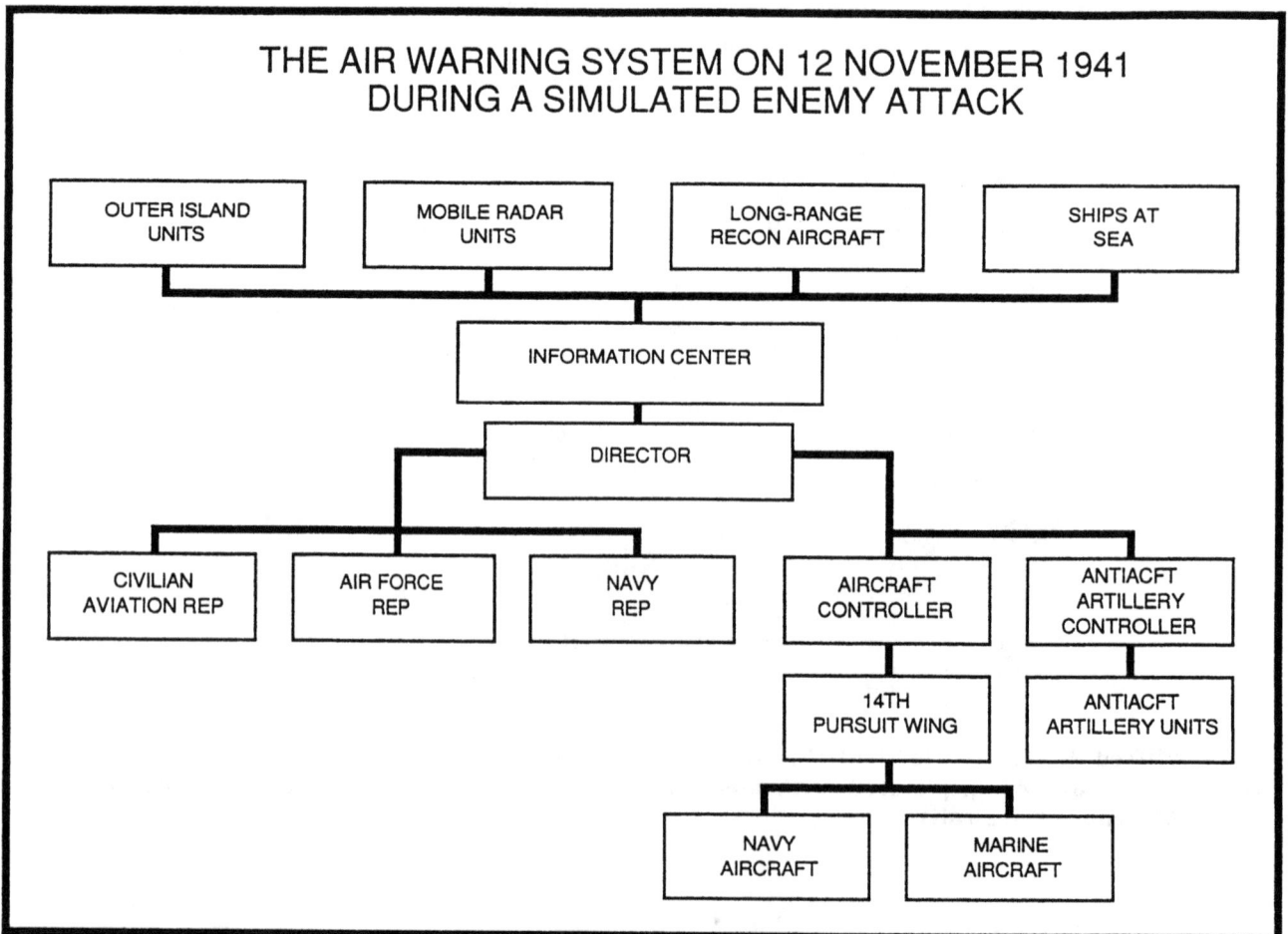

Tyler was there to observe how the system worked and assist the controller with the pursuit aircraft after they had launched. In no way was he responsible for, or for that matter expected to know how to activate, the air warning system. The most he could have done was call Bergquist (now a major) and let him know what was going on. It is unlikely that such a call would have helped the Hawaiian air defense that fateful morning, because the third and final part of the air warning system, aircraft ready to launch, was not set up at all.[18]

The whole purpose of the air warning system was to launch interceptor aircraft against would-be aggressors; yet, no aircraft were ready to launch and attack the enemy that morning. If the Hawaiian Air Force was expected to defend the islands, why were no aircraft on alert? Within the

answer to this question is the basic reason the Japanese attack on Oahu was so successful. Few, if anyone, in the Hawaiian Department felt the Japanese would attack Hawaii despite many indications that an attack on Hawaii was possible. Rather, most people considered the Hawaiian Islands a staging area from which the US Navy would sortie against predetermined targets. It was also commonly believed the Imperial Japanese fleet would attack Singapore or Malaysia, or possibly even the Philippines.

Although some Hawaiian Air Force units held exercise and full alerts on Oahu, and others deployed under field conditions, there was an air of make-believe to the deployments. When they were over, people would carefully clean and put away the equipment and ammunition for the next

THE AIR WARNING SYSTEM ON 7 DECEMBER 1941 DURING THE ACTUAL ENEMY ATTACK

exercise. During the week preceding 7 December, the entire Hawaiian Department, by order of General Short, engaged in a full scale exercise for seven consecutive days. Army units from Schofield Barracks deployed, antiaircraft units drew ammunition and set up stations all over the island, and the Hawaiian Air Force armed aircraft and dispersed them to protective revetments. The warning center was fully operational and launched aircraft against simulated attacking targets.

General Short considered this exercise a great success. After its cancellation on 6 December, personnel returned to the barracks, carefully cleaned and repaired the guns and equipment, removed the ammunition and repacked it in storage containers, and returned the aircraft to their main bases to be reparked close together because Alert One was still in effect. After doing this, each command gave the troops the rest of the day off and told them to report to work Monday. When and if war began, General Short and the other senior commanders in Hawaii felt they would be given plenty of warning to begin long-range reconnaissance, set up communications between the Army and Navy, staff the aircraft warning center, and arm and disperse available aircraft ready for deployment against the enemy. The fleet would sortie, and the Japanese would find a sky full of American aircraft, piloted by well-trained personnel eager to defend the island.[19]

CHAPTER II

ASSIGNMENT PARADISE: BOMBER COMMAND

"Hickam Field . . . this magnificent air base, which is destined to be, when completed, not only the most important unit of aerial defense within the Hawaiian Department, but the largest airdrome in this broad land of ours."

Capt H. B. Nurse, Quartermaster Corps
(Air Corps News Letter, 1 July 1938)

During the 1930s, the thousands of young men who joined the military service and sailed to the Hawaiian Islands for duty considered themselves fortunate indeed to receive such a choice assignment. They enjoyed the beautiful beaches, lush foliage, and year-round pleasant climate that characterized "the Paradise of the Pacific" but, at the same time, they also served as the first line of defense for the United States. Because of its strategic geographical location, Hawaii played a key role in defense plans for the Pacific; and Army Air Forces personnel stationed on the island of Oahu supported those plans as members of either the bomber command or fighter command in the Hawaiian Air Force.[1]

Hickam Field

Hickam Field, the bomber base, was named in honor of Lt Col Horace Meek Hickam, a distinguished and highly esteemed Army Air Corps officer who died at Fort Crockett, Texas, in an aircraft accident on 5 November 1934. It was the nation's largest air base at the time and the showplace of the Hawaiian Department. Army officials, congressmen, and ordinary taxpayers who visited this modern installation were impressed with its potential power and beauty, and left with the feeling that their money had been well spent.[2]

Before Hickam's construction, Army flying activities operated from Luke Field on Ford Island in Pearl Harbor. Constructed in 1918, Luke Field, because of its isolation, soon had one of the most complete post exchanges in the territory, a

Lt Col Horace Meek Hickam (1885-1934)

large and well equipped officers' club, one of the best gymnasiums on Oahu, several hangars, a theater, tennis and handball courts, family quarters, and many other buildings.   Shared by Army and Navy installations, Ford Island became overcrowded in the mid-1930s; to solve the problem, the Navy took over the entire island, including Luke Field, and the War Department found a nearby tract for Army aviation.[3]

The site selected to become Hickam Field consisted of 2,200 acres of ancient coral reef, covered by a thin layer of soil, located between Oahu's Waianae and Koolau mountain ranges. The Pearl Harbor channel marked its western boundary, with Pearl Harbor naval reservation stretching along its northern perimeter, John Rodgers Airport to the east, and Fort Kamehameha on the south. A tangled jungle of algaroba (kiawe) and sugar cane covered the area, providing a haven for mongooses and mynah birds. Along the shore of the Pearl Harbor channel, the plantation village of Watertown spread its shacks among scattered palm and royal poinciana trees.[4]

Capt Howard B. Nurse of the Quartermaster Corps planned, designed, and supervised the construction of Hickam Field, which was to be the home station of not only a bombardment wing but also an air depot capable of accomplishing all the major overhaul work required by Army Air Forces units in Hawaii. The first task confronting him was clearing the land and demolishing the decrepit shanties of Watertown. Next, contracts were let for hangars and other buildings, tons of construction material began pouring in by land and sea, and the air soon filled with the noise of riveting hammers and the rhythmic thud of pile drivers. This mammoth construction project extended over several years and gave employment to many people.[5]

Luke Field on Ford Island, 30 October 1930, with Keystone LB-5 bombers on the right and Thomas Morse O-19 observation planes to the left.

Aerial view of what was originally known as Tracts A and B, acquired on 3 April 1935 at a cost of $1,095,543.78 for the construction of Hickam Field.

While construction was still in progress, an initial cadre of 12 enlisted men, commanded by 1st Lt Robert Warren, moved from Luke Field to Hickam with four airplanes on 1 September 1937. Lieutenant Warren became Hickam's first commanding officer, forming with his men the nucleus of what was later designated as the 17th Air Base Group, the unit responsible for furnishing base services and support.[6]

The 18th Wing, Air Corps (former 18th Composite Wing), at Fort Shafter was the first to relocate to Hickam. Then the exodus of people and aircraft began from Luke Field. Initial plans called for personnel to move as new buildings were completed for them at Hickam; however, the sudden transfer of part of the Pacific Fleet to Hawaii and approval of a $2,800,000 expansion program for the Navy's air station on Ford Island forced Army Air Corps units to leave on short notice. By 31 October 1939, the last troops had departed Luke Field except for the Hawaiian Air Depot, which remained until October 1940 when the new air depot was completed at Hickam.[7]

All of the Luke Field facilities that could possibly be moved were transported to Hickam. Even the gym and basketball court were dismantled and transferred in sections, as were supply huts, the noncommissioned officers' club, chapel, theater, and housing units for enlisted personnel. They were loaded on the ferry Manuwai, carried across the Pearl Harbor channel, and turned over to crews at Hickam Field for reconstruction.[8]

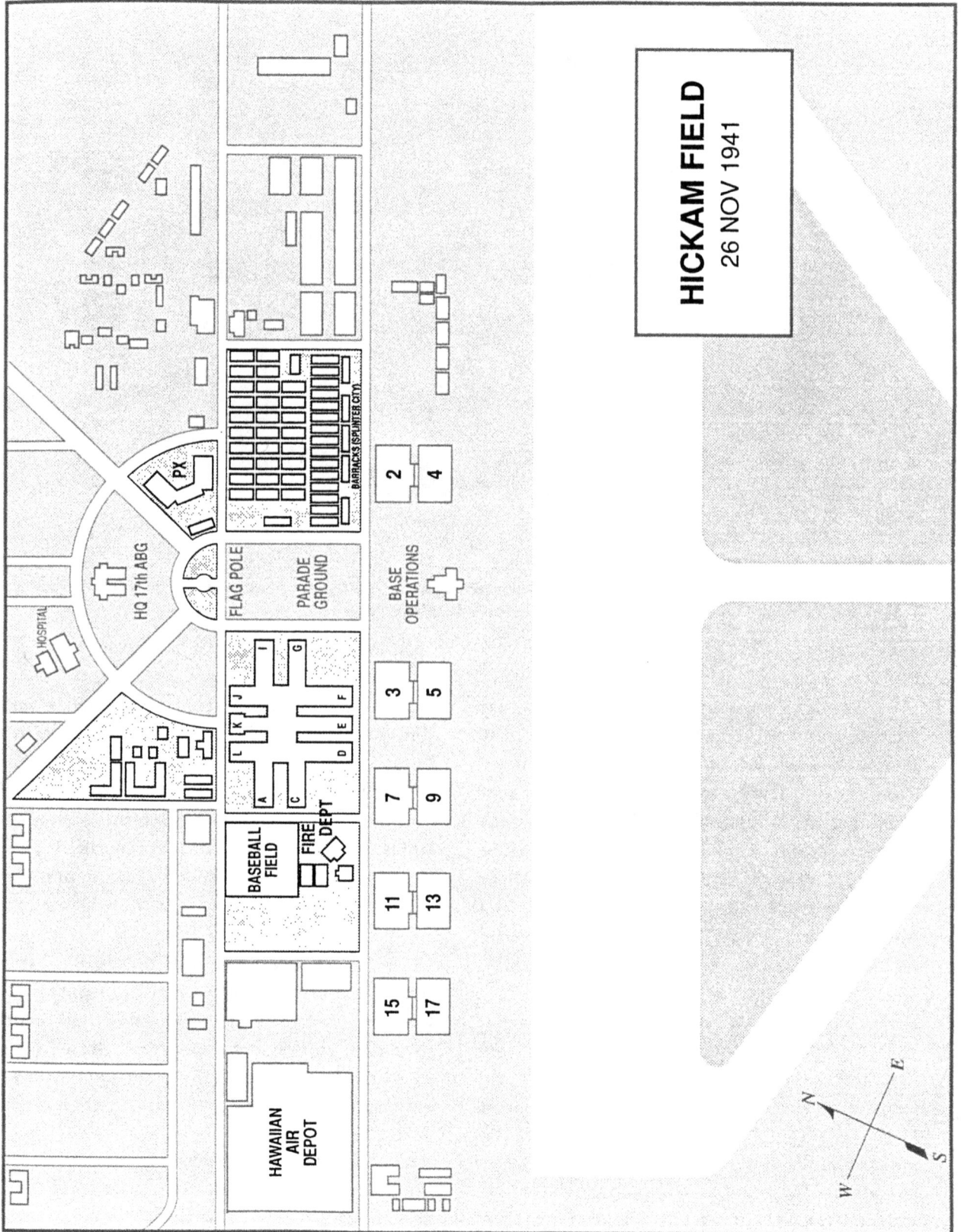

HICKAM FIELD
26 NOV 1941

HAWAIIAN AIR DEPOT

BASEBALL FIELD

FIRE DEPT

HOSPITAL

HQ 17th ABG

PX

FLAG POLE

PARADE GROUND

BASE OPERATIONS

BARRACKS (SPLINTER CITY)

15 17

11 13

7   9

3   5

2   4

A C D E F G I J K L

On 1 November 1940, with activation of the Hawaiian Air Force at Fort Shafter, bombardment and pursuit units became organized into separate wings—the 18th Bombardment Wing (Heavy) at Hickam Field and the 14th Pursuit Wing at Wheeler. The next day, on 2 November 1940, Maj Gen Frederick L. Martin assumed command of the new Hawaiian Air Force, which later became known as the "Pineapple Air Force." The headquarters subsequently relocated from Fort Shafter to Hickam Field in July 1941. Units of the bombardment wing at Hickam were the 5th and 11th Bombardment Groups (Heavy), with the 23d, 31st, and 72d Bomb Squadrons and 4th Reconnaissance Squadron assigned to the 5th Bomb Group and the 26th and 42d Bomb Squadrons and 50th Reconnaissance Squadron assigned to the 11th. Other organizations at Hickam Field included the

"Pineapple Soldier" at Hickam Field, June 1942. (Allan Gunn)

17th Air Base Group, Hawaiian Air Depot, 19th Transport Squadron, and 58th Bombardment Squadron (Light), as well as maintenance companies and various service detachments.[9]

Pending the completion of barracks under construction at Hickam Field, enlisted personnel lived in 50-man tents in a temporary "Tent City" erected near the hangar line. The large tents had wooden sides and floors under the canvas roofs and were equipped with steel lockers and showers. In addition, there were separate kitchen, mess hall, and dayroom tents, the last of these replete with radios, easy chairs, and modernistic smoking stands. The men were relatively comfortable in these temporary accommodations but looked forward to moving into permanent buildings. A dispute in 1938, however, between the Air Corps and the Hawaiian Department's Quartermaster Construction Division over design of Hickam Field's barracks delayed work on the urgently needed troop housing. The Air Corps wanted individual barracks spread throughout the area, while the Quartermaster Corps, to save construction costs, wished to build one huge structure. In the end, the Quartermaster Corps won, and construction finally began early in 1939.[10]

The Robert E. McKee Company submitted a low bid of $1,039,000 to build the massive new multi-winged barracks that faced the parade ground. The three-story reinforced concrete structure was designed to house 3,200 men, and Hickam personnel began moving in to their new home in January 1940 while construction was still in progress. By the time the last coat of white paint had been applied and the project announced as completed on 30 September that same year, the barracks was fully occupied. It was the largest single structure

Above, Tent City as seen from the control tower at Hickam Field in 1939. Here the troops lived until permanent barracks could be constructed for them. (Clifford E. Hotchkiss)

Below, Hickam Field's huge new million-dollar barracks, with Hangars 3-5 and 7-9 in the background, 22 October 1940.

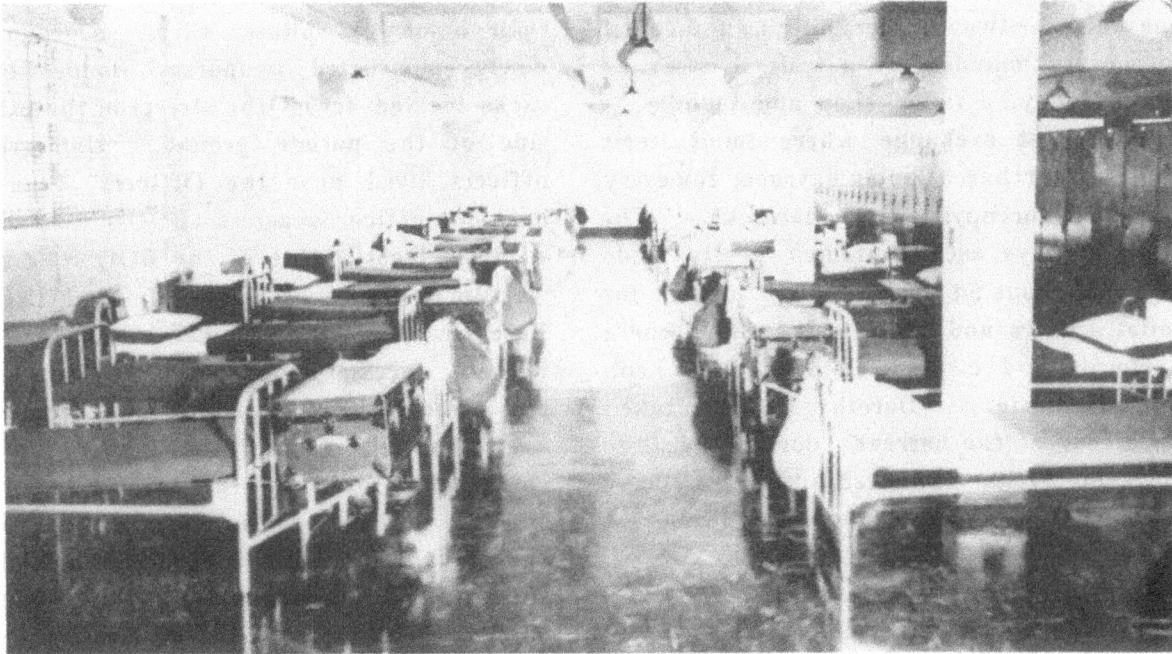

Above, an interior view of the new barracks (sometimes referred to as the "Hickam Hotel—under management of Uncle Sam"). Open bay sleeping quarters contained long lines of neat, orderly bunks made up with "white collars" for inspection.

Below, this huge mess hall, located in the center of the consolidated barracks, fed thousands of hungry enlisted men daily.

of its kind on any American military post and included within its walls every possible convenience—two barber shops, a medical dispensary manned by a trained staff 24 hours a day, a tailor shop and laundry, a branch post exchange where small items could be purchased, and a dayroom for every squadron occupying the barracks. The sleeping bays each contained neatly made beds for about 50 men, with foot lockers for toilet articles and larger wall lockers where uniforms and civilian clothing were kept. Famous movie star Dorothy Lamour, taken on a tour of the barracks during a visit to Hickam Field, remarked, "Why I never dreamed that *men* could keep things so neat!"[11]

The entire barracks centered around a huge consolidated mess hall, with all nine wings connected to it by a series of hallways. Resembling a gigantic hangar, the mess hall could easily accommodate six regulation-size basketball courts. It had the capability of seating and feeding 2,000 at one time. With trays in hand, the tan-clad enlisted men moved along the cafeteria-style line, which included four 40-foot steam tables to keep the food warm. White-uniformed food handlers dished out ample portions of everything on the menu, and personnel ate at the 104 ten-man tables which occupied most of the 26,741 square feet of floor space. Palm trees brightened up the interior of the mess hall, with potted ferns adorning the pillars and paintings of various squadron insignia hanging on the walls. The amount of groceries required daily to feed the hungry troops was staggering—a ton of meat, half a ton of potatoes, 800 pounds of bread, 15 cases of eggs, 100 pounds of butter, and an average of 400 pies. A crew of nearly 200 men working in shifts around the clock was required to operate the facility.[12]

Enlisted men who could not be accommodated in the big barracks made their home in "Splinter City," a group of newly constructed temporary wooden barracks located across the street on the other side of the parade ground. Unmarried officers lived near the Officers' Club in bachelor officer quarters (BOQs) furnished with steel cots. One of the BOQ residents was 2d Lt Denver D. Gray of the 17th Air Base Group. "In a tropical climate it was thought necessary only to screen windows and protect them by overhanging eaves to keep out the rain," he said. "New construction on the base kept the red dust stirred, and my bed had a dusty covering each evening. I bought a roll-down wicker shade from Sears Roebuck for the windows, which partially solved the problem."[13]

Married officers and senior noncommissioned officers enjoyed the luxury of living with their families in spacious stucco houses with red tiled roofs and wide overhanging eaves surrounded by attractively landscaped grounds. Rising above the residential area was the base's landmark—a beautiful concrete tower of Moorish design enclosing a 500,000-gallon steel tank holding an emergency reserve of water. It was a considerable improvement over the familiar ugly tank of bare black steel usually seen on other military posts. Between the water tower and the hangar line was the business and shopping center, which included the hospital, administration building, exchange, and post office. Recreational facilities scattered throughout the area included the gym, theater, tennis courts, swimming pools, and baseball fields. With its broad tree-lined boulevards, street lighting and telephone systems, fire department, public school, and other community facilities, Hickam Field resembled an attractive little city.[14]

Above, the wooden barracks of "Splinter City" at Hickam Field, 1940-1941. (Bernard C. Tysen)

Below, family quarters at Hickam Field, 1940-1941. (Bernard C. Tysen)

Hickam's beautiful moorish-style water tower, at the base of which was a nursery where thousands of tree seedlings and shrubs were propagated to beautify the post.

In the operational center of the base, five immense double hangars lined up along a paved landing mat that looked like a modified letter "A" stretching its length for nearly a mile. Along the street by the hangars was a railroad track which connected Hickam Field with the busy port of Honolulu nine miles away. The railway and street extended past the huge air depot building and shops, continuing beyond rows of warehouses and ending abruptly on a concrete dock where large oceangoing freighters discharged their cargo of supplies. On one side of the dock, a boathouse sheltered high-speed power boats used on rescue missions that included anything from Army or Navy planes forced down in the ocean to capsized commercial or private fishing boats. "The Biggest Little

Navy in This Man's Army" was the term applied to Hickam's fleet of five crash boats and the 28 enlisted men who operated them. Although they were all Army personnel, the men resembled sailors because of their duty uniforms (light blue shirts and blue bell-bottom dungarees) which were very similar to the Navy's but looked like a strange hybrid with their Army stripes and insignia. Nautical experience was a requirement for these Army sailors, who trained until they could board their vessels and get under way within three minutes after the boathouse siren sounded an alarm.[15]

More conventional jobs at Hickam Field ran the gamut from those of the Commanding General, Hawaiian Air Force, and his senior staff, to pilots, engineers, medical

Bishop Point dock at Hickam Field, which not only handled supplies off-loaded by oceangoing freighters but also had a pipeline through which deep-laden tank ships pumped fuel to distant underground storage tanks. Railroad tracks are visible at left, with a boathouse for rescue vessels on the right.

personnel, firemen, mechanics, photographers, clerks, drivers, strikers (enlisted aides), and many others. Assigned personnel reported to the various headquarters and support units which carried out the detailed work of operating a complicated bomber base like Hickam. The bomber command headquarters (18th Bombardment Wing) had the tactical responsibility of launching aircraft on patrol and alert missions, while the post headquarters of the 17th Air Base Group commander handled administrative requirements and provided supervision for the mechanics, shop workers, and other personnel who insured the safe and efficient flying of the big bombers.[16]

Because technical schools on the mainland were unable to provide sufficient skilled specialists to meet the needs of the greatly expanding Hawaiian Air Force, military officials established schools at both

Hickam and Wheeler Fields in 1939. The school at Hickam specialized in training aviation mechanics and armorers, while the Wheeler school provided radio instruction and clerical studies. Hickam later set up a clerical school of its own to meet the mounting demand for "white-collar" personnel to handle the Army's vastly increased paperwork. For the hundreds of young men who received technological education at these schools, it was an opportunity to "earn while you learn." School standards were high and the courses difficult, with a failure rate of about 25 percent. For those completing all course requirements, graduation day was a big event, with each man anxiously waiting to receive the parchment diploma certifying that he had attained "the proficiency required by the United States Army standards of achievement."[17]

Post headquarters at Hickam Field, 1940-1941. (Bernard C. Tysen)

U.S. ARMY AIR CORPS

HICKAM FIELD
17TH AIR BASE

TERRITORY OF HAWAII
TECHNICAL SCHOOL

DIPLOMA

AIRCRAFT MECHANICS

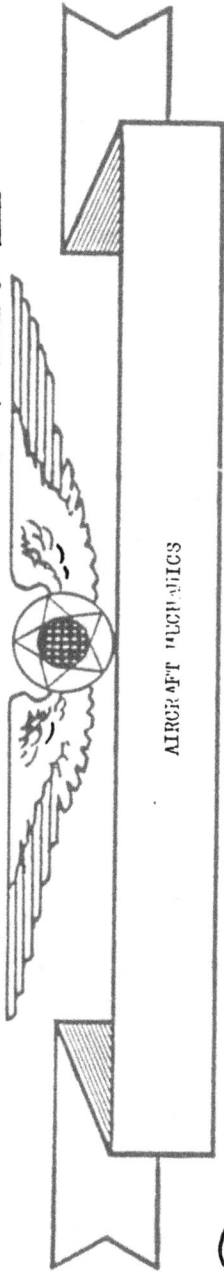

This is to Certify, that _____ Private First Class Herbert J. Kelly, 6931788 _____ has completed the educational course enumerated hereon and has attained in this the proficiency required by the United States Army standards of achievement.

In testimony whereof this Diploma is conferred upon him.

Given at _____ Hickam Field _____ this _____ 5th _____ day of _____ June _____ in the year _____ 1940.

O.I.C. BASE SCHOOLS
W. A. SCHULGEN
Captain, Air Corps.

Diploma awarded to PFC Herbert J. Kelly for successful completion of the Aircraft Mechanics course at Hickam Field, 5 June 1940

At the Hickam Field Technical School, located in one of the hangars, each week brought a new class of 23 students to the mechanics course and every other week a new class of 13 armorers. They attended daily lectures, averaged two hours of study each night, then took oral and written tests on the previous day's lecture. In addition, they received practical experience by working as actual members of maintenance and combat crews before graduating 12 weeks from the date of entry. The school also provided refresher courses or specialized instruction in propellers, hydraulics, and instruments, for crew chiefs, armorers, and other mechanics. This schooling proved its worth as flying schedules increased and more airplanes joined the Hawaiian Air Force's air armada.[18]

The mechanics were a familiar sight on the Hickam flight line, in gray-green coveralls smeared with grease, performing scheduled inspections, daily checks, engine changes, and all but the most major repairs to airplanes and their engines. Major work—reconditioning, overhaul, modifications, and technical changes—on assigned aircraft and aeronautical equipment was the responsibility of Hickam's Hawaiian Air Depot. Col Harry G. Montgomery, the depot commander, had a small staff of officers to help him manage the work of an all-civilian force consisting of personnel hired from the local community or recruited from the mainland, plus a number of former enlisted members.[19]

In addition to the skilled work of trained technicians, the labor of enlisted members on "fatigue detail" was essential to the smooth operation of the base. Unappealing jobs such as post maintenance (keeping lawns trimmed, buildings cleaned, etc.) and the always unpopular KP duty fell in this category, and assigned personnel did their best to avoid them. First sergeants

Members of Aircraft Mechanics Graduation Class 2A pose in front of a Douglas B-18 at Hickam Field, 5 June 1940. (Herbert J. Kelly)

were known to resort to trickery to get the men required for such base details. In one instance reported, the "top kick" lined up his people and asked all those who could do shorthand to fall out. Expecting to be assigned to office work, a number of them stepped forward. The first sergeant then turned to the corporal and said, "March these men to the mess hall. We are *shorthanded* on KPs this morning!"[20]

First sergeants, with the distinctive diamond design at the center of their chevrons, were the top enlisted men in their respective outfits and had a tremendous amount of authority. In many cases, they administered discipline and virtually ran their organizations, with the squadron commander and adjutant handling administrative details and signing necessary paperwork such as the morning report. On payday, it was the first sergeant who sat with the pay officer at a desk in the day room and called out the names of assembled personnel, one at a time. As his name was called, each man stepped up, saluted the pay officer, repeated his own name, received his pay in cash, saluted again, did an about face, and left the room. The pay in those days was $21 a month for privates, and from that amount 25 cents went to the Old Soldiers Home and $1.50 to the quarter-master laundry. After receiving what was left, the men normally had the rest of the day off.[21]

If they wanted to go to Honolulu, a bus ride cost ten cents and taxi fare was a quarter. The bus line ended at the Army and Navy YMCA on Hotel Street in downtown Honolulu where a taxi depot was conveniently located so military members could take cabs to other areas. Across the street was the famous Black Cat Cafe, a favorite hangout for off-duty soldiers and

sailors. A Coney Island atmosphere prevailed there, with hot dogs, hamburgers, sea food, slot machines, and various other concessions. The men especially enjoyed posing for pictures with hula girls and sending the souvenir photos home to their families. The food was plentiful and inexpensive—10 cents for a hot dog, 15 cents for a hamburger, 50 cents for a roast turkey meal, etc.—with the most costly item on the 1941 menu being porterhouse steak and mushrooms for a dollar.[22]

Other well-patronized eating places included the Wo Fat restaurant in Chinatown, a first-class establishment but located in close proximity to the red-light district of the city; Lau Yee Chai in Waikiki; and Kau Kau Korner (at the site of today's Hard Rock Cafe), a drive-in restaurant famous for its "Crossroads of the Pacific" sign that was probably photo-graphed more than any other man-made object in Honolulu next to the Aloha Tower. The Waikiki Theater, with its huge indoor palm trees that reached up to the ceiling, and the Royal Hawaiian and Moana Hotels (the only ones in Waikiki at the time) were other favorite haunts of servicemen spending their leisure time downtown.[23]

Hickam Field personnel also had plenty to keep them busy on the base during nonduty hours. There were movies every night, and the affordable admission price of 10 cents permitted even $21-a-month privates to go to the theater several times a week. The Hickam Hostess Society, a group of officers' and noncommissioned officers' wives, sponsored monthly dances in the large consolidated mess hall, which was decorated with colorful streamers and tropical plants. The hostesses kept an invitation list with the names of over 200 Honolulu girls to whom bids went out for these popular

Above is the Army and Navy YMCA on Hotel Street in downtown Honolulu, patronized by military personnel of all services; and directly across from the YMCA was the Black Cat Cafe (below), where many military members spent their off-duty time enjoying good food at low cost. (Charles L. Tona) Military men pose for a souvenir photo with a hula girl at the Black Cat Cafe (right). The bandage on the arm of the man on the left could indicate that he had just frequented one of the tatto parlors along Hotel Street. (William T. Faulk)

The Black Cat, a popular bar across from the Armed Forces YMCA, 1943

BLACK CAT CAFE
Honolulu, Hawaii

"Do You Remember When"
Sampling Of Items From The 1941 Menu

Breakfast Dishes

Hot Cakes.......................$ .10	
Waffle........................... .15	
Oatmeal......................... .15	
Corn Flakes.................... .15	
Ham, Bacon or Sausage & eggs, Buttered Toast and Hash Browns........................ .35	
Poached eggs on toast.......... .30	
Egg & tomato scramble......... .30	
Oyster omelette................. .45	
Hard boiled egg, pickled egg, or raw egg.................. .05	

24-Hour Specials

Breaded Veal Cutlet........... .35	
Roast Turkey with dressing.... .50	
½ Fried Chicken with bacon.... .60	
Roast Pork & applesauce....... .40	
Swiss Steak & brown gravy..... .25	
Corned Beef & cabbage......... .30	
Spaghetti & meatballs......... .25	
Hot Pork or beef sandwich..... .25	

Steaks, Chops and other meats

Porterhouse & mushrooms:...... 1.00	
T-Bone......................... .60	
Rib steak...................... .40	
Hamburger .30 with onions..... .35	
Liver & onions .30 with bacon. .35	

Fish & Sea Foods

½ doz. Fresh Frozen Oysters, fried, stewed or raw........ .35	
Fried Shrimps on toast........ .35	
Fried Ulua, tartar sauce...... .30	

Salads

Fruit salad with whipped cream............... .25	
Crab........................... .50	
Shrimp......................... .35	
Potato......................... .15	
Alligator Pear (Avocado)...... .10	

Cold Meats with Potato Salad

Boiled Ham.....................$ .35	
Assorted cold cuts............. .35	
Pig's foot..................... .20	
Sardines....................... .25	

Soups

Chicken........................ .20	
Corn Chowder................... .20	
Vegetable...................... .20	
Turtle......................... .20	

Sandwiches
(Any sandwich under .20 - on toast .05 extra) Potato salad with any sandwich .10

Black Cat Special.............. .20	
Bacon & Egg.................... .20	
Cold ham....................... .10	
Bacon & tomato................. .20	
Hamburger...................... .15	
Hamburger & cheese............. .20	
Peanut butter.................. .10	
Club House..................... .50	
Denver......................... .25	
Barbecued Beef................. .15	
Hot dog........................ .10	

Desserts

Strawberry shortcake with whipped cream................. .20	
Pies (per cut)................. .10	
Pie a la mode.................. .15	
Brown bobbies.............2 for .05	
Ice Cream...................... .10	
Banana Split................... .25	

Drinks

Buttermilk..................... .10	
Milk (second glass .05)........ .10	
Postum......................... .10	
Ovaltine....................... .10	
Milk Shakes.................... .15	
Malted Milks................... .20	
Coca Cola & other sodas........ .10	
with meals................. .05	

Courtesy of:

ROBERT STEPHEN HUDSON: AUTHOR-HISTORIAN   "PEARL HARBOR SURVIVOR"

Sampling of items from the 1941 menu of the Black Cat Cafe. (Robert Stephen Hudson)

Right is the famous "Crossroads of the Pacific" sign at Kau Kau Corner on Kalakaua Avenue, at the entrance to Waikiki, circa 1941. (11th Bombardment Group Association) Above, the popular Waikiki Theater in 1941, with a rainbow over the stage, flanked by coconut trees and other tropical flora. (Edward J. White) Below, the Waikiki area and Diamond Head, as photographed on 18 January 1934. (Arthur C. Snodgrass)

events. Dances were also a regular weekly feature at the Hickam Officers' Club adjacent to the Pearl Harbor channel. This beautiful new structure, which replaced club facilities formerly located in the basement of the operations building, contained a large dining room, bar, ballroom, and a fully equipped game room. No officer could go to the club after seven o'clock in the evening without wearing dress whites or a white formal jacket, and everything was signed for with chits rather than paid in cash. The many special programs and activities at the club, such as "Monte Carlo Night" and formal dinner-dances, were well attended by assigned officers.[24]

The Noncommissioned Officers (NCO) Club at the end of Mills Boulevard replaced a wooden frame building that had served as a temporary club ever since the base was built. The old structure fell victim to Hickam's first major fire in March 1940; but work on a new facility had been started months before, so shortly after the disastrous fire, the new club was ready to open. By that time, however, the number of men stationed at Hickam Field had increased considerably, and there were far more NCOs than the club could accommodate. Consequently, it became a first three graders' club, and lower grade NCOs had to content themselves with restaurants and beer gardens operated by the post exchange. Enlisted personnel patronized the "Snake Ranch," a beer hall set up in a wooden building across the parade ground from the big barracks. "I don't know who started that name, 'Snake Ranch'," said Kenneth L. Bayley (former private first class assigned to the 4th Reconnaissance Squadron), "but I suppose if you drank enough of the local beer, you'd see snakes."[25]

HEARD:-- M/Sgt Jessie Martin has got religion. He tried to put in for OCS to be a chaplain - We hope he gets it, too. Imagine Sunday School in the Snake Ranch!

SEEN:--Sgt. John Mullins, holding his own individual 3-day luau - at the Reptile House. Didn't seem to realize (or mind) that there was no roast-pig. Bye-bye, Johnnyboy, understand you're about fed-up on hulas, anyway.

The Snake Ranch (enlisted men's beer hall) was regularly featured or mentioned in Hickam Field's newspaper.

The sports program provided the men at Hickam Field with yet another off-duty activity. In many units, participation in sports was also a regularly scheduled requirement for assigned personnel several times a week during duty hours. Athletes from "Bomberland" (as Hickam was sometimes called) soon made their mark in the Hawaiian Department by winning many interservice and local competitions. The athletic program, set in motion before the last man had vacated old Luke Field, had its first basketball team competing in the Sector Navy League before Hickam was three months old. In the first two years of participation in service sports within the Hawaiian Department, Hickam Field teams won seven major titles in track, baseball, and basketball.[26]

Irrepressible Joe Brimm, Hickam Field artist, obviously took great delight in his work, which vexed the chaplain but endeared him to his buddies. (Toni Gunn Rafferty)

Sports coverage was a major part of *Hickam News* (later renamed *Hickam Highlights*), the base newspaper. In the initial issue published on 15 March 1940, a message from Chaplain James C. Bean stated:

> Hats off to our efficient Base S-2 [intelligence officer] for having the foresight and initiative to see that what this field needed most next to a good five cent cigar is a good news sheet. No matter what they print, as long as it is news, it will add to our acquaintance with the set-up of the field, the current situation of this war, and our acquaintance with each other. Let this letter form the official commendation and blessing of the Base Chaplain.[27]

When talented PFC W. J. (Joe) Brimm later assumed duty as art editor, his drawings of buxom, scantily clad women began appearing on the covers and many inside pages of the base paper. He also added the personal touch of including recognizable drawings of known enlisted men in his cartoons, along with the seductive *wahines* (the word for "women" in Hawaiian). This incurred the wrath of the base chaplain, who repeatedly went to the base commander to complain that Joe was corrupting the morals of personnel on the base. Joe would then put a few more clothes on the women for a while but invariably drifted back to the kind of art that he and his friends liked best.[28]

All was not fun and games, however, for the war situation in Europe had made it evident that an immediate expansion of American air power was vitally needed; and this affected air activity in the Hawaiian Islands. In the spring of 1941, the allocation of a greater number of heavy bombers to the Hawaiian Air Force than to any other overseas garrison was an indication of growing concern over the

Front cover of *Hickam Highlights* (Vol 9, Nr 23, 14 November 1942).

possibility of war in the Pacific. The first mass flight of 21 B-17Ds took off from Hamilton Field, California, on 13 May 1941 and landed at Hickam Field the next morning after an average elapsed time of 13 hours and 10 minutes. Members of the Hawaiian Air Force, who had never flown heavy bombers, began to receive intensive instructions from crew members of the 19th Bombardment Group who had ferried the aircraft to Hawaii.[29]

In the fall of 1941, a War Department decision to send reinforcements to the Philippines adversely affected the ability of the Hawaiian Air Force to perform its mission by assigning a lower priority in allocation of aircraft and requiring a diversion of some of its strength. On 5 September 1941, nine of the Hawaiian Air Force's B-17Ds and 75 crew members under the command of Maj Emmett O'Donnell, Jr., took off from Hickam for Clark Field in the first flight of land-based bombers across the central Pacific. Successful completion of this historic flight proved that the Philippines could be reinforced by air.[30]

On 27 October 1941, Col William E. Farthing assumed command of Hickam Field from Brig Gen Jacob H. Rudolph, who was reassigned as commander of the 18th Bombardment Wing. As base commander, Colonel Farthing managed housekeeping functions, while General Rudolph had the responsibility for tactical defense of the field. As relations between the United States and Japan continued to deteriorate, squadron commanders at Hickam were concerned about their crews being trained and meeting certain essential requirements. Capt Russell L. Waldron, commander of the 31st Bomb Squadron, was particularly frustrated about not having enough people for his gunnery and other combat crew

positions because the Hawaiian Department was demanding that he provide these men for guard duty around warehouses and other facilities in Honolulu.[31]

On Saturday, 6 December, word soon spread through the base that the exercise was over and all restrictions had been lifted. Ira W. Southern, who was on duty that afternoon as Charge of Quarters for the 17th Air Base Group, was busy for two or three hours handing out passes and taking phone calls inquiring about whether the alert was lifted or "Is there a pass for me?" Russell Tener of the 18th Bomb Wing went to Pearl Harbor with Tom Martin, Bill Enos, Stanley Toye, and Lou Kirchner to see the "Battle of Music." He had a proud feeling when the band from the USS *Pennsylvania* (his home state) won the contest. Second-place honors went to the band from the USS *Arizona*.[32]

The Hickam Officers' Club was filled with the usual Saturday night crowd. Lieutenant Gray and 1st Lt Donovan D. Smart finally received the white coats they had ordered from The Hub, a men's store in downtown Honolulu, so they got dates, rented a car, and attended a dinner-dance at the club. Captain and Mrs. Waldron "and probably three-fourths of the pilots who were officers" were also there at a big party. The waitresses serving refreshments that night were, ironically, clad in colorful Japanese kimonos.* A good time was had by all, and it was not until the early hours of the morning that the partygoers finally left to go home, looking forward to sleeping late that Sunday morning, 7 December 1941.[33]

_____

*Information received from Mrs. Yukie Yamashiro, one of the Japanese waitresses working that night at the club, who is the aunt of co-author Leatrice R. Arakaki.

CHAPTER III

ASSIGNMENT PARADISE: FIGHTER COMMAND

"Actually Hawaii turned out to be a great assignment. There was a nice social life, and if you had a good sergeant to handle your ground duties you could fly in the morning and be on the beach in the afternoon. War really messed up the whole thing."

2d Lt Charles E. Taylor, 6th Pursuit Squadron
(*The Pineapple Air Force*, 1990)

Just as Hickam Field was the Hawaiian Air Force's bomber base, Wheeler Field was its fighter base. Periodically, assigned aviators and aircraft would deploy to Bellows Field in Waimanalo or to Haleiwa Field on the north shore for gunnery training.

Wheeler Field

Named in honor of Maj Sheldon H. Wheeler, former commander of Luke Field who died in a plane crash on 13 July 1921, this was the second air station established in the Hawaiian Department. It was located on the old 17th Cavalry drill grounds at Schofield Barracks in central Oahu, bounded on the north by the Oahu Railway, on the east by the main road to Schofield Barracks, and on the west and south by gulches.[1]

Construction of Wheeler Field began on 6 February 1922 under the direction of 1st Lt William T. Agee of the 4th Squadron (Observation), who departed Luke Field with 20 men to start clearing away trees and undergrowth. Within a month, they had completed a landing strip sufficient to handle the relatively slow and light aircraft of the time; and by 30 June 1923, hangars and storage tanks had been built. Originally called the Hawaiian Divisional Air Service Flying Field, this airdrome at Schofield was renamed in honor of Major Wheeler on 11 November 1922. Maj George E. Stratemeyer became the first post commander on the day that construction commenced.[2]

Maj Sheldon Harley Wheeler (1889-1921)

Above, Wheeler Field, before completion of permanent hangars, when it was still part of
Schofield Barracks (circa 1922-1923). And, below, Wheeler, with hangars in place, as well
as barracks, family housing, and other buildings (23 January 1936).

On 10 November 1926, the Hawaiian Department commander appointed a board of officers to study the needs of the Department in connection with the Air Corps Five-Year Program. Three months later, the board recommended the expansion of Wheeler Field into a 400-acre parcel of land immediately east of old Wheeler Field, in a triangle formed by Wahiawa Road, Schofield Road, and the existing Wheeler Field boundary. By 1934, construction had been completed on hangars and other technical structures, family quarters, barracks, and a number of other facilities.[3]

Wheeler Field became the center of world interest in the 1920s and 1930s as the site of several highly significant achievements in aviation history. On 29 June 1927, Army 1st Lts Lester J. Maitland and Albert F. Hegenberger completed the first nonstop Mainland-to-Hawaii flight from Oakland, California, to Wheeler Field in a Fokker C-2 trimotor airplane called the "Bird of Paradise." Two months later, on 17 August, Arthur Goebel and Martin Jensen landed their tiny planes at Wheeler Field as winners of the Dole Derby, an air race from California to Hawaii. On 1 June 1928, Australian Squadron Leader Charles E. Kingsford-Smith landed his Fokker monoplane "Southern Cross" at Wheeler on the first leg of his pioneer trans-Pacific flight from Oakland, California, to Brisbane, Australia, by way of Hawaii and Fiji. Amelia Earhart departed from Wheeler Field in her Lockheed Vega on 11 January 1935 and successfully completed the first solo flight from Hawaii to the mainland in 18 hours and 16 minutes, landing at Oakland, California.[4]

On 5 August 1939, the War Department issued General Orders No. 4

reassigning 1,427.81 acres of Schofield Barracks land to Wheeler Field. Less than four weeks later, on 31 August 1939, it became a separate permanent military post. By this time, the air base had mushroomed into a large and productive facility. Many steel and wooden hangars as well as machine and repair shops had been constructed, and combat units stationed there conducted intensive training throughout the year. For aerial gunnery training, they went to Bellows Field, which had been attached to Wheeler for administrative support since 15 September 1930. Until Bellows became a separate military post on 22 July 1941, Wheeler provided all the manpower, equipment, and supplies required to operate that installation.[5]

On 1 November 1940, the 14th Pursuit Wing activated at Wheeler Field. Assigned units included the 18th Pursuit Group (Interceptor) with its 6th, 19th, 44th, 73d, and 78th Pursuit Squadrons; and the 15th Pursuit Group (Fighter) with the 45th, 46th, and 47th Pursuit Squadrons assigned initially, then augmented later by the assignment of the 72d Pursuit Squadron on 5 October 1941. Other organizations at Wheeler included the 18th Air Base Group (with its 17th Air Base Squadron and the 24th and 25th Materiel Squadrons) as well as various quartermaster, signal, ordnance, and service units.[6]

In February 1941, the Hawaiian Air Force received its greatest single increase in assigned aircraft since its activation. Thirty-one P-36s, with pilots and crew chiefs, sailed aboard the carrier *Enterprise* from San Diego to the Hawaiian Islands, arriving shortly after daylight on 21 February. While the ship was still some 10 to 15 miles off the coast of Oahu, the

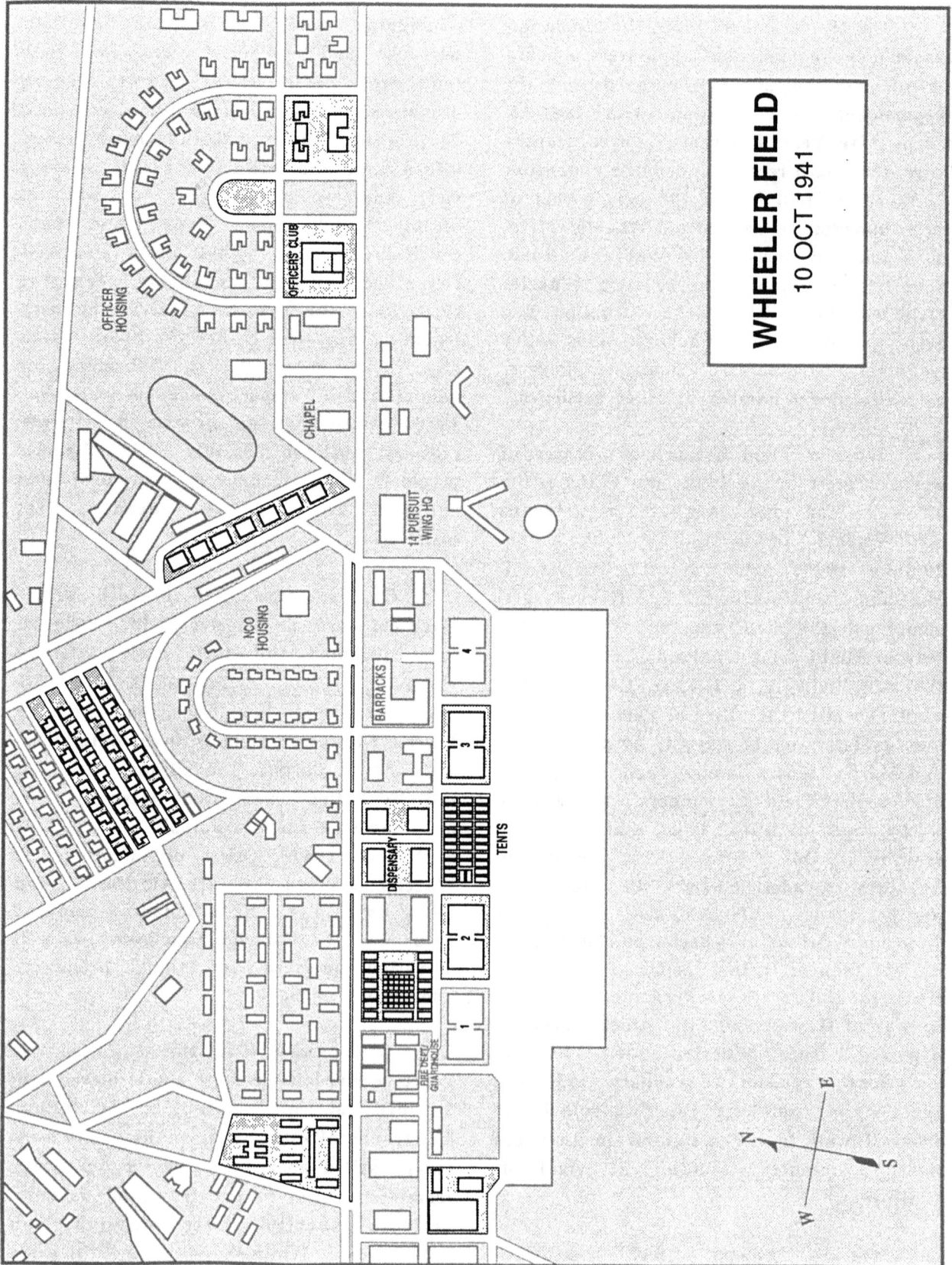

WHEELER FIELD
10 OCT 1941

Above, engineering buildings and parachute shop; left, the flight line; and, below, the fire station at Wheeler in 1940. (Vincent T. Ryan)

planes took off in groups of three from the carrier's broad deck and flew directly to their Wheeler Field destination. This launching of Army fighters from the deck of an aircraft carrier was a historic "first" in military aviation. Led by flight commander Maj George P. Tourtellot, the P-36s were a spectacular sight as they whisked in, three by three, effecting precise and perfect landings. They taxied in front of the hangars and drew up to form a line. Col Harvey S. Burwell, Wheeler's commanding officer, strode to the side of the flight leader's plane to offer his aloha and to extend his post's hospitality. Major Tourtellot returned to the mainland aboard the *Enterprise* the next day, but the 30 pilots who flew in the other planes were absorbed within units of Wheeler's expanding pursuit wing.   Among   the   arriving   pilots   were 1st Lts Kermit A. Tyler and Lewis M. Sanders, 2d Lts George S. Welch, Othneil Norris, John M. Thacker, and George A. Whiteman—who were all destined to have key roles in the drama that unfolded during the Japanese attack on 7 December 1941.[7]

Within the next two months, more modern pursuit planes began arriving. In March 1941, Wheeler pilots welcomed sleek new Curtiss P-40Bs that had come right off the assembly line. They had a top speed of 352 miles per hour, compared to 314 for the P-36 and 234 for the P-26, and also mounted six machine guns while the older pursuits had only two. Those units still operating P-26s were the first to get the new fighters. By mid-April, there were 55 P-40s in the inventory, and more arrived during the ensuing months until the Hawaiian Air Force had a total of 99 P-40 aircraft assigned.[8]

Intensive training became a way of life for the pilots. Lieutenant Sanders, who

had been appointed commander of the 46th Squadron, cautioned his men to "Learn something every time you fly. There's a war coming on. I don't know just when, but knowing what you're doing is your life insurance." Air raid alerts became a regular part of the flying routine, and between March and October 1941 assigned personnel participated in seven exercises, two of which were alerts directed by Washington. The intense training took its toll in flying mishaps that resulted in a number of deaths and serious injuries, but it was the younger, inexperienced pilots who usually made up the accident statistics.[9]

It took good pilots to fly the modern military warplanes, but it also took other men, just as good in their own line of work, to keep those planes flying. The mechanics, sheet metal workers, and other unheralded ground support personnel were conscientious and serious about their responsibility to insure safe and efficient flying at all times. Edward J. White, a young recruit from Concord, New Hampshire, learned this firsthand. When he arrived in Hawaii after sailing from New York aboard the *Chateau Thierry*, he and other Army Air Forces personnel assembled at the pier for roll call. Those with last names from "A" to "part of the S" went to Hickam Field, while he and others in the remaining group were put on the "Oahu Express" train and transported to Wheeler. After completing basic training, they were interviewed for the duty they desired.   Most of the men wanted to be aircraft mechanics, but Ed White chose sheet metal work instead and was assigned to the 18th Air Base Group's sheet metal shop at base engineering.[10]

Capt Jack Gibbs, the base engineering officer, was well liked by his men; and SSgt "Ace" Snodgrass, who ran the sheet metal

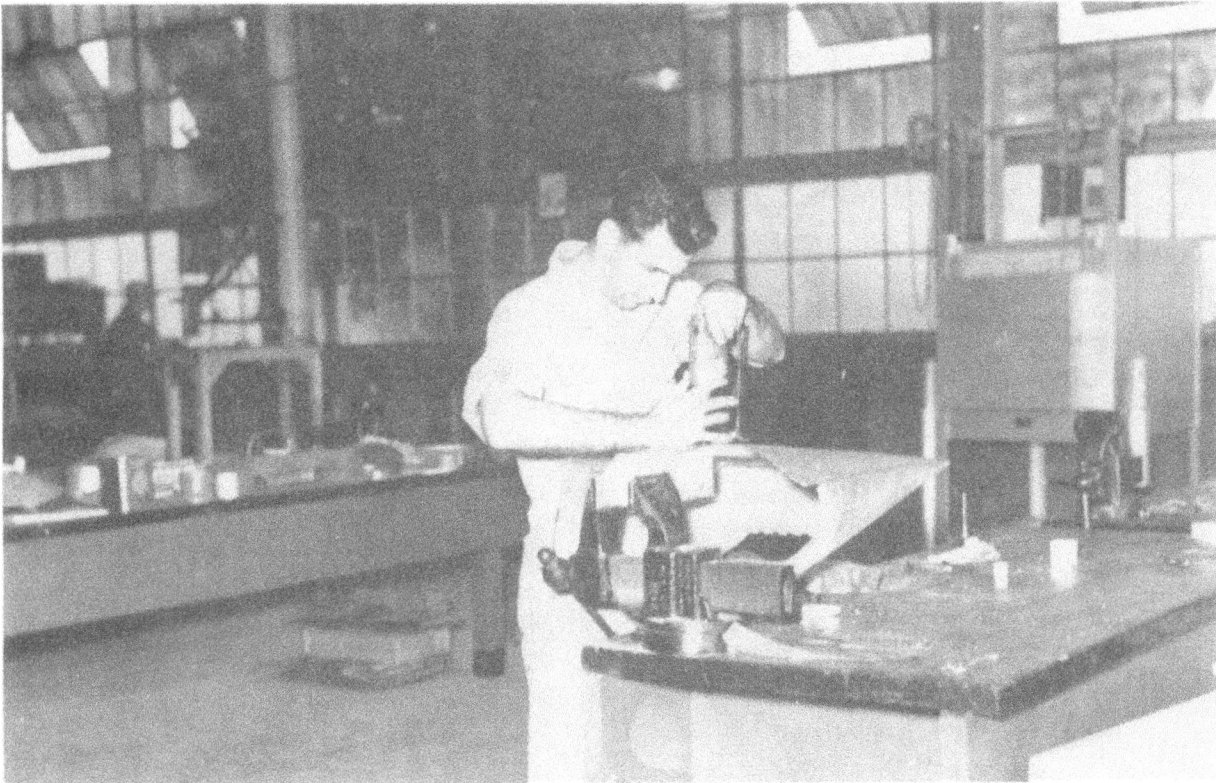

PFC Edward J. White in Sheet Metal Shop at Wheeler Field, 1940.

shop, was highly respected. The Wheeler shop was unique because of the depot-level work accomplished there, far above and beyond that normally expected of an airfield sheet metal shop. Sergeant Snodgrass, known as "a natural born mechanic [who] could do almost anything," conducted a school for those interested in learning about aircraft sheet metal. This was not compulsory, but those who attended qualified as aircraft mechanics; and their "AM rating" entitled them to the same pay as a staff sergeant, regardless of whether they wore private, private first class, corporal, or sergeant stripes. When they attained the rank of staff sergeant, they lost the AM rating but received the same pay. The maintenance of their planes was of prime concern to these men, and they took great pride in their work. White recalled a new apprentice completing a job

and saying, "Oh, it's good enough." He was quickly asked, "Would you want your life hanging on that repair you're making?" When he answered, "No," he was told, "If it isn't good enough for you, it's not good enough for anyone either—fix it right."[11]

The enlisted troops were extremely serious about their work but managed to have their share of fun and found ingenious ways to make life more comfortable for themselves. In 1940 for example, following the big Thanksgiving dinner for enlisted personnel, held in the final assembly hangar, the men knew that the mess fund had been hit hard for this lavish feast and they could expect only sparse meals for the next few days. Unwilling to suffer such a cruel fate, they raided the hangar and took the leftover food to the sheet metal shop, keeping it refrigerated in a container that

Left, Thanksgiving feast in the final assembly hangar at Wheeler Field, 21 November 1940 (Edward J. White). Below, the dinner menu, with "Cigars" and "Cigarettes" listed right after the desserts. (Donated by W. W. Collins and Douglas Van Valkenburgh)

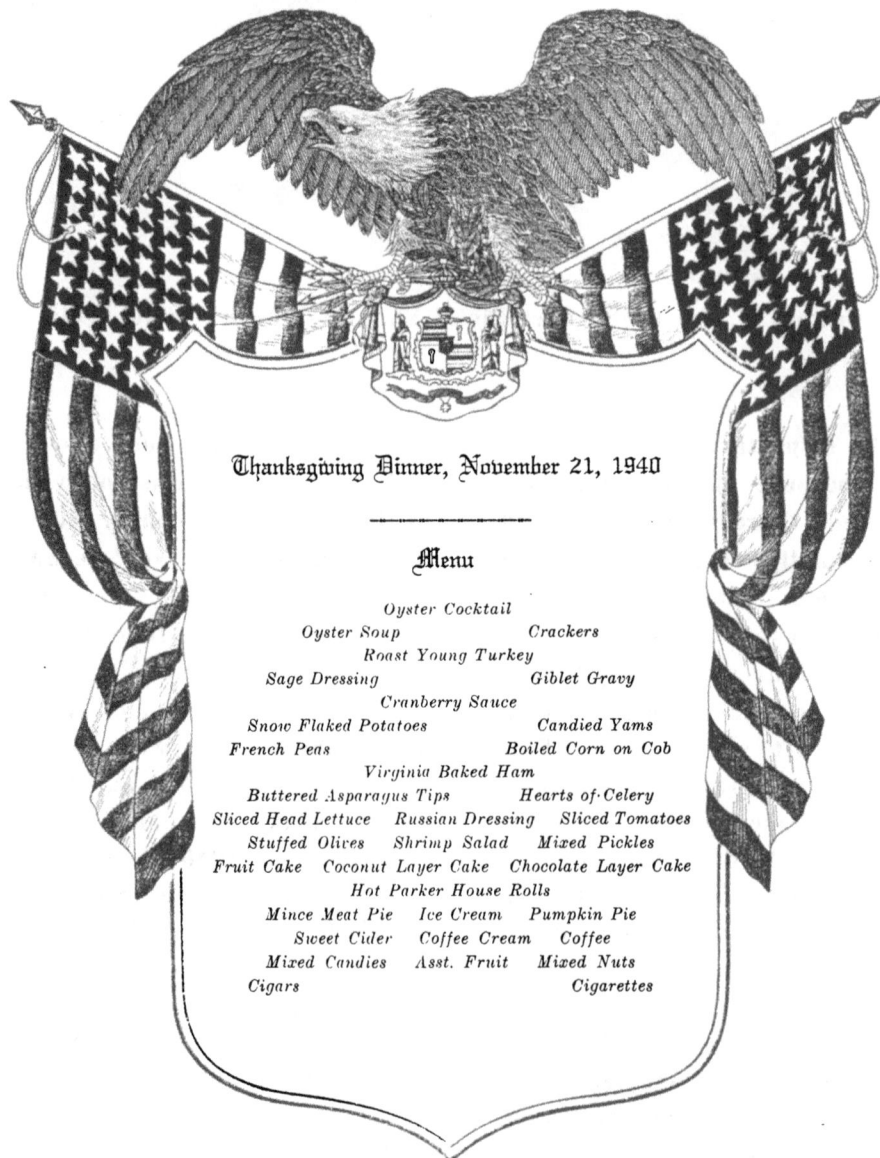

Thanksgiving Dinner, November 21, 1940

Menu

Oyster Cocktail
Oyster Soup   Crackers
Roast Young Turkey
Sage Dressing   Giblet Gravy
Cranberry Sauce
Snow Flaked Potatoes   Candied Yams
French Peas   Boiled Corn on Cob
Virginia Baked Ham
Buttered Asparagus Tips   Hearts of·Celery
Sliced Head Lettuce   Russian Dressing   Sliced Tomatoes
Stuffed Olives   Shrimp Salad   Mixed Pickles
Fruit Cake   Coconut Layer Cake   Chocolate Layer Cake
Hot Parker House Rolls
Mince Meat Pie   Ice Cream   Pumpkin Pie
Sweet Cider   Coffee Cream   Coffee
Mixed Candies   Asst. Fruit   Mixed Nuts
Cigars   Cigarettes

held Dry Ice. For the next few days, instead of going to the mess hall, they heated and ate the roast turkey. Using an oven in the shop that was set at 1200 degrees for heat treating aluminum alloy, they placed the turkey on a piece of aluminum, with one man raising the oven door and another shoving the turkey in for a count of eight to ten, then pulling it out. The system worked well, and the men enjoyed a second, third, and fourth Thanksgiving that year.[12]

During their off-duty time, Wheeler personnel enjoyed the same recreational activities and places of interest as their counterparts at Hickam Field. In addition, they patronized many of the restaurants and bars in nearby Wahiawa, Hawaii's second largest city. Especially popular was Kemoo Farm Restaurant located across the street from Schofield Barracks' Funston Gate. It was a common sight to see long lines of people waiting to dine in the eucalyptus-framed building overlooking Lake Wilson. On Sundays, buck privates and generals alike would line up outside the restaurant door for a home-style breakfast of pancakes and waffles.[13]

As war clouds gathered over the Pacific and the intensity of alerts, exercises, and other training activities increased, Hawaii's military community as a whole still maintained a peacetime mentality and continued to operate with a business-as-usual attitude. On 7 August, just four months before the blitz, Wheeler Field held a big "GALADAY" to commemorate the dedication of the Wheeler Field airdrome and post office. The program included a welcome by General Davidson, 14th Pursuit Wing commander; presentation to the wing commander of the key to the new post office by Mr. Albert P. Lino, Postmaster of

Dance held in the consolidated mess at Wheeler Field, sponsored by the 18th Air Base Group, circa 1940-1941.
(W. Bruce Harlow)

Honolulu; presentation of athletic awards and trophies, an aerial demonstration, and an all-star baseball game. Incredibly, the public was invited to visit Wheeler for this occasion, unrestricted except for a ban against cameras. Needless to say, "Tadashi Morimura" (alias of Takeo Yoshikawa, a trained intelligence agent who was the Japanese Navy's top spy) took advantage of the invitation and wandered freely around Wheeler Field, missing nothing. He watched the P-40s in flight, observing that "they were very fast" and the pilots' "flight technique most skillful." He noted such things as the number of hangars, direction of runways, their length and width, and the fact that three aircraft took off at once, then recorded his observations when he returned to the Japanese consulate.[14]

On 27 October 1941, Col William J. Flood assumed duty as post commander of Wheeler Field from General Davidson, who retained tactical responsibilities as

Active participants in Wheeler's sports program: Members of the 46th Pursuit Squadron's championship basketball team, pictured here with Athletic Officer Lt Bill Southerland, circa 1940-1941. (Clarence Kindl)

commander of the 14th Pursuit Wing. With the buildup of men and planes in the Hawaiian Air Force, a housing shortage surfaced. A wooden barracks was hastily erected for junior bachelor officers, and many enlisted men were billeted in tents located between Hangars 2 and 3 along the flight line.[15]

In late November, Colonel Flood reported to General Martin's office, along with the other base and tactical commanders, was briefed on a message outlining the strained relations between the Japanese and the United States, and instructed to implement Alert One for sabotage. Earlier, earthen bunkers had been built all around Wheeler for about 125 aircraft so they would be suitably dispersed and protected from air attack. Colonel Flood asked if he could keep the aircraft dispersed, but General Short disapproved his request. He therefore had all the aircraft pulled in and parked together on the ramp, then increased the guards around the aircraft and around the perimeter of the field.[16]

On Saturday, 6 December, following a classic peacetime parade, all but essential Wheeler personnel received the weekend off. The aircraft of all but two squadrons, however, remained lined up on the ramp in front of the hangars. The 47th Squadron was at Haleiwa Field on the north shore and the 44th Squadron was at Bellows Field in Waimanalo for gunnery practice. The officers and enlisted men at Haleiwa and Bellows, who had their fill of the primitive living conditions, lost no time heading back to Wheeler for a hot shower and a night of partying at the Officers' Club or in Honolulu.[17]

Above, Tent City, located between Hangars 2 and 3, along the Wheeler Field flight line. (Harry P. Kilpatrick).

Below, Cpl William H. Roach, 45th Pursuit Squadron, in front of his tent quarters on Wheeler's hangar row.

Bellows Field

Originally called the Waimanalo Military Reservation when established by Presidential Executive Order in 1917, Bellows Field was renamed in 1933 in honor of 2d Lt Franklin B. Bellows, a World War I hero who was killed in action near St. Mihiel, France. This 1,500-acre installation on the southeast coast of Oahu, located about five miles south of what was then called the Kaneohe Naval Air Station, had Waimanalo Bay bordering its eastern perimeter and Waimanalo town to the southwest. Wailea Point marked its northern boundary along the seacoast, with the sugar mill village of Lanikai extending above.[18]

Bellows Field occupied a stretch of white coral sand and rock that varied from 10 to 20 feet above sea level, with a central knoll about 55 feet high. Near the northern boundary, a rise of volcanic rock jutted into the sea and formed Wailea Point. Approximately three miles from shore, the Koolau Mountains ran northeast to

2d Lt Franklin Barney Bellows (1896-1918)
(Wilmette Historical Museum, Illinois)

southwest as a solid wall back of the reservation, with rich sugar cane acreage and some marshland stretching between the sandy shore and the steep slopes of the mountains. Rainfall was abundant, and dust was not a problem despite the strong prevailing winds.[19]

At first, Bellows was a satellite of Wheeler Field and served as a training camp, providing a bivouac area for the Infantry, a target practice area for the Coast Artillery, and a strafing and bombing practice range for the Army Air Forces. Sugar cane and guava bushes covered the land except where cleared away for training areas and for tents in which the men slept while at Bellows for gunnery training. There was also a single asphalt runway, 75 feet wide and only 983 feet long (later lengthened to 3,800 feet), and a wooden air traffic control tower.[20]

In early 1941, the small group of enlisted men who maintained the installation were members of the 18th Air Base Group at Wheeler but on detached service at Bellows, under the supervision of TSgt Salvatore Torre, the first Bellows camp commander. They were primarily responsible for base maintenance, which included upkeep of the rifle pits, pistol range, and strafing targets. In addition, they monitored the use of barbecue pits and shelters along the beach.[21]

The beach at Bellows was one of the finest on the island and a favorite picnic ground and swimming spot where Hickam and Wheeler Field personnel frequently spent their free time. There were also reports of "good pheasant hunting from the beach to the mountains" (although the legality of this activity was never mentioned).[22]

Aerial view of Bellows Field, 27 October 1941

As the commanding officer, Sergeant Torre lived in a small stone building, which was the only permanent structure on the installation at the time. The other assigned personnel lived in tents set on wooden frames located in a flat grassy area lined with palm trees. There were two rows of about 30 tents, with the entrances to the tents facing each other and separated by perhaps a hundred feet. This open space was used as the squadron formation area. At the south end was the mess hall, a wooden building which also served double duty as the dayroom. Behind the west row of tents was a latrine and shower facility, a little further north was the guard house, and on top of "Headquarters Hill" was the officers' club. A small two-room shack nearby served as the dispensary. The focal point of activities at Bellows was the operations shack located at the bottom of the hill adjacent to the flight line. It served as a combination radio room and armament facility.[23]

March 1941 marked the beginning of many changes and a program of expansion at Bellows. On 23 March, Lt Col W. V. Andrews succeeded Sergeant Torre as camp commander. During the month, both the 86th Observation Squadron with its O-47B aircraft and the 58th Bombardment Squadron with B-18s moved from Wheeler Field to Bellows. A month later, on 29 April, the 58th Bomb Squadron transferred to Hickam Field, because its newly assigned A-20 aircraft could not be accommodated with the facilities existing at Bellows. Squadron

Above, tent area at Bellows Field, 1940. (Gene Taylor)

Below, headquarters building at Bellows in 1941. (Jean K. Lambert)

Operations shack at Bellows, located at the bottom of "Headquarters Hill" and adjacent to the flight line.

personnel at first hated their new duty station at Bellows. The tents which housed them were old and rotten, so equipment and personal belongings sometimes suffered considerable damage during heavy rainfall. Hordes of mosquitoes that bred in cane field ditches around the camp made life miserable and caused Colonel Andrews to issue orders on 26 March 1941 decreeing that "between retreat and reveille the members of the guard, while on post, will wear the campaign hat and mosquito headnet."[24]

Despite the discomfort and inconveniences, morale remained high and the men gradually began to enjoy their Bellows assignment. Cpl Chuck Fry of the 86th Observation Squadron found that "living was quite pleasant, with good food, excellent beach for swimming and walking, and perhaps a 30-40 minute ride to Waikiki in Honolulu when you were off-duty." Transportation was scarce in those days,

however, so the men spent most of their off-duty hours on the base or in the adjacent community of Waimanalo, where they had limited use of the tennis courts and the gymnasium. Participation in sports competitions between officers and enlisted men also filled much of their leisure time; and with an outstanding beach in their own backyard, most personnel sported a fine suntan and generally maintained a good physical condition. A unique one-time benefit enjoyed by Bellows personnel on 11 June 1941 was an extra day off in memory of King Kamehameha I. This was a legal holiday observed by the Territory of Hawaii; and Bellows published General Orders No. 5 proclaiming Kamehameha Day a holiday for Bellows Field also, "with all activities suspended except for necessary guard and police duties."[25]

Members of the 86th Observation Squadron bore the brunt of guard and fatigue duties at Bellows Field during the summer and fall of 1941. With pick-and-shovel labor, they moved tons of coral to level off several shoulders of land for field operations. The squadron's communications personnel laid several miles of telephone wire for the base system, but grass cutters continually severed these wires, adding to the headaches of the communicators. The primary function of the 86th Observation Squadron, however, was air-ground liaison work, and assigned personnel received numerous commendations for their cooperation and spirit in supporting the ground forces' maneuvers. On 14 June 1941, seven new officers reported to the squadron for observation training, to fill a requirement for trained observers to participate in forthcoming maneuvers. Several squadron members, on the other hand, went to Wheeler Field for their training at radio, photography, and clerical schools, while others attended the mechanics and armament schools at Hickam Field.[26]

On 22 July 1941, Bellows Field became a separate permanent military post under the jurisdiction of the Commanding General, Hawaiian Department; and Wheeler Field was relieved of any further responsibility for its operation. Three days later, on 25 July, Colonel Andrews' official title changed from camp commander to base commanding officer.[27]

An accelerated construction program began. A contractor moved in south of the tent billeting area to build two-story wooden barracks around a large oval area, with orderly rooms and supply and other buildings located in the center of that oval. Bachelor officer quarters and many other structures seemed to spring up overnight, and work also started on a new and bigger runway. The barracks facilities were finished first, and assigned personnel moved into them in the fall of 1941. During the first week of December, a civilian contractor began work on a project to install a sanitary system. Using a trenching

An O-47B aircraft of the 86th Observation Squadron at Bellows Field in 1941. (William E. Simshauser)

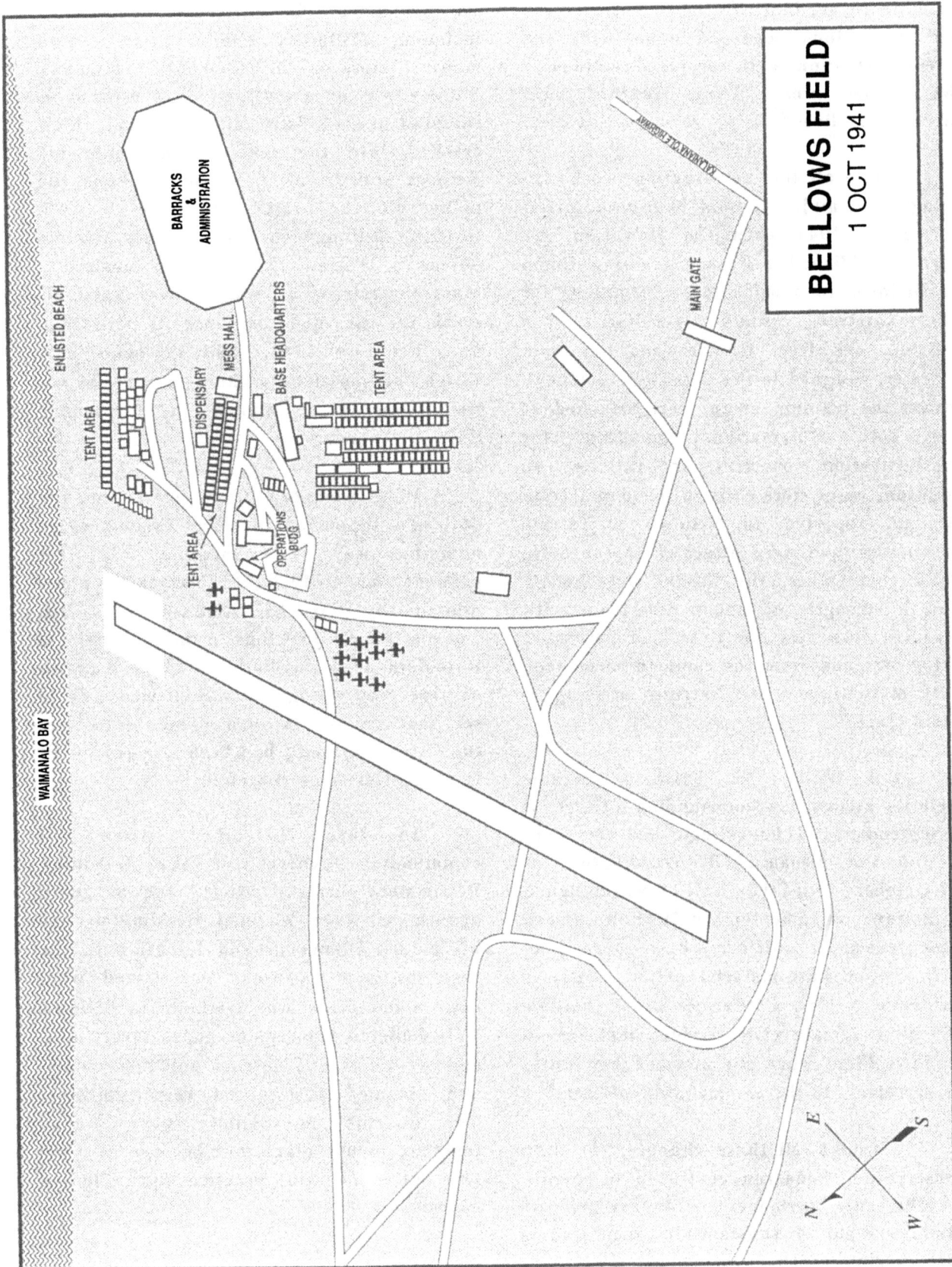

BELLOWS FIELD
1 OCT 1941

machine to dig into the sandy soil, he soon had excavations about 24 inches wide and 4 feet deep running in various directions in the bivouac area. These trenches later saved many lives.[28]

While all this construction work was going on, a major mission change occurred in August 1941 when the Hawaiian Air Force established a Casual Training Camp at Bellows to provide basic training for newly arrived casuals (recruits). Ten enlisted men from Hickam and ten from Wheeler, assigned to the Casual Detachment to run the training camp, were attached to the 86th Observation Squadron for administration, quarters, and rations. In addition, eight more enlisted personnel from Hickam reported to Bellows as recruit instructors and were attached to the 86th. By 27 September, the Casual Detachment had a strength of about 500 men, with frequent turnovers due to trained personnel being assigned from the camp to permanent duty stations and new recruits arriving in their place.[29]

Col William E. Farthing became Bellows Field's new commanding officer on 1 September 1941 but relinquished command to Lt Col Leonard D. Weddington on 27 October. Maj Clyde K. Rich was assigned to Bellows on 15 September 1941 and named base executive officer, base operations officer, and base materiel officer. Also in September, Mrs. Catherine Brush became the first female civil service employee at Bellows Field when she assumed her duties as secretary to the commanding officer.[30]

Through all these changes, the 86th Observation Squadron continued to operate as the only permanent unit assigned to Bellows Field. It substantially increased in size, beginning on 13 September 1941 with the assignment of 25 second lieutenants, including Millard C. Shibley, Jr. Two months later, on 17 November, Lieutenant Shibley was on a routine patrol mission as the pilot of O-47B aircraft No. 39-84, which crashed into the sea one-half mile off Bellows shortly after takeoff. When the plane hit the water, it broke in two, instantly killing Lieutenant Shibley and his observer, Warren French of Swampscott, Massachusetts. This was the first fatal air crash for the squadron since its activation on 1 February 1940. Bellows' main gate, which led directly to the tent area at the time, was later named in Lieutenant Shibley's honor.[31]

In addition to military operations, the 86th also supported the local community in numerous ways. In November 1941, for example, an O-49 light observation plane piloted by 1st Lt Richard L. Allen transported Santa Claus to the polo field at Kapiolani Park in Waikiki, where a crowd of wide-eyed youngsters waited anxiously to see Santa arrive in an airplane. This was the first time Santa had been brought by air to the children of Honolulu.[32]

In late November, when the commanding general of the Hawaiian Department ordered Alert One to guard against sabotage, Colonel Weddington had his trained 50-man ground defense unit take their assigned positions and issued what little ammunition was available at Bellows. This depleted the regular guard force, however, so the ground defense unit reorganized and assumed post guard responsibilities. The aircraft at Bellows were parked together in one place, not because of Alert One but as a routine practice due to limited space.[33]

Above, the main gate at Bellows Field, named in honor of 2d Lt Millard C. Shibley, Jr., who died in an O-47B plane crash on 17 November 1941.

Below, one of two O-49 aircraft at Bellows Field in 1941. This was the type of plane used to bring Santa Claus by air to the children of Honolulu for the first time in November 1941. (John J. Lennon)

Earlier, beginning on 7 November 1941, personnel and P-40s of the 44th Pursuit Squadron (Interceptor) at Wheeler Field began deploying to Bellows for a month's aerial gunnery training. This involved the squadron's twelve P-40 aircraft and a complement of crew chiefs, assistants, armorers, radio men, and other support troops. They flew a practice mission on Saturday, 6 December, but did not immediately refuel their aircraft afterward. This was in line with the normal practice of the various squadrons conducting aerial gunnery training at Bellows. When they finished on a Saturday afternoon, they usually waited until Sunday to refuel their airplanes. Also, during the week, they normally cleaned the guns on the aircraft and armed them the next morning when they were ready to go; however, on Saturday afternoons, they removed the guns from the aircraft to do a more thorough job of cleaning. Consequently, on 7 December 1941, the P-40s at Bellows were parked wing-to-wing, low on fuel, and some had their guns removed.[34]

On Saturday evening, 6 December, the week-long exercise was completed. This meant a reduction of restrictions, with 50 percent of personnel allowed passes. Most of the 44th Pursuit Squadron's officers returned to their home base at Wheeler Field to enjoy the remainder of the weekend with their families. Only four of the officers remained at Bellows.[35]

Howard Taylor, who was the Provost Sergeant and responsible for ground defense of Bellows recalled: "We had .50-calibre, .30-calibre, and 20-mm artillery for perimeter overhead defense, and heavy artillery on beaches. On Saturday, 6 December, we were told to take down all arms and lock [them] in [the] Armory and take our passes to Honolulu." Cpl Clarence McKinley of the Signal Section was one of the many who went to town on pass Saturday night. He returned to Bellows about two o'clock in the morning on Sunday, 7 December, and went to bed in his tent.[36]

CHAPTER IV

7 DECEMBER 1941: A DAY THAT WILL LIVE IN INFAMY

"All the publicity is 'Remember Pearl Harbor.' They should take a look at Hickam Field or what was Hickam Field. Twenty-seven bombs hit the main barracks. They dropped about 100 bombs on Hickam, practically all hits. The papers say they are poor bombardiers! They were perfect on nearly all their releases."

Charles P. Eckhert, Major, Army Air Forces, 10 December 1941.

At approximately 0755 on 7 December 1941 the first Japanese aircraft struck the Territory of Hawaii. In less than two hours they inflicted upon the Hawaiian Air Force the most terrible destruction it had ever received. All the anti-saboteur alerts, mock battles, and practice deployments proved to be of no avail during the actual attack. Only the individual courage and sacrifice of personnel acting in fear and desperation prevented the Japanese from completely destroying the Army Air Forces on Oahu.

The Japanese Attack

The Japanese planned to hit Pearl Harbor just after sunrise on a Sunday morning. They reasoned, correctly, that defenses would be at their weakest at this time due to the American tradition of taking Sunday as a rest day. The attack's primary purpose was to inflict sufficient damage on the US Fleet so it would be unable to interfere with their conquest plans in the Pacific for at least six months. Six carriers—the *Akagi, Kaga, Soryu, Hiryu, Shokaku,* and *Zuikaku*—would transport a

360-aircraft* attack force to a point 220 miles north of Oahu. The Japanese believed their carriers, concealed by darkness during the final approach, could steam no closer without risk of being spotted by American reconnaissance aircraft. So worried were they about the air defenses on Oahu, they committed over a third of the attacking aircraft just to provide air cover for the remaining force. Another 39 aircraft would take off and fly top cover for the carrier force, just in case the Americans tried to attack.[1]

Three types of aircraft were used in the attack: 143 Nakajima Type 97 three-place bombers (B5N2 model 11), 129 Aichi Type 99 two-place dive bombers (D3A1 model 11), and 78 Mitsubishi Type 0

---

*Several publications, including the Congressional Investigation Report, give different figures for the number of aircraft used by the Japanese during the attack. Our thanks to David Aiken of Irving, Texas, for sharing his work in translating and interpreting the Japanese history series Senshi Sosho: Hawai Sakusen (BKS Vol 10), pp 596-616, which contains, we feel, the most accurate information on actual aircraft used in the attack.

To the left is the Japanese carrier *Akagi*, flagship of VAdm Chuichi Nagumo, who headed the task force which attacked military installations on Oahu. Above, a Nakajima B5N (Kate) bomber heading toward Pearl Harbor with its deadly load of bombs; and below, a Mitsubishi A6M2 (Zero) fighter launching from a carrier deck as the ship's crew waves and yells "Banzai!"

single-place fighters (A6M2 model 21).* The Nakajima was used with three different bomb loads. Forty aircraft were loaded with 800-kilogram modified torpedos for use against large naval targets. Another 49 Nakajimas were loaded with 800-kilogram, specially modified, armor-piercing 16-inch naval shells, also for use against large ships. The remaining 54 aircraft carried a mixed load; 18 had two 250-kilogram bombs for land targets, and 36 had one 250-kilogram and six 60-kilogram bombs, also for land targets. In addition each aircraft carried a hand-operated, rear-mounted, 7.7mm machine gun. The Nakajima delivered its bomb load primarily from the horizontal position, either at high altitude (around 10,000 feet) for those carrying the modified artillery shells or at low altitude (50 feet) for those with torpedoes. Bombers with multiple bomb loads could drop them either singly, in pairs, or all at once depending on the targets attacked.[2]

The Aichis carried a 250-kilogram land target bomb during the first attack and a 250-kilogram ordinary bomb for use against naval targets during the second attack. In addition, each aircraft could carry two 60-kilogram bombs under the wings. According to eyewitness accounts several dive bombers made multiple bombing runs, and these may have had the additional 60-kilogram bombs on board, although no Japanese records have been found supporting this claim. Each aircraft had two fuselage-mounted, forward-firing, 7.7mm machine guns and a hand-operated, rear-mounted, 7.7mm machine gun. After completing its bombing attack, the aircraft could make repeated strafing attacks.[3]

The Zeros were the Japanese Navy's best aircraft. On the morning of 7 December they could outmaneuver anything stationed on Oahu. Armed with two wing-mounted 20mm cannons and two 7.7mm machine guns mounted in the engine cowling, they also outgunned anything that would be sent up against them. Their primary job was to protect the other aircraft against American fighters. After gaining air superiority, or in case there was little to no fighter resistance, the Zero pilots were free to attack targets of opportunity anywhere on the island.[4]

Ideally, all the aircraft would strike their assigned targets simultaneously, thus assuring complete surprise. To launch and assemble that many aircraft in the dark would be difficult and would consume large quantities of fuel needed for the actual attack. The Japanese then modified the plan. Half the force, or 189 aircraft, would attack in the first wave and the remaining 171 would hit 30 minutes later. Thirty-nine fighters would take off and remain above the carriers to provide protection in case of attack. All the torpedo bombers were in the first wave because they were the most vulnerable and needed the surprise element to insure success. The launch was accomplished almost exactly according to plan. All the first wave aircraft except one horizontal bomber, three dive bombers, and two Zeros launched within fifteen minutes, a record for the Japanese. All the aborts from the first wave were for mechanical problems that developed prior to takeoff. The second wave, although delayed due to rough seas, made it off with the loss of only four aircraft. Two dive bombers aborted on takeoff, while one dive bomber and one Zero aborted for mechanical problems.[5]

Roughly twenty minutes ahead of this attacking armada flew two Zero type scout planes launched from the heavy cruisers *Chikuma* and *Tone*. It was their job to make last-minute observations of Pearl Harbor and the alternate fleet staging area at Lahaina, Maui, and notify Lt Cmdr Mitsuo Fuchida, airborne commander, of any changes. This meant breaking radio silence, but Fuchida considered this information so critical he was willing to take the chance that the Americans would not discover the scout aircraft. Not only were the scout planes spotted, five different radar stations on Oahu tracked one of them across the island. Unfortunately, these stations had no idea how important this contact was and did nothing about it. The scout planes encountered no opposition and radioed back that the weather over the target was clear, no ships were anchored at Lahaina, and no changes in the ships at Pearl Harbor had been made.

Just north of Kahuku Point the first wave formed into attack formations, turned west, and paralleled the island for several miles. On reaching the Haleiwa area, the force split into two groups. Fuchida took direct command of the horizontal bombers and the torpedo planes under the command of Lt Cmdr Shigeharu Murata and headed toward Kaena Point. Just short of the Point, Fuchida again changed direction, heading south, staying west of the Waianae Mountains. These two groups of aircraft split again before the actual attack on Pearl Harbor; so they hit the facility from the west and south. Other than uncoordinated strafing passes on Hickam Field and other targets of opportunity, none of these aircraft directly attacked the Hawaiian Air

Force facilities on Oahu; their targets were the Navy ships in the harbor.

Lt Cmdr Shigeru Itaya's fighters escorted various units including the dive bomber force under Lt Cmdr Kakuichi Takahashi. After separating from Fuchida, Takahashi's bombers flew straight down the center of Oahu, with the fighters providing top cover. Their route took them over Wheeler Field, where they divided and part of the force attacked the field from the east and west, while the rest continued on down the island to Hickam Field and Ford Island, where they again divided and attacked from several directions. From there they moved on to Pearl Harbor, Ford Island, and finally Ewa Field Auxiliary Base.

The first Hawaiian Air Force installation to be hit by this attacking force was Wheeler Field. Approaching the field from the north, the dive bombers split into two groups. Takahashi took 26 aircraft and continued south to hit Hickam and Ford Island, while Lt Akira Sakamoto took the remaining 25 into Wheeler. Part of Sakamoto's force turned west and then south, paralleling the Waianae Mountains until abreast of the base, then headed east and began diving on the base from the west. The rest of his aircraft turned east, then south, then west, and hit the field from the east. No one on the ground sighted these aircraft until they had made the final turn for the attack. Eyewitness accounts would claim the aircraft coming in from the west had flown through a pass in the Waianaes called Kolekole. To someone standing on the ground, they would indeed have appeared to approach through the mountains, but all the aircraft that hit Wheeler Field came from the north and stayed east of the Waianaes.

JAPANESE AIRCRAFT DEPLOYMENT
FIRST ATTACK

LEGEND
———— FIGHTERS
·········· DIVE BOMBERS
— — — HORIZONTAL BOMBERS
—·—·— TORPEDO BOMBERS

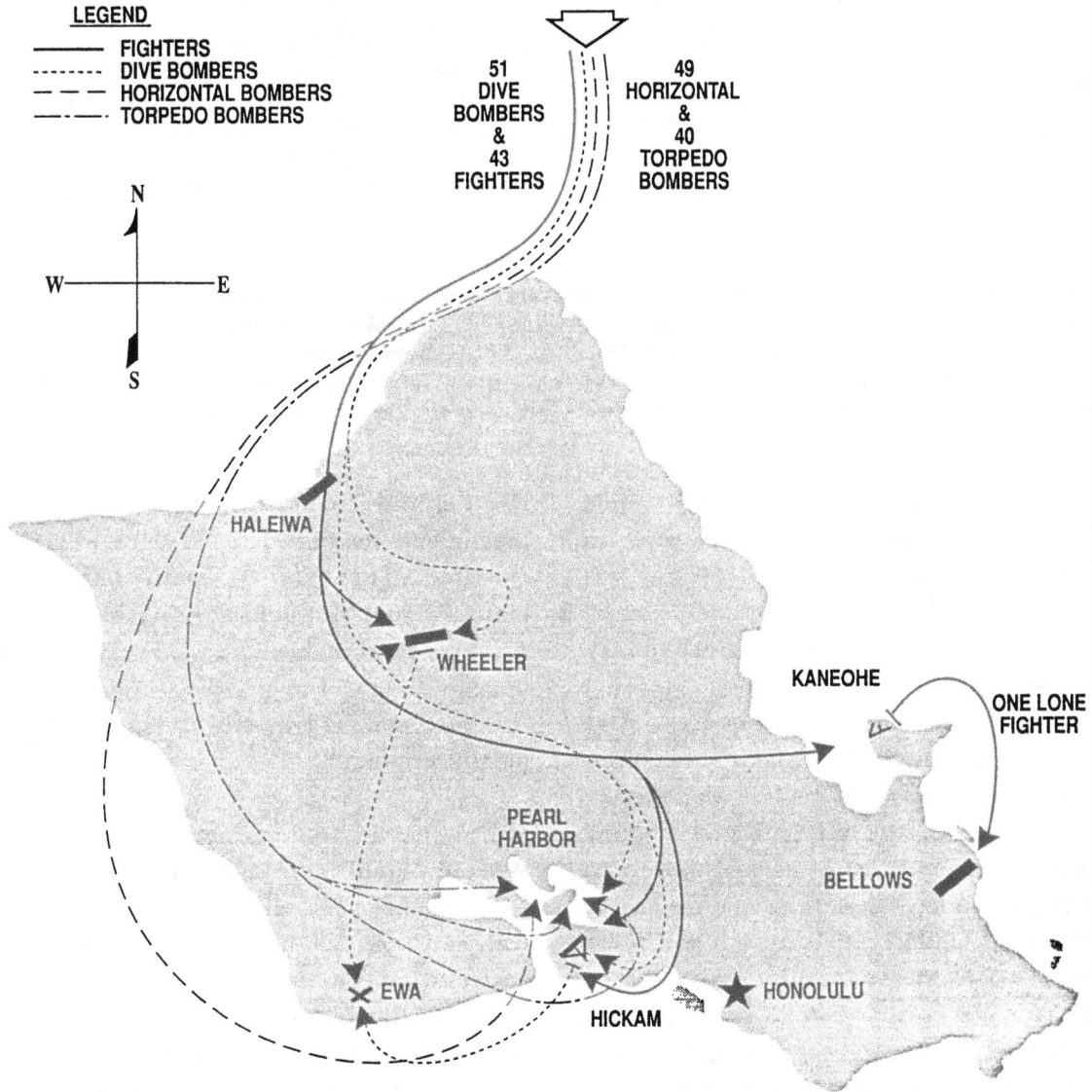

51
DIVE
BOMBERS
&
43
FIGHTERS

49
HORIZONTAL
&
40
TORPEDO
BOMBERS

N
W———E
S

HALEIWA

WHEELER

KANEOHE

ONE LONE
FIGHTER

PEARL
HARBOR

BELLOWS

EWA

HICKAM

HONOLULU

WHEELER, EWA, FORD ISLAND, AND HICKAM HIT BY DIVE BOMBERS.
PEARL HARBOR HIT BY HORIZONTAL, TORPEDO, AND DIVE BOMBERS.
43 FIGHTERS ESCORTED BOMBERS DOWN THROUGH CENTRAL OAHU, THEN
BROKE OFF AND ATTACKED ALL INSTALLATIONS EXCEPT HALEIWA.
BELLOWS HIT BY ONE LONE FIGHTER.

Wheeler Field in 1941, with hangar row at extreme left across from the concrete barracks that housed pursuit squadron enlisted personnel. The Waianae mountain range is in background, and the deep cut is Kolekole Pass. This natural cleft took its name from a large stone which Hawaiian legend depicted as a beneficial guardian of the pass to whom offerings of flowers and maile were made by travelers. (Harry P. Kilpatrick)

The Japanese took Wheeler Field completely by surprise. The first wave of dive bombers lined up on the hangars paralleling the aircraft parking area. Releasing their bombs from 500 to 1000 feet, they scored direct hits on Hangars 1 and 3 and additional buildings in that area. One bomb struck the 6th Pursuit Squadron barracks, destroying it. After completing their bomb runs, the pilots began making strafing passes on the parked aircraft. Once Itaya realized that they had taken the Americans completely by surprise and there would be no fighter opposition, he released the fighters from their role of protector and they began strafing ground targets. The 20mm cannons of the Zero fighters would do considerable damage to ground targets. To increase the amount of damage caused during the strafing runs, the Japanese had loaded their machine gun ammunition in the following order: two armor-piercing, one tracer; two armor-piercing, one tracer; two armor-piercing, one incendiary. With this loading the bullets would puncture things

like gasoline tanks, and then the tracer and incendiary rounds would explode or set them on fire. They started many fires in this manner, and a thick pall of black smoke quickly covered the area. From the air it appeared that they had severely damaged the base and had destroyed all the aircraft on the ground.[6]

Aircraft and maintenance facilities at Wheeler Field were the primary targets of the attack. The pilots had been too well trained to waste their bombs and ammunition on insignificant targets. One bomb did land in the front yard of a house, but it probably resulted from a miss rather than a deliberate attack on the housing area.* At times there were over 30 fighters

*The authors, along with Maj John W. Boozer III, Commander, 15th Air Base Squadron, located the bombed area using photographs taken immediately after the attack. The crater was located on a line running east to west through an aircraft hanger and a large building used as a barracks at the time of the attack. The attacking aircraft was probably aiming at one of these two buildings when he overshot his target and hit the housing area.

Above, burning hangars and aircraft at Wheeler Field, as photographed by a Japanese pilot participating in the attack. The thick black smoke that covered the area served to conceal some of the parked aircraft from the Japanese attackers.

Below, bomb crater in the front yard of family quarters at 540 Wright Avenue, across the street from the Wheeler flight line. (Joe K. Harding)

and dive bombers attacking Wheeler from every direction. In the confusion a missed target or a long strafing run was to be expected. Schofield Barracks, located next to Wheeler Field, also appeared to be under attack with all the aircraft flying in the area; however, other than a possible isolated individual strafing attack or two, on targets of opportunity, the Japanese did not specifically target Schofield.[7]

After making several strafing attacks on Wheeler, Lt Akira Sakamoto led the dive bombers south to the Marine Corps base at Ewa. The fighters continued a little longer and then left for other targets. While they were attacking Wheeler Field, the remaining dive bombers and fighters of the first wave continued south, where they again split and headed for either Kaneohe Naval Air Station or the Hickam Field and Pearl Harbor areas. During the attack on Kaneohe, Lt Tadashi Kaneko flew off and made a single strafing pass over Bellows Field then rejoined his unit. Why he made this lone strafing attack is not known, because Bellows Field was not on the initial target list for his group.[8]

The dive bombers and fighters that struck Hickam Field were not the first indication that personnel there had of the attack. When some of Murata's torpedo bombers hit Pearl Harbor, they flew directly over Hickam on their way out from the targets. Before anyone had a chance to react to the noise coming from Pearl Harbor or identify the low flying aircraft, the dive bombers and fighters were upon them. As at Wheeler Field, the first targets were those in and around the hangar area. The attack then widened to include supply buildings, the consolidated barracks and dining hall, the base chapel, the enlisted men's beer

A Nakajima B5N (Kate) horizontal bomber flying over Hickam's burning flight line.

garden, and the guardhouse all in just the first few minutes. This was in addition to machine gun attacks by both the dive bombers and the fighters on all visible aircraft and personnel in the area. Within minutes the base was ablaze with many fires, and the Americans lost any chance of launching aircraft to attack or quickly locate the attacking carriers.[9]

Approximately 30 minutes later the second wave of 35 fighters, 54 horizontal bombers, and 78 dive bombers sighted the coast of Oahu. This group also approached from the north but was several miles east of the first attack. Roughly ten miles east of Kahuku Point, the second wave split into various attack groups. The dive bombers, under the command of Lt Cmdr Takashige Egusa, banked slightly to the right and approached Oahu just to the west of Kaneohe Bay, heading directly for Ford Island. Later, this group, after completing their bombing runs over Ford Island and the Pearl Harbor area, made strafing runs on Hickam Field and the Marine Corps base at Ewa.[10]

Lt Cmdr Shigekazu Shimazaki's horizontal bombers split into three groups, with 18 aircraft coming straight in to hit Kaneohe Naval Air Station. The other two groups continued flying south, passing Diamond Head to the east and circling out over the ocean, where 27 struck Hickam Field and the remaining 9 hit Ford Island. Several individuals on the ground spotted this group approaching Hickam from the south, reinforcing rumors that the enemy carriers lay to the south of the island.

A B-24, serial number 40-237, en route to the Philippines from the 44th Bomb Group, was caught on the ground and destroyed by the Japanese during the attack. (Denver D. Gray, US Army Military History Institute)

JAPANESE AIRCRAFT DEPLOYMENT SECOND ATTACK

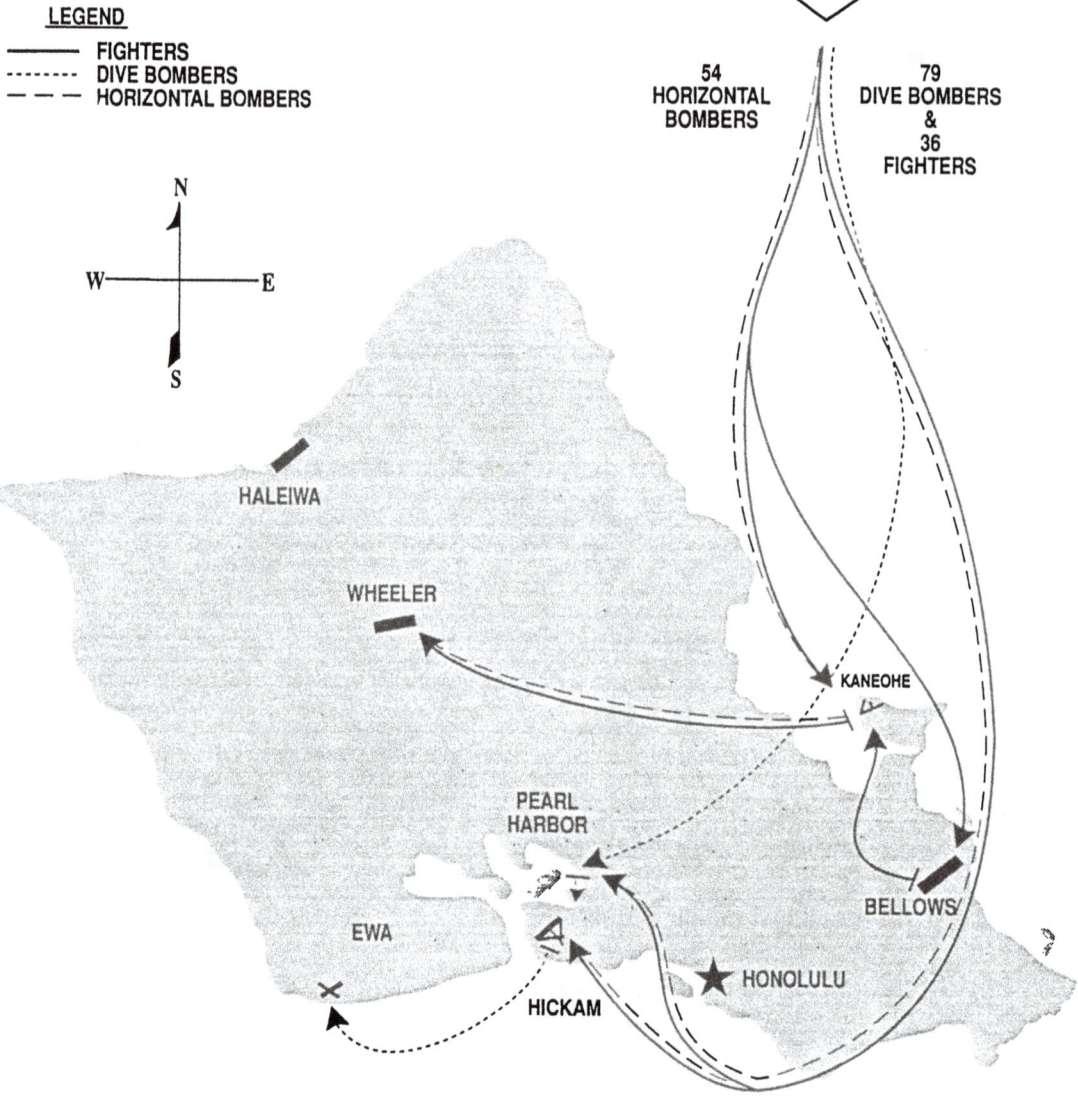

LEGEND
—— FIGHTERS
········ DIVE BOMBERS
— — HORIZONTAL BOMBERS

54
HORIZONTAL
BOMBERS

79
DIVE BOMBERS
&
36
FIGHTERS

N
W   E
S

HALEIWA

WHEELER

KANEOHE

PEARL
HARBOR

BELLOWS

EWA

HONOLULU

HICKAM

WHEELER, KANEOHE, BELLOWS, HICKAM, AND
PEARL HARBOR HIT BY FIGHTERS.
HORIZONTAL BOMBERS HIT KANEOHE, HICKAM,
AND PEARL HARBOR AND STRAFED WHEELER.
DIVE BOMBERS HIT PEARL HARBOR AND
STRAFED HICKAM AND EWA.

Dividing again into two groups, the horizontal bombers hit Hickam from both low level, around 150 feet, and high level, about 1,000 feet. Targets of this attack continued to be buildings close to the flight line, the consolidated barracks, and the baseball diamond located next to the fire department facility.*[11]

Staying with the horizontal and dive bombers, the fighters under Lt Saburo Shindo struck Kaneohe, Hickam, and Pearl Harbor. Seeing no resistance, Lt Sumio Nono led nine fighters away from Kaneohe toward Bellows Field. Attacking from the ocean side of the base, the fighters made repeated strafing attacks, destroying or damaging most of the aircraft parked there, the tent city area, and hitting several buildings. After completing their attack on Bellows, the fighters returned to Kaneohe and from there, worked their way back to their carriers.[12]

In less than an hour the Japanese had destroyed or damaged more than fifty percent of the Hawaiian Air Force's aircraft, many buildings and support facilities, and left over 600 casualties on the three main airfields. The only people who saw the attack coming were the radar operators, and even they were not exactly sure what they were looking at.

Radar Intercepts

The radar systems in use on 7 December were SCR-270-B radio sets. They were mobile units housed in two trucks. The unit's heart was the oscilloscope that gave a picture similar to a

heart monitor in hospitals today. The operator would move the antenna through a given arc until the line across the bottom showed a small spike or "pip." By adjusting the antenna and the controls on the set, the pip was enhanced until the operator could tell the approximate distance to the target. Next, the operator would look out the window to a plate mounted on the antenna base, with an arrow on it that would give the direction of the contact. Unlike today's radar scopes the antenna did not oscillate and there was no constant repainting of the picture on the scope. This system could not tell an incoming target's altitude, its size or number, nor could it differentiate friend from foe.[13]

In July 1941 these radio sets began arriving on Oahu. Signal Company personnel began assembling them at Schofield Barracks and then began learning how to operate them. Once assembled, personnel moved them to prepared sites throughout the island. The Signal Corps planned to put up six sets. On the morning of the attack, five were operational, with the sixth still at Schofield. The five operational sets were at Kaaawa, Opana, Kawailoa, Fort Shafter, and Koko Head. The sets began operating at 0400 on 7 December except at Opana, which came on the air at around 0415 due to a delay for maintenance on the generator first thing in the morning. The operators had been on duty since noon Saturday. They divided their tour between standing guard, maintenance, and operating the sets. The schedule called for each site to have a crew of three: one operator, one plotter, and one person to maintain the power generators. Because several units worked off commercial power and used the generators as standby power, some crews cut back to two people per shift on the weekend. Opana had two crew members that Sunday morning.[14]

*See Chapter V for an explanation why the baseball diamond was targeted.

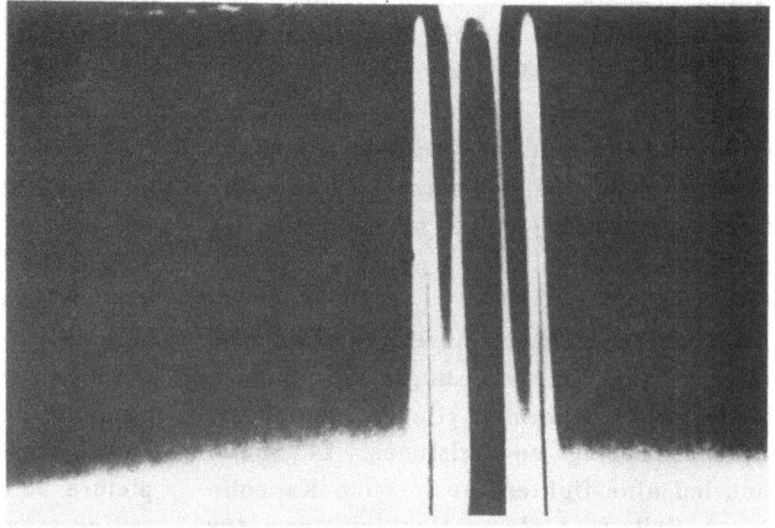

Above, an oscilloscope display at Opana radar site, showing the pip resulting from contact with the island of Kauai 89 miles away. Only distance and relative size of the target could be determined. A large flight of incoming aircraft would have generated a similar picture on the morning of 7 December. To the right, Pvt Joseph LaRue Lockard, the young Signal Corps member who was on duty at the Opana radar site with Pvt George E. Elliott (no photo available) the morning of the attack. Below, temporary information center built on top of Building 307 (a Signal Corps warehouse) at Fort Shafter to coordinate activities of the SCR-270-B radar sites. (All three photos courtesy of the US Army Museum of Hawaii)

During the first two hours, no radar contacts were made. At 0613, Koko Head and Fort Shafter began picking up sightings south of the island. Then at 0645, Kaaawa, Opana, and Kawailoa picked up a target approximately 135 miles north of Oahu heading south. All three stations called the Information Center with the targets, which were then plotted on the master plot board. Personnel at the center included five plotters (one for each radar site), a historical information plotter; PFC Joseph P. McDonald, the switchboard operator; and Lt Kermit Tyler, a pursuit pilot. The radar sites phoned the plots to the five plotters, and no one present found anything unusual with the information. McDonald had worked the switchboard for several months and knew the radar operators, while Tyler had been to the Information Center only once before. On 3 December he had worked from 1200 to 1600 with just the switchboard operator. On that occasion nothing had happened, because the sites were not operating. Therefore this was the first time he had actually seen personnel plot targets. When the reports began coming in, Tyler went to the historical plotter's position and talked with him about how he recorded the information. These first plots were probably the scout planes sent ahead of the main attacking force.[15]

At 0700 all the radar sites began shutting down. At the Information Center the five plotters and the historical information plotter shut down and left the area, leaving McDonald and Tyler behind. At Opana, Pvts George E. Elliott and Joseph L. Lockard had been scheduled to work until noon, but the next shift had come back early from a pass to town so they could relieve them at 0800. This meant that when the truck arrived to take them to breakfast, they would be through for the day.

However, the same call that informed them about getting off early also let them know the truck would be late picking them up. Lockard was a trained radar operator and had been with the 270s since they arrived on the island, while Elliot had just transferred into the Signal Corps from the Hawaiian Air Force and only knew how to operate the plotting board. Because the breakfast truck would be late and they were going to be off for the rest of the day, the two decided to use the time to work on Elliot's training. A few minutes after seven, Elliot got a large spike on the screen; thinking he had done something wrong, he immediately began to check the settings. Lockard then took over the operation and also rechecked the controls. This was the biggest sighting he had ever seen since learning how to operate the system. Elliot then tried to call the Information Center, using the phones connected directly to the plotters. No one was there to take the call. He then called on the administration line and got McDonald. The switchboard operator knew both of the radar operators and tried to explain to them that there was nobody on duty in the Center after 0800. McDonald then spotted Lt Tyler and called him over to talk to Elliot; meanwhile, Lockard got on the phone and tried to explain that this was a large target and might be significant. McDonald interjected at this point that if the targets were so large, maybe they should call back the plotters so they could practice handling a big aircraft movement. Tyler thought about this for a moment and then told Lockard and McDonald not to worry and closed the conversation.[16]

Because the breakfast truck still had not arrived, Elliot and Lockard continued tracking the incoming target until about twenty miles from the coast of Oahu. At that point ground interference blocked the signal, and the target was lost. This was around 0745. Just then the breakfast truck pulled up, so the two young radar operators shut their unit off and headed down the mountain to breakfast, not yet realizing that they had discovered the first wave of the Japanese attack.[17]

Why had Lt Tyler told the operators not to worry, and why had he not followed McDonald's advice to call back the plotters? Tyler saw no reason to change the normal operations that morning. First, there was no alert or warning of an impending attack. Second, the US Fleet's carriers were at sea and the sightings could well have been the carrier's aircraft returning to port.* Third, a bomber pilot friend had explained just a few days before that one could always tell when aircraft were arriving from the US because the local radio stations would play Hawaiian music all night. The incoming aircraft would use the music to tune their directional finders and thus locate the islands. (This was exactly what the Japanese did.) On the way to the Center, Tyler had heard the Hawaiian music, so he assumed a flight was coming in. Finally, although Lockard had said this was the biggest flight he had ever seen, he did not say how many aircraft he thought it might contain. Later, Lockard would claim he knew the flight had to number over 50 aircraft to make that large of a pip on the screen, but at the time he did not give that information to anyone. Had Tyler known that the sighting was over 50 aircraft, he might have reacted differently; but with the information on hand, second lieutenants do not wake up commanding officers at seven o'clock Sunday mornings with wild speculations.[18]

Lockard and Elliot heard about the attack when they returned to their camp. After a quick breakfast, they returned to Opana and helped keep the site operating 24 hours a day for the next several months. The first Lt Tyler heard about the attack was a telephone call from someone at Wheeler Field shortly after 0800. The plotters were immediately called back, and soon a full complement began to arrive. Tyler would stay in the Center except for short rest breaks for the next 36 hours. During the morning's activities, two plots began to form 30 to 50 miles southwest of Oahu.* Not knowing what these were and thinking they could be the retiring Japanese circling before landing on their carriers, the senior controller passed this information on to bomber command as the possible location for the Japanese attack force. No one remembered to check the early reports coming in before 0700 or the Opana sighting after 0700. It wasn't until several days later that people assembled this information and realized the radar stations had located the direction from which the attack had come.[19]

B-17 Arrivals

As part of the American buildup in the Pacific, Washington scheduled 16 B-17s to deploy to the Philippines through Hawaii in late November 1941. The 38th Reconnaissance Squadron from Albuquerque, New Mexico, would supply eight aircraft and the 88th Reconnaissance Squadron from Fort Douglas, Utah, would furnish the remaining eight. The aircraft would take off from Hamilton Field, California, for the long flight to Hawaii. Modifications to the aircraft, installing long-range fuel tanks in

---

*The Navy would launch their carrier aircraft prior to arriving in port and have them land at one of the airfields so they could be used while the carriers were tied up in port.

---

*The plots may have been American aircraft looking for the Japanese or even an atmospheric phenomenon; no one was ever quite sure where they came from.

the bomb bay, and high head winds combined to delay the flight until the evening of 6 December. General Marshall became alarmed over the delay, and sent General Hap Arnold to California to impress upon the crews the urgency of their mission and the potential danger they faced. Maj Truman H. Landon, flight leader for the 38th, questioned General Arnold about why—if the flight was so dangerous—were they not carrying ammunition for their guns. Arnold explained that the distance to Hawaii was so great, the B-17s needed to carry as much fuel as possible. The real danger would be during the second leg of the trip. It was a calculated risk that war would not start until after the aircraft arrived in Hawaii, where the protective grease would be removed from the guns and the aircraft armed for the final flight into the Philippines.[20]

As the flight prepared to leave Hamilton Field, two aircraft from the 38th experienced engine trouble and didn't make the mission. One aircraft from the 88th also developed problems and aborted the takeoff. Once airborne, another aircraft from the 88th had problems and returned to Hamilton Field. In all, four B-17Cs and eight B-17Es, spaced about ten minutes apart, made the flight to Hawaii.*

The long flight over the water was uneventful, and no one experienced any major difficulties. The Navy had positioned ships across the Pacific for the aircraft to use as directional indicators, and as they neared Hawaii, radio station KGMB was playing Hawaiian music for them to use in

locating the island. Capt Richard H. Carmichael from the 88th contacted the Hickam Field tower at 0745 but was still too far away, and the transmission was too garbled for anyone to understand.[21]

A few minutes later the B-17s from the 38th sighted the Hawaiian Islands and spotted a flight of fighter aircraft coming out to meet them. Thinking they were Americans, the pilots were glad to have escorts for the remaining miles into the field. Suddenly, what they had thought to be friendly aircraft began firing at them, and each bomber took whatever evasive action it could. The Japanese attacked at least five aircraft, destroying two. 1st Lt Robert H. Richards tried to land his B-17C at Hickam, but the Japanese harassed him so badly that he aborted the landing and headed east out to sea. He then turned the aircraft and attempted a downwind landing at Bellows Field, but came in too fast and ran off the end of the runway into a ditch. Zeros repeatedly strafed the aircraft after it was on the ground. Initially maintenance personnel thought they could repair the aircraft, but they eventually used it to supply replacement parts for other aircraft, and it never flew again. Capt Raymond T. Swenson managed to land his B-17C at Hickam, but a strafing Zero hit the flare storage box in the middle of the aircraft, igniting the flares and causing the aircraft to burn in two. The crew all reached safety except for the flight surgeon, 1st Lt William R. Schick, mortally wounded by a passing Zero while he was riding in the observer's seat. Maintenance crews pushed the separated back portion of the aircraft away from the taxi area and eventually salvaged all four engines from the front half. The four remaining aircraft landed at Hickam Field, having experienced various attacks which caused minor damage. Maintenance

---

*Appendix D lists the aircraft serial numbers, pilots, crews, and landing locations in Hawaii on 7 December 1941.

Above, two Aichi D3A (Val) dive bombers photographed over Hickam Field by SSgt Lee R. Embree, a combat photographer aboard one of the 38th Reconnaissance Squadron B-17Es that arrived from California in the middle of the attack.

Below, the wreckage of Captain Swenson's B-17C which burned in two after a strafing Japanese Zero hit its flare storage box.

Closeup view of front half of the burned B-17C. In left foreground is a straw helmet which identifies this as a picture taken by well-known photographer Tai Sing Loo, Pearl Harbor's main cameraman from 1918 to 1948.

personnel worked around the clock to have all four repaired within 24 hours.[22]

The 88th arrived shortly after the 38th and met a similar fate. Capt Carmichael and later 1st Lt Harold N. Chaffin passed up Hickam Field, flew over Wheeler and landed their B-17s at the small auxiliary field at Haleiwa. 1st Lt Frank P. Bostrom attempted several landings at Hickam, only to be attacked each time by the Japanese, so he headed over to Barbers Point and eventually flew to the northern part of the island where he was again attacked by the Japanese and forced to land at the Kahuku Golf Course. General Martin had planned to build an emergency air strip in that area, but it had not been completed when Bostrom landed there. Two more aircraft from the 88th eventually landed at Hickam Field, timing their landings between

Japanese attacks. The sixth aircraft's route was a bit more confusing.[23]

The maintenance records for Hickam Field on that day show three aircraft from the 88th in commission at Hickam Field. Still, several eyewitnesses, including General Davidson and 2d Lt Henry Wells Lawrence, claimed a B-17E landed at Wheeler Field (see Chapter VI for the eyewitness accounts). They described how the aircraft came in cross-wind over the highway and landed along the width of the grass field at Wheeler, stopping just short of the hangars. General Davidson stated that when he asked the pilot why he landed at Wheeler Field, the pilot replied that by then all he was looking for was a flat piece of land to set the aircraft down. Lt Lawrence described the aircraft perfectly and added that when he came down from his mission later that morning, he did not remember seeing it again. In fact no one remembers seeing the aircraft after it landed. At the same time this B-17 was landing, a B-18 that had flown from the island of Molakai landed at Wheeler. It is possible that the personnel at Wheeler mistook the B-18 for the B-17. Even Capt Brooke E. Allen, a B-17 pilot at Hickam Field, admitted that when he first saw the B-17s arriving, he thought they were Japanese. The Hawaiian Air Force had kept the flight from the coast a secret, and the B-17E model was new to the islands so most people had never seen one before. If a B-17 pilot could become confused during the attack and misidentify an aircraft, so could fighter pilots under attack. A second more plausible explanation is that the B-17 did land at Wheeler Field but sometime during the morning took off and flew to Hickam. This would explain the eyewitness accounts of its landing, why no one remembers seeing it after the attack, and why the maintenance records written at 1300 recorded three B-17Es at Hickam.[24]

Regardless of where this sixth aircraft initially landed, the 88th was extremely lucky, with five out of six aircraft in commission by the next day. Maintenance personnel repaired Bostrom's aircraft at the Kahuku Golf Course and flew it back to Hickam Field within a week.[25]

Air Force Opposition

The Japanese caught the Hawaiian Air Force completely by surprise. There was no coordinated, systematic, island-wide air defense that morning. Instead, 14 individual pilots attempted to engage the enemy with varying degrees of success. Later in the morning, after the attacks, another dozen pilots took off not knowing the Japanese had left the area. Those involved in the attack considered it quite an accomplishment just to get a fighter in the air that morning, much less to do any damage to the attackers.[26]

The first confirmed takeoffs by American pilots against the attack occurred at Haleiwa Auxiliary Field. 2d Lts George S. Welch and Kenneth M. Taylor traveled by automobile from Wheeler Field to Haleiwa when they realized the island was under attack. Their squadron had deployed to Haleiwa for gunnery practice, and the Japanese had not attacked there. Ground crews got the P-40s armed and ready to go when Welch and Taylor arrived so they could immediately take off. The time was around 0830. Ground control directed the two pilots to head for the southern tip of the island where the Japanese from the first wave were still strafing the Marine base at Ewa. Spotting a group of enemy planes in a long line, both pilots jumped into the line and began shooting down aircraft, each getting two confirmed kills during this first engagement. Taylor fired on a third plane but did not see the crash. Both pilots were running out of ammunition and low on fuel, so they returned to Wheeler Field to rearm and refuel.

At Wheeler, things were in turmoil. The Japanese attack had destroyed or damaged most of the P-40s. One hangar had received a direct hit and secondary explosions from the ammunition stored in it continued for several hours. As ground personnel reached the flight line, they began pulling the aircraft away from the immediate area into the protective revetments around the field. Once the aircraft were clear, they returned to the hangar area to gather up as much ammunition as they could find and returned to the aircraft to arm and prepare them for flight. By this time there were many more pilots available than aircraft ready to fly, so it became a contest as to who would get which aircraft. 1st Lt Lewis M. Sanders picked three experienced pilots and told them to grab the first available aircraft and follow him for a four-ship attack. Lts John M. Thacker and Philip M. Rasmussen stayed by their aircraft until they were ready to go and then jumped in and began to taxi. Lt Othneil Norris assisted in getting an aircraft ready, but left it to go get a new parachute; 2d Lt Gordon H. Sterling, Jr. spotted the unattended aircraft, jumped in, and taxied out to join Sanders and the other two pilots. This practice of grabbing any aircraft ready to fly would happen several more times before the day was over.

Once airborne, around 0850, Sanders led the flight east toward Bellows Field. Spotting the Japanese second wave over Kaneohe, the four P-36s immediately engaged. Sanders got on the tail of an enemy aircraft and shot it down. Coming off the attack, he spotted Sterling in hot pursuit of a Japanese plane that was diving toward the water. Behind Sterling another Japanese had gotten into the fight and was shooting at Sterling. Sanders came up behind this aircraft and opened fire. Rasmussen observed the four aircraft: the plane that Sterling was attacking crashed; Sterling, close behind, also plunged into the sea, shot down by the Japanese on his tail; Sanders meanwhile had set fire to this fighter, but Rasmussen did not know whether it, too, went into the water. Just before witnessing Sterling's death, Rasmussen had charged his guns, only to have them start firing on their own. While trying to stop the guns from firing, a Japanese aircraft passed directly in front of

him and exploded. Things began to happen fast after that, and he soon had two Zeros on his tail. Taking evasive action, he lost them in some cloud cover. Meanwhile, Thacker dove into the battle, only to discover his guns had jammed and would not fire. He kept making passes at the Japanese until hit several times, then broke off the engagement and returned to base. Sanders found himself alone with a Zero and was quickly losing the flying contest. Deciding that discretion was the better part of valor, he broke off the one-sided contest and headed back to Wheeler Field. So far the Americans had managed to get six aircraft airborne and had shot down seven Japanese with two more probables at the cost of one P-36.

From that point on, the story became confusing; and, because pilots were taking off individually from two different fields and then joining up after getting airborne, takeoff times were difficult, if not impossible, to verify. About the same time Sanders' flight was mixing it up with the Japanese over Kaneohe, Welch and Taylor were ready to head out on their second flight that morning. Welch got off first, and just as Taylor was ready to go, another Japanese attack hit Wheeler Field. Taylor waited until what he thought was the last in the line of Japanese aircraft and took off after them, guns blazing. Just after he became airborne, another Japanese got on his tail and opened fire. For a few seconds it looked grim; but Welch had stayed in the immediate area, saw what was happening to Taylor, and came to the rescue. He jumped behind the aircraft that was shooting at Taylor and scored his third kill for the day. This allowed Taylor to break free and gain altitude. Although wounded in the action Taylor was still able to fly, so he continued attacking Japanese aircraft wherever he could find them, damaging at least one more. Welch, meanwhile, headed back to Ewa and got a confirmed kill on another Japanese, bringing his total for the day to four.

Meanwhile, at Bellows Field, 1st Lt Samuel W. Bishop and 2d Lt George A. Whiteman attempted to take off to join the defense. Whiteman was hit as he cleared the ground and crashed just off the end of the runway. Bishop managed to get his P-40 into the air; but before he could gain altitude, several Zeros attacked him, and he crashed into the ocean. Whiteman was killed instantly, but Bishop was only wounded and managed to swim to shore. While this was going on, Haleiwa launched aircraft as fast as pilots showed up. Lts John Dains and John Webster both got off at different times in P-40s, while Lts Harry Brown and Robert Rogers each took off in P-36s. From Wheeler Field, Lts Malcolm Moore and Othneil Norris entered the fight, also flying P-36s. Brown and Rogers headed out to Kahuku Point, where they engaged

the enemy without any confirmed kills, but Rogers damaged one enemy aircraft. From there they joined up with Moore and Webster and headed west. At Kaena Point, Webster damaged one aircraft, but could not confirm a kill. Rogers was cornered by two Japanese; and Brown plowed into the fight, shooting down one attacker. As the action started to wind down, Moore opened up on one retreating Japanese aircraft but failed to down it. Brown spotted the smoking ship and also fired but, like Moore, could not hit a vital spot, and the aircraft got away. Rogers started to run low on fuel, so he returned to Haleiwa where he took off on his second mission in a P-36. Dains also returned to Haleiwa and got off on a second mission in a P-40.

By this time the Japanese had completed their attack and were returning to their carriers as fast as they could. Wheeler Field and Haleiwa kept launching aircraft for the next hour with little coordination or direction for the pilots. No additional combat with the Japanese

Five Army Air Forces pilots from Wheeler Field who downed a total of nine Japanese planes the morning of 7 December 1941. Left to right: 2d Lt Harry W. Brown, 2d Lt Philip M. Rasmussen, 2d Lt Kenneth M. Taylor, 2d Lt George S. Welch, 1st Lt Lewis M. Sanders.

occurred. One mystery still remains concerning the action that occurred in the air that Sunday morning. Radar operators at the station at Kaaawa watched a P-40 shoot down a Japanese Zero during the height of the battle. The operators were positive the American aircraft was a P-40, and they identified it both from its distinctive silhouette and the sound of its engine. None of the pilots that survived that morning's action remembered flying in the Kaawa area. The only pilot whose action was unaccounted for was Lt John Dains, who flew two missions that morning in a P-40. Both times he was separated from the other American fighters and fought by himself. After landing the second time, he switched to a P-36 and joined up with George Welch for a third mission. Neither pilot spotted anything because by that time the Japanese had cleared the area, so they decided to return to Wheeler Field.

On the return flight, antiaircraft guns at Schofield Barracks opened up on the two aircraft, killing Dains. There were three plausible explanations. First, the radar operators could have been mistaken in what they saw; second, some other P-40 pilot downed the Japanese plane and was unaware where the action occurred; or third, we suspect that Dains did get the enemy plane as the ground personnel observed and just never got the chance to tell his story.

The Japanese would concede the loss of twenty-nine aircraft from all causes that morning. The Hawaiian Air Force claimed ten of those losses with four more probables and two Japanese aircraft damaged. If Dains' kill is added to the list, the score comes out to eleven Japanese aircraft destroyed in air-to-air combat with a loss of four American planes, which were flown by Whiteman, Sterling, Bishop, and Dains.

Japanese plane shot down by Lt George Welch, crashed at 711 Neal Street, Wahiawa, located next to Wheeler Field. Photo by CWO Joe K. Harding, USAF, Retired. He was a master sergeant at the time he took this picture.

Sterling was the only pilot lost in actual combat with the enemy; the Japanese downed Whiteman and Bishop during takeoff, and friendly fire shot down Dains. Could the American fighter forces have made a difference that morning had they known about the attack? The above information would certainly seem to suggest they could. But it is important to remember that the Japanese had committed over half their force just to deal with the American fighters. They abandoned their whole fighter defense system when they encountered no initial reaction from the Americans. This meant that the few aircraft that did get airborne that morning hit an almost unprotected attacking force. Welch and Taylor's encounters over Ewa during their first flight provided an example of this. Had the American forces met the Japanese from the beginning, the formation over Ewa would certainly have had Zeros flying top cover for them. As Sanders discovered over Kaneohe, the P-36 was no match for the Zero; and without special training or good luck, neither was the P-40. But these are matters of speculation. More important under the circumstances that morning, however, was how the personnel of the Hawaiian Air Force in fact responded. From the lowest ranking ground personnel to the hottest fighter pilot in the command, everyone did the best they could with what they had. The men of the Hawaiian Air Force might have been caught by surprise, but they most certainly did not give up.

CHAPTER V

HELL IN PARADISE: BOMBER COMMAND

"As a member of the Pearl Harbor Survivors Association, I am often asked what ship I was on. When I reply that I wasn't on a ship but was stationed at Hickam Field, I am usually asked, 'Where is Hickam Field?' .... The Japanese certainly knew!"

Former Master Sergeant Thomas J. Pillion
400th Signal Company, Hickam Field

The Japanese not only knew precisely where Hickam Field was, they also knew where Wheeler and Bellows Fields were located, because land-based US planes on Oahu were priority targets on 7 December 1941. The Japanese intended to destroy as many American aircraft as possible, preferably on the ground at the outset of the attack, not only to eliminate air opposition when their bombers struck the fleet at Pearl Harbor but also to preclude US planes from following their aircraft back to their carriers and bombing the task force.[1]

The death and devastation resulting from the surprise attack transformed the "Paradise of the Pacific" into a veritable hell on earth. For Army Air Forces personnel and others stationed in Hawaii, the horrifying sights they witnessed that day were unforgettable.

Hickam Field

To those at Hickam, the Japanese seemed to strike in three waves. The first indication of an attack was at 0755 when

The first bombs to strike Hickam Field were dropped on Hawaiian Air Depot buildings and the hangar line, causing thick clouds of smoke to billow upward. (John W. Wilson)

nine enemy single-engine, low-wing monoplanes carrying torpedoes flew south-east of the hangar line toward Pearl Harbor at an altitude of 50 feet. Observers noted that they were in two echelons, five in the first and four in the second. Although these planes did not attack Hickam Field, dive bombers came in shortly afterward and hit the Hawaiian Air Depot buildings and the hangar line. After a lull, the Japanese bombers returned around 0825 and struck again, then once more at about 0900.[2]

When the attack began, Hickam's base commander, Colonel Farthing, was in the control tower awaiting the arrival of the B-17s from California. With him was Lt Col Cheney L. Bertholf, adjutant general of the Hawaiian Air Force. The tower provided a panoramic view of the surrounding area; and, while watching what they believed to be Navy planes taking off from nearby Ford Island and going around toward the Pearl Harbor Naval Base to the east of the island, they heard "a bunch of airplanes diving in, coming from about 10,000 feet." They knew these were not Army planes and thought they must be Marines. The planes dived down on Pearl Harbor, and Colonel Farthing saw a black object leave the first and hit with an explosion. That plane then zoomed upward, and he could see the rising sun insignia on its wings as it headed directly toward Hickam. Colonel Bertholf immediately rushed down from the tower to sound the alarm. Farthing followed right behind him and saw the Japanese plane approaching at about 25 feet, firing all its guns. It hit the No. 3 engine of a B-17, setting it on fire, and setting some B-18s ablaze at the same time. These aircraft were parked so close together that when one was hit, they all caught fire. The enemy plane flew on, then turned and came back across the field, firing at Colonel Farthing,

B-18 wreckage on the Hickam flight line.

who was the only person in the area at that time. The colonel hit the dirt and stayed there for the remainder of the first wave attack. By then, other Japanese planes joined in, dropping bombs and firing their machine guns.[3]

Capt Gordon A. Blake, Hickam's base operations officer, had been in his office in the operations building since 0700, preparing for the B-17 arrival. His good friend Maj Roger Ramey was there, too, partly in his capacity as A-3 (operations officer) of the Hawaiian Air Force but mostly because his classmate and close friend, Maj Truman H. Landon, was leading the incoming flight of 38th Reconnaissance Squadron B-17s. They were sitting there "chewing the fat" and listening to reports coming in to the tower when they suddenly heard a loud explosion. Dashing outside, they saw a dive bomber with the rising sun of Japan on the underside of its wings pulling up almost directly overhead after bombing the Hawaiian Air Depot.[4]

Captain Blake's first thought was to get the incoming B-17s down safely, so he ran up to the tower to guide them in. The pilots of the Flying Fortresses had maneuvered through heavy antiaircraft and enemy machine-gun fire to reach Hickam Field. When they asked for landing instructions from the tower, a calm voice gave wind direction, velocity, and the runway on which to land, as though it were any other day, occasionally reporting that the field was under attack by "unidentified planes." After the B-17s landed, Blake left the control tower to go over to see Landon, whom he had known as a cadet, so he could pass on instructions to get their planes ready in case higher authority assigned them a mission. He rode out to Landon's revetment on the back of a fancy motorcycle driven by a large Hawaiian man wearing a big, wide, studded leather belt. The cyclist and other members of the Honolulu Motor Club had appeared on the scene to offer their help.[5]

Earlier, General Rudolph of the 18th Bomb Wing had scheduled a flight of B-18s for "some of the youngsters who had not completed B-18 training." He had more pilots than airplanes assigned, so this Sunday morning flight provided the opportunity to give them an extra hour of training. Twenty-four men were in the hangar, moving the bombers out in preparation for an 0800 takeoff, when the Japanese attacked and killed 22 of them outright, seriously injuring the other two. Outside, MSgt Dave Jacobson was changing a B-18 tire on the ramp. He disappeared without a trace when a bomb hit.[6]

The first wave of enemy planes to attack Hickam approached over Fort Kamehameha and scored direct hits on the Hawaiian Air Depot's engineering building,

leaving only the framework and destroying its contents. The depot restaurant was a total loss, but supply buildings were untouched except for scattered machine-gun bullets, shrapnel, and flying debris. After the first raid, all Hawaiian Air Depot officers came in and assisted with fire fighting, salvaging material, and other requirements. Approximately 100 civilian employees also reported for duty, including Mr. Phillip W. Eldred, purchasing clerk for supply, who was strafed and killed on his way to the depot. Another employee, Mr. John B. Gordon Bankston, suffered temporary paralysis in his left arm, when hit by a piece of flying shrapnel.[7]

Hangar 15, which housed the base engineering function, suffered considerable damage, with many personnel injured and killed; but Hangar 17 had only minor damage. Bombs wrecked Hangar 11, killing nearly all of the 11th Bomb Group's armament and aircraft maintenance technicians. The attack shattered Hangar 7 and slightly damaged Hangar 9, but left Hangars 3 and 5 intact. The Japanese also destroyed all the tugs and several gas trucks in the gas storage area but failed to damage the underground fuel tanks. A target folder later discovered in a downed Japanese plane showed the tanks in the area where the baseball diamond was located. That area was in fact the original site planned for the tanks; however, over a year before the attack, a change in plans resulted in placing them elsewhere and building a baseball field in that location. Consequently, the ball field was bombed instead of the underground fuel storage tanks. The same target folder identified the base operations building as the officers' club, so the nerve center of the base was spared, as were Hangars 2 and 4, which had been completed just a few months before the attack.[8]

Above, smoke pouring from Hickam Field's Hawaiian Air Depot shops, which were struck by attacking Japanese planes. Below, rear view of wrecked Hangar 11, with B-18 of the 18th Bombardment Wing on the right. The two men near the hangar are Capt Roland D. Boyer of the Signal Corps and Pvt Elliott C. Mitchell, Jr., 50th Reconnaissance Squadron. This was taken just as a Japanese plane swooped down, machine-gunning the field. Cpl Vincent P. Dargis, another photographer, snapped this picture, then ran for cover. All were safe.

Clockwise from top: Closeup view of bullet-riddled walls and twisted window frames of Hangar 11; aircraft wreckage inside Hickam Field hangar, including (at left) a B-18 assigned to the 5th Bombardment Group; and Hangar Avenue, looking *makai* (toward the sea), with Hangar 35 in background.

Hickam's big new consolidated barracks was a major target. PFC Robert P. Chase, an aircraft mechanic assigned to the 23d Bomb Squadron, awoke from a deep sleep to the thunderous roar of exploding bombs and watched in utter disbelief as enemy aircraft repeatedly strafed the barracks. Pvt Ira W. Southern got up to the sound of what he thought was heavy artillery gunfire. This was not unusual, since target sleeves were regularly towed close to Hickam; but the noise seemed louder, sharper, and more erratic than usual. After grumbling that target practice should be held sometime other than a Sunday morning, he strolled over to the windows to look outside. He could see a plane, flying at an altitude of about 500 feet, coming toward the barracks but thought nothing of it until he saw a large object drop from the plane. The next thing he knew, there was a terrible explosion, and the engine repair depot across the street seemed to disintegrate. At the same time, he noted with horror that the plane pulling out of the dive was clearly marked with the Japanese rising sun insignia. A sudden explosion drowned out the roar of the plane overhead. A low-flying plane had dropped a bomb through the window, tearing a huge hole in the floor and filling the barracks with flying shrapnel.[9]

Chaos reigned as panic-stricken men milled around in all directions. More and more earthquake-like shocks rattled the building as the enemy planes expended their bombs. The racket of explosions, shouting, and yelled orders to vacate the barracks was deafening. Southern went to his locker to get his gas mask but was so nervous, he couldn't work the combination to the lock. He finally got the locker open, slung his canister gas mask across his shoulder, and headed down the stairwell toward the supply room to get a gun and some ammunition. As he reached the ground floor landing, he saw that several dying and wounded men had been dragged inside the building for protection. The supply room was locked, so the men broke open the door, only to find that the rifles were all neatly

Hickam Field's big barracks, still burning from the Japanese attack, with Hangar 3 visible to the right of Wing D and Wing C at extreme left.

Fiercely burning fires like this one devastated Hickam Field's consolidated barracks. (11th Bomb Group Association)

locked in the racks. They somehow broke the locks, grabbed Springfield rifles and Colt .45 automatics, found ammunition stored in boxes on the shelves, and dragged several boxes to the floor. Bombs that hit nearby were sending fragments of shrapnel flying through the windows of the supply room, so they lay on the floor while filling their bandoliers, then dashed outside the barracks and began firing fruitlessly at the bombing, strafing enemy planes.[10]

Others who fought back included Sgt Stanley McLeod, who stood on the parade ground firing a Thompson submachine gun, alongside Cpl William T. Anderson. Both men lost their lives. A soldier, kneeling near some bushes, took potshots at the attacking planes with a bolt-action Springfield rifle. SSgt Doyle King fired his submachine gun from under a panel truck. MSgt Olef Jensen of the 72d Bomb Squadron directed the emplacement of machine guns, and one of his crews under SSgt R. R. Mitchell claimed credit for shooting down an enemy plane.

TSgt Wilbur Hunt set up twelve .50-caliber machine guns in bomb craters near the barracks, then unexpectedly got the gunners he needed. A bomb had blown off a corner of the guardhouse, releasing all the prisoners, who dashed over to Hunt and said they were ready to go to work. He immediately put them on the guns. On the ball diamond, two men set up a machine gun on a tripod between home plate and some trees along the edge of the field. Suddenly a wave of high-level bombers dropped their deadly projectiles right on the ball field, scoring a direct hit on the gun and killing both men instantly. By the time the third wave of the attack came, ground defenses were going full blast. In addition to the parade ground and the barracks area, guns were set up on the hangar line and even around the flagpole at post headquarters. Green troops under fire acted like veterans and displayed amazing courage. A corporal sped across the parade ground to help man a machine gun that was entirely in the open without any protection whatsoever.

Above, gun emplacement (center) on parade ground at Hickam Field, with the big barracks burning in background.   Serving today as headquarters of the Pacific Air Forces, this building has been known since 1948 as the *Hale Makai* ("Home by the Sea" in Hawaiian).

Below, Old Glory continues to wave over Hickam Field, bearing silent witness to the brutality of the Japanese attack.   This same flag later flew above the United Nations charter meeting in San Francisco, over the Big Three conference at Potsdam, and rippled above the White House on 14 August 1945 when the Japanese accepted surrender terms. It was part of a historical display at the Air Force Academy until returned for permanent display at Hickam Air Force Base in 1980.

Above, damaged post exchange at Hickam Field, looking from the parade ground and consolidated barracks; and below, complete devastation inside the big barracks at Hickam Field.   (Denver D. Gray, US Army Military History Institute)

Halfway there, he was strafed by a low-flying Japanese plane. Mortally wounded, he kept on trying to reach that machine gun but fell dead on the way. Time and again, as the machine gunners fell, others rushed to take their places. One man managed to lug—no one knows how—a machine gun to the top of one of the unbombed hangars and was perched up there, popping away at the strafing planes. On the apron in front of the hangars, a "mild-mannered private first class who was an orderly room clerk" climbed into a B-18 and mounted a .30-caliber machine gun in the nose. It was unstable, because the mount was made for an aerial gun; but he braced it against his shoulder and kept up a steady stream of fire. An enemy plane flew low, strafed the B-18 with incendiary bullets, and set it on fire. There was no way for him to escape, and spectators nearby said he did not even seem to try but kept on firing. Long after the leaping flames had enveloped the nose of the plane, they heard his screams and saw the tracer bullets from his machine gun mounting skyward.[11]

The valiant men who fought to defend the base were exceptional individuals, well deserving of the honors they later received (posthumously in many cases). The average and very normal reaction to the attack, however, was fear, confusion, and panic. There were a few extreme cases, such as the "Little Lord Fauntleroy of a second lieutenant" found hiding in a bomb dump, crying with fear and nerves; an unnamed officer of fairly high position who "went all to pieces after the attack and had to be sent back to the states on a stretcher"; and a PFC who also had to be evacuated to the mainland, "crying and combative," for years of neuro-psychiatric care. These individuals just did not have the temperament to withstand the horrors of battle and were probably more

deserving of pity than scorn. On the other hand, unbelievable as it may be, there were a few who took advantage of the chaos resulting from the attack. After the post exchange (PX) was shattered by bombs, for example, a small group of men who had taken shelter under a nearby building were shocked to see an airman looting the place. He emerged from the PX with a case of beer and cartons of cigarettes, started across the parade ground, but was mowed down by a strafer. As he fell, beer cans and packs of cigarettes flew in all directions. Even at the consolidated barracks, amid all the death and destruction, looters helped themselves to items belonging to others. When Ira Southern returned to his third-floor bay after the attack, he found several of his personal things missing, including his new portable Zenith radio.[12]

William Melnyk of the 17th Air Base Group and two friends were sitting around one of the beds in the big barracks, relaxing and chatting after eating an early breakfast. They heard the noise of a low-flying plane; and someone remarked, "It looks like the Navy is practicing dive bombing us again." Less than a minute later, there was a loud explosion. They rushed outside to see what was going on. While standing on the stair landing, looking toward Wing F, they saw a bomb hit Hangar 7 and explode. The resulting concussion blew all three of them off the landing onto the ground. As they got up, they heard the squadron first sergeant yelling for everybody to get out; so they ran toward the parade ground, which soon began to fill up with men coming out of the barracks, some clad only in their underwear. Then a Japanese plane, flying so low that the pilot and rear gunner were clearly visible, began strafing the area. Men were soon falling or running in all directions.[13]

Russell Tener of the 18th Bomb Wing jumped into a pair of trousers and scurried down the stairs from his second-floor squadron bay with many others, heading toward the grassy parade ground. The whistling of falling bombs was clearly audible, as were the frightening sounds of machine-gun fire and exploding bombs. Tener recalled thinking at the time that he had joined the Army and chosen an assignment in Hawaii as a vacation at government expense, but he would be lucky to get through this alive. As he made his way across the parade ground, pandemonium erupted when low-flying aircraft with machine guns blazing began streaking toward the mob of men while dive bombers were unleashing their bombs. He ran toward the base chapel, only to find that it was no longer standing. It had been leveled by a direct hit, leaving only the concrete entry steps. He thought immediately of his friend, Joe Nelles, who was the Catholic chaplain's assistant and went there early every Sunday to prepare the altar for mass. Later, what he feared was confirmed—Joe had been killed in the chapel.[14]

In the meantime, Melnyk dashed for the shelter of the new wooden barracks in Splinter City across the way. He stayed there for a short time, watching some men shooting at the Japanese planes with .45-caliber pistols, then left the area to return to the big barracks and report to the supply room where he worked. While en route, looking at the burning aircraft along the hangar line, he saw a flight of high-level bombers come over and start dropping bombs again. He dashed for the protection of the barracks and later learned that some of the bombs had landed in Splinter City, close to where he had been standing, killing several people. The nearby Snake Ranch beer garden took a direct hit and was demolished, incurring the wrath of a truck company first sergeant. He had bravely endured the first two waves of the attack, but this was too much. Shaking his fist at the sky, he screamed, "You dirty SOBs! You've bombed the most important building on the post!"[15]

When Melnyk reported to the supply room, he was put to work passing out rifles and ammunition to the men of his squadron. Another wave of bombers flew over, and a bomb exploded between Wings E and F, shaking the building. A moment later, someone came running in, shouting, "I need some help; the lieutenant has been hit!" Melnyk went with him to pick up 1st Lt Malcolm J. Brummwell, their squadron adjutant.* He was bleeding across the chest, moaning with pain. They carried him to the supply room and laid him on a counter while someone called the hospital for an ambulance. It arrived a short time later at the front of the building, and they were instructed to bring the lieutenant out. As they slid him off the counter, he fell toward Melnyk, who grasped him, with his bleeding chest against his own. They carried him to the ambulance, laid him on a stretcher, and slid him inside. The ambulance driver and assistant then turned toward Melnyk, thinking he was wounded also because of all the blood on his shirt, and said, "Take it easy now and get into the ambulance." Melnyk protested, saying there was nothing wrong with him. The driver soothingly said, "I know, I know," and kept forcing him

---

*Lieutenant Brummwell was actually in command of Headquarters Squadron, 17th Air Base Group, at the time. He had relieved 1st Lt Howard F. Cooper, the regular commander, who was seriously injured by flying shrapnel at his residence earlier that morning. Concerned about broken mains and loss of water pressure on the base, Brummwell and two airmen had just obtained aluminum kitchen containers to get water before the supply failed, when he was struck down.

Wing L of Hickam Field's big barracks, with its fire-blackened, bullet-scarred walls and wrecked roof, was devastated by the attack. Mess hall is at left.

inside until Melnyk finally climbed into the vehicle but then crawled over the driver's seat, went out the front door, and started to walk away. The ambulance driver, believing he was in shock, began chasing him, yelling at him to come back. He finally gave up, returned to the ambulance, and drove the injured man to the hospital. Lieutenant Brummwell later died of his injuries.[16]

With both Lieutenants Cooper and Brummwell seriously injured, Lieutenant Gray succeeded to the command of the squadron. He had never felt so inadequate. Everyone, including airmen twice his age, looked to him for guidance, which he felt he did not have to give. Nevertheless, he did his best* during his "baptism of fire," rendering aid to the wounded in and around the barracks throughout the attack. The consolidated barracks, reported to be the

most heavily bombed building on Oahu, shook with the force of explosions for what seemed like an eternity. Infantry-trained airmen ordered all personnel to disperse to lessen the possibility of multiple deaths from a single explosion, but many who left the building were killed by strafing or by bomb fragments. The concrete-reinforced barracks actually offered the best protection and was the most resistant to fire. However, bombs that crashed through the roof of the big mess hall located at the center of the barracks took a heavy toll. The first bomb instantly killed 35 men eating breakfast. Trays, dishes, and food splattered everywhere; and, the injured survivors crawled through the rubble to safety. More bombs hit and exploded, and the concussion killed all the Chinese cooks who had sought protection in the freezer room.[17]

Two bombardier cadets from Texas were newly assigned at Hickam Field. They wore blue cadet uniforms with wing insignia

---

*"His best" was good enough to win for Lieutenant Gray the Bronze Star Medal, which was awarded by the Decorations Board in Washington, DC, on 26 October 1944.

Above, sunlight streams through the splintered mess hall roof where bombs entered, inflicting heavy casualties and leaving the place in a shambles.

Below, wall-to-wall debris covers the floor of the mess hall following the attack. (Denver D. Gray, US Army Military History Institute)

on their caps and were soon to be commissioned as second lieutenants. When the attack began, they had no assigned place to report but felt they should "do something," so they headed toward the consolidated barracks to see if they could help. While crossing the baseball field, they looked up and saw bombs falling directly at them; so they hit the ground, and the bombs exploded close by. Falling debris struck and injured one cadet, who wore his arm in a sling for awhile and later received a Purple Heart. The other man was not hurt but lost his cadet cap for which they looked high and low after the attack, because he had promised his Texas girl friend she could have the insignia on it when he was commissioned.[18]

PFC Gabriel W. Christie of the 19th Transport Squadron lived in the two-story wooden barracks of Splinter City. He thought nothing much about it when he heard the first explosion, because he had become accustomed to the sound of blasting dynamite from construction projects in the Navy area. Going out the back of the barracks, he joined some men standing around outside watching Japanese planes circling over Pearl Harbor, then saw one of them drop a bomb. How could the Navy practice so close to their home quarters without endangering their men, he wondered. Upon seeing the rising sun on the wings of another plane that dived lazily down, dropped a bomb, then pulled away in a right bank, his thought was that it didn't seem right for the Navy to be using a foreign power's emblem in their war games. When a third plane dived, dropped a bomb, then flew over Hickam Field strafing personnel, it finally dawned on him that they were actually under hostile attack![19]

Members of the Hawaiian Air Force's Headquarters Squadron, 17th Tow Target Squadron, and 23d Materiel Squadron watch Japanese high-level horizontal bombers heading toward Pearl Harbor. (John W. Wilson)

In the chaos that followed, conflicting stories emerged as to what happened next. Most of the 19th Squadron personnel remembered running to the supply room for guns and ammunition. PFC George J. Gabik stated that when they arrived there, the supply sergeant refused to give them anything, so they "just eased him aside with a little force," broke down the door to the weapons room, and grabbed .45-caliber pistols and ammunition, which was all they had. Christie, on the other hand, recalled one of the lieutenants being in the supply room when they got there and said they were issued .45-caliber pistols and the few Thompson submachine guns that were available. In any event, the actions of "the lieutenant" after that became the subject of numerous but widely differing recollections. Identified as the squadron adjutant, who was a first lieutenant and ROTC graduate from the University of Hawaii, he ordered all the troops to assemble on the parade ground in the direct line of fire, resulting in the loss of many men, according to some sources. First Sergeant Carlos F. McCuiston, on the other hand, unaware of the lieutenant's order, told men approaching him to scatter, take whatever cover was available, and try to stay alive. He stated later that had he known, he most certainly would not have countermanded the lieutenant's order. Another individual reported that the lieutenant called everyone together on the edge of the parade ground, "made the great statement 'Men we are at war,' as if we did not already know it," posted a couple of men on the east and west sides of the parade ground, and instructed them to yell when they saw an aircraft coming. He no sooner said that then the enemy aircraft were upon them, and "we lost several men because of this." According to Christie, however, the officer asked them to assemble in the middle of the parade ground in order to distribute .45-caliber ammunition which had been loaded in a small panel truck. He also asked for a volunteer to drive the truck to the parade ground, so Christie offered to do so. After the ammo was distributed, the lieutenant told Christie to stay with the truck in case he needed it and to drive it off the parade ground and park it along the curb. There were several other such references to the lieutenant; and, regardless of which story was the most accurate, he must have been quite a prominent figure that day to be remembered for his actions by so many people in so many ways.[20]

Russell J. Tener (left) and his friend Bill Enos (far right), while on guard duty at this PX warehouse, escaped harm when the building was shattered from the concussion of a bomb which left a crater (partly visible in left foreground) about 20 feet in diameter and 5 feet deep. (Russell J. Tener)

As the Japanese planes commenced their bombing and strafing runs, most of the men on the parade ground scattered. Many ran back toward Splinter City. A PX warehouse was one of the buildings in that area, and facing it was a little fruit and vegetable stand operated by a Japanese couple during the work week. Christie was momentarily paralyzed with fear as he stared at the approaching enemy planes, but then twisted around and ran for his life. He passed the parked truck that he had been instructed to stay with, and leaped under a metal sink located at one end of the fruit and vegetable stand. The bomb bursts were getting closer and closer, and the concussion from one blast caused the corner of the building to collapse over the sink. Looking across the way, he saw that his truck had been hit and was burning furiously. Nearby, five 55-gallon drums had been perforated by shrapnel from exploding bombs, and their position had protected him from injury. He then saw PFC James I. Lewis, a member of his squadron, lying on his back under the

PX warehouse. He looked so calm that Christie envied his courage, wishing at the time that he could be like him. Later, he found that Lewis was dead, killed by shrapnel which had hit him in the back.[21]

First Sergeant McCuiston, from his position between the street and the 19th Squadron barracks, heard one explosion after another; and the last was a deafening blast which seemed to lift him off the ground. He jumped up and turned to run, hoping to find better shelter before the next bomb fell. A few feet away, two dead airmen were lying face down. One had both legs severed at the buttocks, and his blood had soaked the ground. The other had a massive head wound from an object which had passed through him from the left temple to just above the right ear, and his brains were lying on the ground. In the horror of the moment, McCuiston failed to notice that his own left shirt sleeve and the front of his shirt were bloodstained from wounds which, fortunately, turned out to be

Mangled truck, still burning, parked on F Street next to the parade ground (today's Headquarters Pacific Air Forces parking lot).

Blood-stained stretchers, awaiting the next load of casualties, grimly attest to the severity of injuries suffered by Army Air Forces personnel at Hickam Field. (Denver D. Gray, US Army Military History Institute)

minor. Other squadron members injured near the parade ground were Private First Class Gabik, who was struck on his left leg by a piece of shrapnel, and SSgt Sidney C. Howe of the radio section, whose left arm was nearly blown off. An ambulance picked up both men during a lull in the attack and transported them to the base hospital, where they received a shot of morphine before going on to Tripler Hospital located at Fort Shafter. Another 19th Squadron member, Sgt Jack O. Ehrke, helped carry injured personnel from the parade ground despite being wounded himself by several pieces of shrapnel in his back. He was later awarded the Distinguished Service Cross for this action.[22]

Vehicles of every conceivable type—bread wagons, milk wagons, hand carts, trucks, private cars—were commandeered at Hickam to augment the ambulance fleet and transport wounded personnel to the base hospital; and all available airmen in the immediate area were pressed into service to help load the injured. At the parade ground, they stacked the most badly wounded on top of each other in the back of an ambulance and rushed them to the hospital. PFC Raymond L. Perry of the Army's 29th Car Company was on temporary duty at Fort Armstrong in downtown Honolulu when the first attack occurred, and everyone was scrambling around trying to get away from the antiaircraft shells that were coming down. As they were using contact fuses on the shells, which were not making contact with aircraft, they were exploding upon contact with the ground. Perry was "tired of getting shot at" and they needed vehicles at Hickam to transport wounded to Tripler, so he quickly volunteered to go. Two military policemen on motorcycles escorted their convoy of five trucks to Hickam Field; and they proceeded along Hangar Avenue, past the consolidated barracks, and pulled into the area between Hangars 9 and 13. With the help of Army Air Forces personnel, they began loading wounded men into their trucks. Then at 0845, someone shouted, "Here they come again!"; and everyone took cover in the closest hangar doorwell. After the explosions and firing subsided, they went out and found all their trucks completely demolished. Of the 17 men they had picked up, only three were still alive. Earlier, someone had taken a bedsheet, painted a large red cross on it, and attached it to the top of the center truck; but all it proved to be was a target for the attackers.[23]

From the first moments of the attack until the close of the day, Hickam's small new hospital, which had opened only a few weeks before, was the focal point of activity on the base. Capt Frank H. Lane, the acting hospital commander, was an Army Air Forces flight surgeon who lived with his wife, Carmen, and their two sons in family housing located only a short distance from the Pearl Harbor boundary. He awoke shortly before 0800 that Sunday morning to take his family to church and had just finished dressing when he heard a loud explosion. His first thought was that one of the oil storage tanks on the hill just inland from Pearl Harbor had exploded. When he looked out the bedroom window, a cloud of black smoke in that direction seemed to confirm his guess. He ran downstairs and out the back door, just in time to see a small plane marked with the rising sun insignia of Japan flying slowly by, slightly above the level of the tops of the two-story houses. He could plainly see the pilot and thought at the time that a Japanese carrier must be in Hawaii on a diplomatic mission. As the plane flew toward Ford Island in Pearl Harbor, more explosions occurred; then another plane flying in front burst into flames and fell in the water. Only then did Captain Lane realize that a real attack was underway. He called to his wife to stay inside, ran to his car parked behind their quarters, and drove to the hospital about four blocks away. By then, the air was filled with the high-pitched whine of diving planes, the chatter of machine-gun fire, and the roar of exploding bombs.[24]

The Hickam hospital, located about three blocks away from the flight line, was built of reinforced concrete three stories high, with wide, tropical screened porches on three sides. In the back, and connected to it with a ramp, was a building that housed medical department personnel, a kitchen, and mess hall. The hospital had a capacity of only 40 beds, about 25 of which were occupied at the beginning of the raid. Seriously ill patients were normally sent to Tripler General Hospital. Hickam's hospital staff consisted of about seven medical

Hickam's small new 40-bed hospital received its "baptism of fire" on 7 December 1941 when its medical staff treated hundreds of casualties. (Bernard C. Tysen)

officers, five dentists, seven nurses, and forty enlisted men.[25]

As Captain Lane parked his car on the street in front of the hospital, the medical officer of the day, Capt Andre d'Alfonso, arrived in an ambulance with a wounded soldier. The captain had been at the flight line to meet the incoming flight of B-17s, to get them sprayed for bugs, and certainly did not expect to treat victims of an enemy attack. About the same time, a severely wounded soldier came in, carried on a door, conscious, but with a good part of his abdomen and one hip cut out by a piece of shrapnel. Captain Lane felt he was probably beyond hope but, to reassure him, sent him on to the operating room, telling him he would be fixed up. By this time, all available personnel had been pressed into service. The entire hospital staff came in, even those who had been on night duty and just relieved at 0700 that morning. Three Filipino orderlies—Maguleno H. Jucor, Torihio Kendica, and Cosme R. Echanis—ran through a hail of bombs and machine-gun fire to get to their jobs. Hospital patients left their beds and either went home or joined in to help with the flood of casualties. All the phones in the facility were busy with calls for help. The trucks and drivers augmenting the fleet of seven ambulances began a regular pickup of injured at the consolidated barracks, mess hall, and the flight line, where most of the casualties were occurring, then made regular runs to Tripler.[26]

When the first of the injured started coming in, they found the hospital staff prepared and waiting. Surgeons performed numerous emergency operations to remove bomb fragments. One of the dentists, Lt Robert Lee Kushner, turned surgeon that day, working alongside Lieutenants White

and Garret and all the other medics who put in long, continuous hours of labor. Not knowing how long the raid would last, they did not attempt to fill the beds in the Hickam hospital but evacuated the wounded to Tripler as fast as they could after administering first aid (which was limited to applying tourniquets, splints, bandages, and giving morphine). The pharmacy prepared morphine in syringes holding ten doses each, and they did not have the time to change needles between patients. Every few minutes, a medical officer would go out and check the corpses that were being stacked in back of the hospital to make sure that none of the living was among them.[27]

Sometime during the attack, a delayed-action 500-pound bomb landed on the front lawn of the Hickam hospital, about 60 or 70 feet from the building. Shortly afterward, the air was filled with the acrid smell of the explosives from the bomb, and a number of people yelled "Gas! Gas!", adding to the tumult and confusion. Hickam's nurses, including Monica E. Conter and M. Kathleen Coberly, provided a calm, steadying influence and won the praise and admiration of all for their hard work, seeing to the needs of the patients. This was the first time that Army nurses had been on the front line of battle; always in the past they were in evacuation hospitals at least 10 miles behind the lines. Annie Gayton Fox, who was the nurse in charge that day, later received the Purple Heart, not for wounds but for bravery. She was believed to be the first woman receiving the medal since it was revived as an award of honor by President Roosevelt in 1932.[28]

Hundreds of casualties arrived at the hospital on 7 December 1941, but two made a special impression on Captain Lane. The first was a soldier who walked in the front

One of the more than 200 men killed on Army Air Forces installations on Oahu.

door under his own power with one arm completely gone but waving his remaining arm in greeting, still managing to wear a big smile on his face and make a joking remark. The other was a young flight surgeon, 1st Lt William R. Schick, from one of the B-17s arriving in the middle of the raid. He was sitting on the stairs leading to the second floor of the hospital and drew Captain Lane's attention because of his winter uniform (which was never worn in Hawaii) and the insignia of a medical officer on his lapels. He had a wound in the face but, when approached for treatment, said he was all right and pointed to the casualties on litters on the floor, saying "Take care of them." Captain Lane told him he would be placed in the next ambulance going to Tripler. He was, but died after arriving there. Schick General Hospital, which occupies 160 acres in the northern limits of the city of Clinton, Iowa, was later named in his honor.[29]

The 31st Bomb Squadron Commander, Captain Waldron, was at his quarters when the "fireworks" began. His six-year-old daughter ran into the bedroom where he and his wife were and said, "Dad, they're firing at Fort Kam!"* He listened to the racket and, at first, told her to go on back to bed. Then, hearing more explosions, he got up and looked out the window. The first thing he saw was an airplane going by, right at about eye level, with a rising sun on it. He shook his head—"I was kind of foggy"—and waited for a moment, then saw another one. He pulled on his pants, ran downstairs, looked outside, and saw more planes. His next reaction was, "They're having an exercise here, and they never told us about it!" Watching the planes circling overhead, he saw their "fish" (big torpedoes) being released and, although Pearl Harbor

---

*This was Fort Kamehameha, the Coast Artillery base to the south of Hickam Field.

couldn't be seen from where he was, heard loud explosions from that direction and witnessed a lot of black smoke billowing upward. Then he realized, "This is for real! The Japanese are attacking us!" He quickly pulled on his shirt and hat, jumped into his Buick, and headed for the line. The aircraft were all parked there like sitting ducks and, by the time he arrived, were on fire. Only two or three of them could be dispersed; the rest were hit and damaged so severely, they couldn't be moved. As he crossed the hangar line, he saw the Japanese planes flying overhead and strafing people in the area.[30]

Captain Waldron's next thought was for his men in the barracks, so he started running in that direction, thinking maybe he should get his people out of there. Crossing through one wing of the consolidated barracks trying to get to the second, he heard the whistling sound of falling bombs. He looked up through the open archways and could see the bombs coming, so he dived

Looking out toward the flight line from the courtyard between heavily damaged Wing E (left) and Wing D of the big barracks at Hickam Field.

through that open space on his belly. One of the men running with him was hit by shrapnel, and Waldron never saw him again. He then went to the squadron supply room and was there when that wing was hit by bombs on the third floor. After talking to some of his people, he concluded that the barracks was probably the safest place for them to stay. Since there was nothing he could do there, he started thinking about his wife and children, then began running toward his quarters with the idea of getting his family off the base. He was on foot all this time, because his car had been hit while parked near the flight line. Passing the base hospital, he saw more high-level bombers overhead and a string of bombs coming down, one of which looked like it had his name on it. So down he went again on his belly, beside the curb by the hospital building. A bomb missed the hospital but landed on the front lawn, shaking the ground, and shrapnel flew right over the place where he lay. He then got up, ran on down the road to his quarters, and found a large group of women and children gathered there. He went out into the street, commandeered a truck, got everyone aboard, then said to the driver, "Take these women and children to the hills up behind Honolulu, back up in the hills there. And God bless you."[31]

On the flight line, 19th Transport Squadron personnel acted to save their two C-33 aircraft, one of which was riddled so badly by enemy machine-gun fire that it later acquired the name "Patches." Lt L. A. Stoddard received the Silver Star for taxiing that aircraft to the safety of a revetment while it was being strafed. The other C-33 was just out of maintenance and had no fuel in its tanks, so PFC Samuel D. Rodibaugh and some other squadron personnel pushed it across the runway to the

Hickam Field personnel man this gun emplacement set up in a bomb crater between Hangars 11-13 and 15-17.

grass area. No sooner had they done this than three Japanese planes came strafing across the field. A ditch had been dug nearby, but the dirt pile was on their side, making it difficult to hide behind, so they just hit the ground and lay motionless. In the meantime, TSgt Arthur C. Townsend obtained a small truck, asked 2d Lt John E. Roesch to help him get some ammunition and a machine gun, after which they both headed out to the bunkers. After dropping off some of the ammunition, they proceeded across the runway, which was under heavy bombardment and machine-gun strafing, and reached the far side of the field, where they set up their machine gun and commenced firing at the Japanese. To cool the weapon, Sergeant Townsend shot a hole in his World War I metal helmet, making a funnel out of it, so that water on the ground nearby could be scooped up and poured into the small hole in the water jacket of the machine gun. This permitted them to fire away until all the ammunition was exhausted. Sergeant Townsend and Lieutenant Roesch later received the Silver Star for heroism in action.[32]

Another gun emplacement, hastily constructed in front of Hangar 5, was manned shortly after the raid by PFC Raymond Perry (left, with binoculars) and Cpl Howard Marquardt of South Dakota. A burned-out aircraft engine, sand bags, table, and debris from the attack made up the construction material for this bunker.

The 23d Bomb Squadron Commander, Capt Laverne G. ("Blondie") Saunders, had been at his quarters (located a block east of the Pearl Harbor channel) dressed to go to mass. As he stepped outside to pick up the Sunday paper, he heard a big blast. That's pretty loud for dynamite, he said to himself, thinking the Navy was doing some construction work again across the channel. Just then two Japanese torpedo bombers flew over his quarters at about a 50-foot altitude, low enough for Saunders to plainly see the pilots' faces. His wife and two sons came running out of the house, so he ordered them to get back inside and lie down. He had seen the rising sun on the planes overhead and "knew we were at war." He jumped in his car and drove down to the hangar line, only to find that a bomb had exploded in the hangar housing his B-17 and set the bomber afire. He then drove down to the consolidated barracks, parked, and ran to the far end where his men were quartered to tell them to get out to the hangar line to save the airplanes. Upon arrival, however, the men found the airplanes locked and the keys in the armament section, which had been bombed and blown sky high. They shot the locks off the aircraft, taxied them out to a dispersed position, then loaded bombs by hand with the help of ropes since the bomb-loading equipment had been damaged. They finally got three B-17s loaded.[33]

In the BOQ area, 2d Lt Lee E. Metcalfe of the 23d Bomb Squadron had dressed early, was standing on the second floor balcony of his quarters looking out toward the Officers' Club, and was planning to go to the Junior Officer's Mess for breakfast. He looked up and saw planes diving on the end of the Hickam runway, then saw smoke coming up from that area.

He thought at the time that the Navy flyers were certainly making their practice runs look realistic. Just then, one of the planes pulled out of a dive and made a steep climbing turn close to and just above where he was standing. He could see the pilot's face and the red balls painted on the wings of his plane. Next he saw flames coming from Hangar 17, so he headed out to the flight line to see what was going on. There wasn't much he could do, since he had just graduated from flying school and received his wings only a little more than a month before. As he crossed the railroad tracks along the street, he saw pieces of bodies where a bomb had hit. Then a B-17 appeared on the scene, with gear down for a landing, trying to outrun a Japanese fighter that was right on its tail with blazing guns. It was going too fast to land, so it pulled up and went around for another approach. The fighter stayed on its tail, firing a burst whenever in position to do so, but the B-17 managed to land. As it braked to a stop, a burst of machine-gun fire set it ablaze just ahead of the vertical stabilizer. The crew ran from the plane as it burned in two and sagged in the middle. Shortly afterward, the first wave of the attack was over, leaving Hickam with burning aircraft and smoking buildings. Lieutenant Metcalfe started to head back toward his BOQ, wondering what to do next, when a loudspeaker announcement directed all personnel to report to the flight line. He walked to Hangar 4, where his squadron commander was talking to a small group of personnel on the ramp. Someone looked up and saw a formation of aircraft coming in from the ocean over the end of the flight line, and the commander ordered everyone to get off the hangar line at once. The Japanese planes started strafing the B-18s lined up wingtip to wingtip on the taxi strip, setting them afire.[34]

Above, smoke pours from burning
aircraft and buildings at Hickam
Field   following   the   Japanese
attack.   Right, B-18 wreckage on
the Hickam flight line.   Below,
broken water main on 6th Street at
Hickam Field with upended car on
the left and tilted lamp post on the
right.

The skill of the Japanese pilots and the incredibly low altitudes at which they flew made an indelible impression on many survivors of the 7 December 1941 attack. From his BOQ room, 2d Lt Vernon H. Reeves saw a Japanese plane speeding by his window with its wingtip almost touching the ground. It appeared to him to be targeting the door of the Officers' Club and, he thought, "the guy is awful good to be able to do that. He must be an expert. I couldn't do it. I don't know anyone who could do it." Jessie Reed, wife of 2d Lt Stanley J. Reed, looked out the front door of her on-base quarters and saw the planes flying so low, the pilots' goggles were clearly visible. Sgt Robert G. Crouse, a supply sergeant, said he could almost see the expression on their faces. Several people witnessed one Japanese pilot skimming along the parking ramp so low that his aircraft's propeller tips flicked the asphalt and the belly tank scraped off, scooting down the ramp. He finally pulled up, hitting the hills beyond the field, according to one man; crashing into the sea, according to another; getting away with it completely, according to a third. Radio operator Harold S. Kaye observed a similar incident, which he said was also viewed by three other men. Looking between the operations building and Hangars 3 and 5, he saw a Japanese plane touch down on Runway 3, sit there for a fraction of a second, then take off again. "It was as if the Japanese pilot wanted to touch American soil and go back to his carrier with a good story. Whatever his reason, it was a remarkable and brilliant feat of flying," said Kaye.[35]

In response to an order to "Disperse those planes!", scores of men rushed around on the Hickam flight line to do so, heedless of the rain of bullets. A general's aide was trying to taxi one of the B-18s when strafers put an engine out of commission. It was no easy job to taxi such a heavy plane with only one engine going, but he did it by racing the one engine until it pulled its side of the plane forward, then slamming that brake on hard, which forced the other wing up. Waddling and crawfishing along in this manner, all the time under enemy fire, he finally brought the plane across the landing mat to comparative safety. While fire department personnel fought flames at the tail end of some of the planes, daring crew members jumped upon the wings, disconnected the engines, and pulled their 800- or 900-pound weight to the edge of the apron. Their quick thinking and action saved the expensive engines.[36]

Base fire department personnel responding to the scene faced a formidable task, with fires blazing in the hangars, aircraft, barracks, and numerous other facilities. Broken water mains from bomb blasts, which also hit the fire station itself, crippled their efforts. PFC Howard E. King, a hoseman, had just manned one of the fire engines when his crew chief, Sgt Joseph J. Chagnon, suddenly yelled, "Look out!" Before he could move, there was a blinding flash, and something hit him like a ton of bricks. From his prone position, he peered through the smoke and could barely make out the twisted engine, Chagnon dying, and his own shattered leg. Fire Chief William L. Benedict also suffered injuries when blown 60 feet by a bomb, then strafed by a Japanese pilot. Searchers at first couldn't find him. Then one young soldier told a chaplain that the fire chief had died in his arms; so Mr. Benedict's name appeared on the list of dead. He was finally found, bleeding in 23 places from shrapnel about two hours after the attack began, and later read his own death notice when a doctor at

Tripler showed him a newspaper clipping prematurely announcing his death.[37]

Under a mutual aid pact, 22 firemen from Honolulu Fire Department companies* responded when the alarm rang, calling for help at Hickam Field. When they reached Hickam's main gate on Kamehameha Highway, the first wave of the attack was over. The fire fighters saw dead, dying, and wounded bodies lying everywhere; the multi-story concrete barracks off the main street was burning fiercely; an underground gas main at the base's entrance had been hit and was spewing flame dozens of feet into the air; and aircraft hangars and a quarter-mile long row of planes parked outside were also ablaze. They reported to the Hickam fire station upon arrival but discovered that the station had been bombed and was a shambles. One fire engine had been driven about 20 feet out onto the ramp, apparently trying to respond, but it was badly strafed and the driver was dead, slumped over the steering wheel. The other engine never got out of the station. Thus, the firemen from Engines 4 and 6 (Palama and Kalihi stations) suddenly found themselves to be

The Hickam fire station, wrecked by bombing and machine-gun fire.

the only fire-fighting force available. Shortly afterward, however, Engine 1 from Honolulu's Central station on South Beretania Street arrived to assist.[38]

Hickam's primary water main had been struck by a bomb, leaving an enormous crater which was filling rapidly with water, and no hydrants were functional. Lt Frederick Kealoha, who was in charge of the Honolulu Fire Department companies on the scene, had just decided to try drafting water from the bomb crater when more Japanese planes appeared overhead. He screamed at the fire fighters to take cover, and they scattered in all directions. For the next 15 minutes, "hell rained down from the skies in the form of whistling bombs and screaming machine gun bullets, seemingly strafing everyone and everything in sight." That quarter hour seemed to last forever, as the firemen tried to make themselves invisible to the Japanese. When the second wave of the attack was finally over, the fire fighters hesitantly emerged from their hiding places and began to assess the latest round of death and destruction. Capt

_____

*A "company" in fire department terminology was defined as a single specialized operational unit consisting of one or two pieces of apparatus and the personnel who manned the vehicle(s). Companies were designated according to their function; e.g., engine company (to supply water), ladder company (ventilation and salvage), rescue company, etc. In everyday usage, the term "company" was often deleted, so Engine Company 6, for example, was referred to simply as Engine 6. All of Honolulu's engine companies in 1941 were "two-piece companies" consisting of a pumper (or engine) and a hosewagon. Thus, Engine Company 6 consisted of Pumper 6 and Hosewagon 6.

Above, Honolulu Fire Department pumper with suction hose drawing water from bomb crater next to Hangar 7. (Denver D. Gray, US Army Military History Institute) Below, firemen battled these oil flames and numerous other fires around the base.

Thomas S. Macy, Capt John Carreira, and Hoseman Harry Tuck Lee Pang were dead. Lieutenant Kealoha and Hoseman Moses Kalilikane were critically wounded; and three others—Hoseman John A. Gilman, Solomon H. Naauao, Jr., and George Correa —were also injured.* The remaining firemen did little fire fighting for awhile, concentrating instead on providing aid to the injured men.[39]

Honolulu Fire Department apparatus sustained considerable damage from repeated strafings and from bomb fragments. The chemical tank of Wagon 1 was pierced by shrapnel, Pumper 6 had too many bullet holes to count, Wagon 6 was afire, all six tires of Pumper 1 were punctured, and radiators of several units were spewing miniature geysers of water through bullet holes. The resourceful fire fighters got their damaged equipment functioning by using brown soap and toilet paper from nearby latrines to plug holes in the radiators, then began attacking the fires. Three pumpers dropped their suction hoses into the bomb crater that by now was filled with water from the ruptured main, and this was their primary source of water until Hickam's water system was restored in the afternoon. Civilian employees of the Hawaiian Air Depot also helped fight fires in Hickam's shops and hangars. General Mechanic Helper William Garretson quickly converted a gas tanker to a water truck, which was driven to nearby Bishop Point, filled with seawater, and returned in time to help fire fighters save the main shop building. Another mechanic helper, Clifford Oliver, drove a truck into a burning repair building to remove valuable aircraft engines. James Mahr, Robert Awong, Nicolas Lenchanko, Volney McRoberts, and Charles Baker prevented fires in the engineering building from spreading to the adjacent repair hangars. It took many hours of backbreaking labor to finally quell all the fires on the base, and the last Honolulu Fire Department company left at about midnight Sunday.[40]

Earlier, when the attack began, members of the 58th Bombardment Squadron (Light) immediately reported to the flight line where their disarmed A-20A aircraft had been carefully lined up on Friday. To get the planes flyable required a trip to the Hawaiian Air Depot for machine gun mounts and landing gear tires to replace those being shot up by the strafing Japanese aircraft. The A-20s also had to be loaded with bombs. Sgt William H. Heydt and other ordnance personnel, following established emergency procedures, had gone out to the ammunition storage area, loaded 600-pound bombs on trailers, and pulled them with tractors to the flight line to arm all available aircraft. The sight of "busted fuselages, wings dropping on the ground, tires flat, [and] engines falling out of the wings" stunned them; and Heydt was momentarily at a loss to know what to do, because he could see no planes in any condition to be loaded with bombs. A major then directed him to "take these bombs back and get 300-pound bombs, because they're going to bring out the A-20s." As he spoke, bullets sprayed the area, and they all flattened themselves under one of the trailers. After the enemy aircraft vanished, they crawled out; and the captain of Heydt's outfit, who had appeared on the scene, said that they had to go back and unload the 600-pound bombs. Instead, Heydt drove the trailer alongside a B-17, ordered his men to

---

*Another fire fighter, Patrick J. McCabe, suffered leg injuries at Hickam Field when a bomb exploded and, like the others involved, later received a Purple Heart; however, in his case, he was injured two days after the attack.

dump the bombs, then returned to the ammo storage area to get 300 pounders, which they then loaded into the A-20s. The men, fearing more strafing attacks, worked faster than they had ever done before. When the Japanese planes returned with machine guns blazing, everyone ran for the grassy area on the other side of the field and hit the ground. A private first class who was "one of the best men on the crew" fell dead right in front of Heydt, a line of bullets running up his back, almost splitting him in two and transforming what had once been a fine young man into a bloody mass of shattered bones and flesh. The 58th Bombardment Squadron subsequently received orders from General Martin to search for and attack a Japanese carrier reported south of Barbers Point. At 1127, the first four A-20As led by Maj William J. Holzapfel, Jr., taxied out and took off. The flight of these Douglas twin-engine bombers was the most inspiring sight of the morning for the downtrodden Hickam troops.[41]

Douglas A-20 in flight.

CHAPTER VI

HELL IN PARADISE: FIGHTER COMMAND

"It was the first time I had ever seen a plunging dive bomber and it was an awesome sight. Nothing in warfare is more frightening. Hurtling down on us was the dive bomber being followed by another, while six or seven more in echelon awaited their turn. The leader pulled out right over us in a spectacular climbing bank. We could clearly see the rising sun of Japan on his wings and fuselage."

Pvt Wilfred D. Burke, 72d Pursuit Squadron
Wheeler Field, 7 December 1941

Wheeler Field

The Japanese hit Wheeler in two waves, the first shortly before 0800 and the second about an hour later. Principal targets of the first attack were aircraft and buildings along the hangar line and people in the immediate area. In the second raid, seven enemy planes approached from the south and fired machine guns at aircraft being taxied onto the airdrome. This attack, which lasted less than five minutes, was made by fighters and horizontal bombers expending the remainder of their ammunition after attacking the Kaneohe Naval Air Station. Wheeler had little protection against aerial attack, with no antiaircraft guns, no trenches, and no air raid shelters. The base had only five machine guns, which were mounted on top of the hangars and the big barracks; and the perimeter guard was armed with rifles.[1]

Colonel Flood, the base commander, was in front of his quarters talking to some people when the attack began. He saw a bomb hit near the Wheeler depot area and at first thought someone out on maneuvers must have accidentally dropped it. Immediately afterward, a group of low-flying airplanes sped by, only 50 to 75 feet off the ground. "You could almost hit them with a rock if you had it," thought Flood. When he saw the insignia of the Japanese rising sun, he knew what had happened and hurried down to the flight line. By then, hangars and aircraft were in flames, and a thick pall of black smoke hung over the area.[2]

The bombs struck and burned Hangars 1 and 3, in addition to wrecking a PX storehouse and a warehouse filled with cement. One bomb hit the 6th Pursuit Squadron's barracks, entering a window on the second floor, where it exploded and caused considerable property damage and personal injuries. Another landed in an open area and made a crater 15 feet in diameter and 6 feet deep. After expending their bombs, the enemy planes dropped down to a very low altitude and machine-gunned aircraft parked in front of the hangars and also fired incendiary bullets through the

Wrecked planes on Wheeler Field flight line, with Hangar 2 in background and (on the right) tent quarters where many enlisted men were killed.

windows of buildings, attempting to set them afire. The tent area between Hangars 2 and 3 came under heavy attack.[3]

Around 0700 that Sunday morning, Pvt Wilfred D. Burke, an aircraft armorer assigned to the 72d Pursuit Squadron, reluctantly got out of bed in one of the tents on the hangar line. He had been awakened by his boss, Sgt Forest Wills, and resented being disturbed so early on the only morning he could sleep late, even though he had promised to go to church with Wills. A deeply religious man, "Deacon" Wills had become a good friend and, as Burke put it, "was sincerely concerned with my spiritual welfare, having observed that I was a worthless fellow given to drinking beer."

After eating breakfast in an unusually empty mess hall, Burke still had some spare time before church so he joined a group of

Splintered building filled with bags of cement. (Joe K. Harding)

men in the open quadrangle in the middle of the tent area "shooting the bull." As they talked, a flight of planes passed by to the west of Wheeler, heading toward Pearl Harbor. "It's the Navy," said someone; but they were surprised to see black puffs of antiaircraft fire fill the sky over Pearl Harbor. Their astonishment soon turned to stark terror when Japanese aircraft almost directly overhead began diving down toward them.[4]

According to some sources, the first place hit was the gas storage dump on the southwest corner of the base, where all of Wheeler's flammables such as gas, turpentine, and lacquer were kept. Most witnesses, however, reported that the first bomb struck Hangar 1, where the base engineering shops were located. The tremendous blast caused skylights to blow out and clouds of smoke to billow upward, making it appear as though the entire hangar was lifted off its foundation. The sheet metal, electrical, and paint shops in the front half of the hangar were decimated; but the machine and wood shops and the tool room in the back were spared, protected by a concrete block, dividing wall.[5]

The diving planes released their bombs from one end of the hangar line to the other. No one was in sight at first except weary guards who had maintained an all-night vigil against possible sabotage, but

Badly damaged barracks of the 6th Pursuit Squadron, which suffered heavy casualties. (Joe K. Harding)

others quickly began arriving on the scene. Sgt Mobley L. Hall, crew chief assigned to the Headquarters Squadron, 18th Pursuit Group (Interceptor), was at his quarters in the new defense housing area at Kemoo Farms when he heard the first explosion. Knowing that something was wrong, he immediately drove to his duty station at the hangar. When he arrived, the bombing was still going on and "everybody was there . . . doing everything as rapidly as possible." Officers and enlisted men alike were

Above, Hangar 1, devastated by the Japanese attack, with block dividing wall visible on left. This saved many of the base engineering shops from destruction.

Below, A severely damaged P-36 sits in the rubble of Hangar 1 at Wheeler.

battling fires, tending the wounded and dying, dragging equipment and supplies from burning hangars, and pushing or towing undamaged aircraft toward dispersal bunkers. General Davidson was in the midst of his troops, pushing airplanes around. Capt James O. Beckwith, 72d Pursuit Squadron Commander, concentrated his efforts on relieving the suffering of his men, whose tent complex had been strafed and burned. All of his new P-40 aircraft were ablaze and could not be saved. Sergeant Hall's squadron had three planes assigned—two AT-6s and an OA-9. One AT-6, in the hangar following installation of a new engine, was destroyed by fire when the hangar took a direct hit; but the two other aircraft, parked on the ramp in the open, escaped damage. Wheeler personnel who rushed to move aircraft out of burning hangars included SSgt Charles A. Fay of the 72d Pursuit Squadron, who managed to run into a blazing hangar and pull out a plane even though he was wounded. Pvt Donald D. Plant of the 46th Pursuit Squadron (Fighter) was killed while assisting in the removal of injured. The men on the line experienced great difficulty in separating aircraft that were afire from those that were not because many of the otherwise undamaged fighters had flat tires due to all the strafing and flying debris in the air. The biggest problem of all, however, was trying to get the aircraft guns loaded; because the hangar where much of the ammunition had been stored was on fire, and the ammunition was exploding like firecrackers.[6]

Burke and his friends, as well as many other Wheeler personnel, fled from the strafing attack in the flight line area, scattering in all directions. Burke headed for the married NCOs' quarters a block away, thinking the attackers were unlikely to waste their ammunition on family homes. As he ran across the street corner nearest his tent, a bomb struck the pavement behind him and killed several fleeing men. When he reached the first row of family housing, he placed his back against the wall of a house and looked back toward the hangars. He was on higher ground and could clearly see the extent of the carnage and devastation. By then, the dive bombers had dropped all their bombs, regrouped, and were methodically strafing planes of the 14th Pursuit Wing which were lined up by squadron, wingtip to wingtip, in precise rows on the ramp. The thick pall of oily black smoke from burning planes and hangars stretched over the flight line and was hanging almost as low as the tent tops. This dense smoke cover served as a screen for the 46th Pursuit Squadron's P-36 aircraft parked in the last row on the west end of the Wheeler flight line, preventing the Japanese from pinpointing them as targets.[7]

After the firing ceased and the dive bombers had gone away, Burke headed back toward his tent. Reaching the corner where the bomb had exploded, he was horrified to see six or seven torn bodies lying around, one of which had been completely denuded by the bomb blast, its head and one arm missing from the torso. Reaching his tent, Burke went inside to pick up his helmet and found two other men getting theirs. The helmets had only recently been issued and were the old World War I "tin hats." They all had to stop and take the time to lace in the helmet linings, indicating how unprepared they were for an attack. A corporal ordered Burke to assist with casualties in the next tent, which was riddled with holes. The first man he saw was beyond help, crouched down on the floor in a bizarre position of death with

Above, the roar of flames in Hangar 3 was punctuated by firecracker-like explosions from the great quantity of ammunition stored there; and below is another view of blazing fires in the twisted remains of Hangar 3 at Wheeler Field. (Joe K. Harding)

Above, when the flames died down and the smoke cleared, all that remained was the skeleton of Hangar 3; and below, total devastation in Hangar 3. (Joe K. Harding)

part of his head knocked away. A seriously wounded soldier lay on his bunk with his abdomen ripped open by a bomb fragment, exposing his intestines. He was conscious and stared at them but said nothing. They carried him on a stretcher to the dispensary, where several other wounded men had already been brought in and were lying on the floor awaiting medical attention. They were all silent and uncomplaining.[8]

Returning to the flight line, Burke was just in time to hear a shouted alarm that the Japanese were attacking again. He dashed toward the NCO housing area once more and got a clear view of the enemy planes firing their machine guns at aircraft on the ramp. He could not help but be impressed with the skill and daring of these adversaries, who were so badly underestimated by the Americans. "They had been portrayed as little near-sighted

men wearing glasses, [and] this arrogance led to this debacle. The enemy . . . was not to be considered lightly," he thought. When the last of the Japanese planes had flown off, Private Burke went back to the flight line and saw the first sign of military organization. An armed sentry had been posted, giving orders to returning personnel: "Colonel says everyone on the flight line!" They could hear the constant pop of exploding ammunition, which continued for two or three days. This came from Hangar 3, which along with the base engineering hangar had suffered the most damage. It held a tremendous amount of ammunition, including several million rounds of .50-caliber ammo that had been taken out of the planes on the ramp and stored in the hangar as another antisabotage measure.[9]

The immediate task at hand was to salvage whatever planes were still flyable or repairable. The operational planes were

Many enlisted members of the 72d Pursuit Squadron were killed or seriously injured in these tent quarters along Wheeler's hangar line.

Hangar row at Wheeler Field, with Hangar 3 on the right and the burnt remains of tents which were hit hard by the attacking Japanese.

taxied to the east end of the field, where mechanics and armorers began to work frantically, checking them out in preparation for flight. There were many more pilots than available aircraft, so a simple system evolved in which the pilots ran for the planes when a call came through to scramble them. The first one arriving got the cockpit. One pilot accused another of not running very fast, and a fist fight ensued. Burke saw the humor of the situation and took comfort in knowing that he was not the only one with "cold feet." In the middle of the chaos, personnel on the line saw a large bomber flying in very low and landing crossways on Wheeler's grassy, rectangular airfield. The plane seemed doomed to crash into the hangars, even if it got through the obstacle course of burning aircraft, but it managed to spin around and pull up short. Crew members hastily scrambled out of what turned out to be a B-17 Flying Fortress. Nervous Wheeler

personnel had greeted this huge plane with rifle fire, but, according to Burke, "Fortunately, our people were notoriously poor marksmen and I don't think any of the crew was hit by the hostile welcome."[10]

First Lieutenant Teuvo ("Gus") Ahola of the 19th Pursuit Squadron was present when General Davidson went over to welcome the tall, slender lieutenant who had piloted the B-17 from Hamilton Field, California, and managed to bring it safely down in the midst of the Japanese attack. Earlier, when the attack began, Ahola was in his on-base BOQ located on Lilienthal Road. Upon hearing machine-gun fire and a loud explosion, he peered out through the venetian blinds and saw a cloud of smoke over the western end of the field, then spotted a Japanese Zero overhead. He immediately headed out toward the flight line in his 1939 Ford covertible but ran over a Coke bottle and got a flat tire, so he sped

Above, resourceful crews remove parts from a demolished P-40 for use on repairable aircraft.

Left, aircraft wreckage on the Wheeler flight line, in front of a fire-blackened Hangar 3 and a virtually undamaged Hangar 4 (with radio tower on roof). In the foreground is a demolished amphibian plane. (Joe K. Harding)

Below, looking through a heap of wrecked planes at Wheeler Field for salvageable parts.

off on foot the rest of the way. Reaching his P-40, which was in the first row of fighters on the eastern end of the ramp, he climbed aboard and yanked off the collar device which locked the controls. The engine of his aircraft was intact, so he started it up and taxied out of the line of aircraft, intending to get it away from the flight line area. Just then he saw a Japanese plane coming straight toward him. With no ammo in his guns, he thought, "I'll ram the SOB!" and tried to get his P-40 off the ground, but there was no lift since the fabric covering the control surfaces had been burned off. All he could do was get out of the middle of the field, taxiing at high speed to the far side, where he got the plane into a revetment.[11]

Before the attack began, Pvt Henry C. Woodrum was at the mess hall, pleased to see only four people in line ahead of him. The mess hall was as empty as the 500-man consolidated barracks had been when he woke up early that morning and saw only a few bunks occupied. Obviously, most of the GIs hadn't returned from Honolulu where they headed as soon as the island-wide alert ended at noon the day before. As Woodrum reached for a food tray, the deep roar of a diving plane filled the air, blotting out all other sounds until it was absorbed by a loud explosion which shook the windows and echoed through the high-ceilinged room. A newcomer behind him, thinking it was a crash, commented, "Boy, that lieutenant sure hit hard!" Turning to look out the window, Woodrum saw a mustard-colored airplane making a climbing turn, revealing a huge red disk on the underside of its wings. "That's no crash," he shouted. "It's the Japs!" Others crowded around the window for a look, then tried to rush outside at the same time, jamming the main entrance. Woodrum took a shortcut by

vaulting over a steam table and running through the rear of the kitchen, as a cook screamed obscenities at him. He dashed out the doorway onto a loading dock, paused to look upward, and saw a low-wing monoplane that seemed to be diving directly toward him. He froze as a bomb detached itself from the fuselage and arched downward, exploding nearby. The shock wave hurled him from the doorway, back into the building, across a hall, and through the open door of a walk-in storage area. Wet, smelly vegetables spilled on top of him from crates on the shelves. He made his way through the clutter back to the doorway, jumped off the dock, and ran toward the 14th Pursuit Wing headquarters.[12]

As Woodrum dashed up a steep slope leading to a construction site, where foundation trenches had been dug and lumber stacked ready for use, machine-gun slugs raked the dirt in front of him, so he scrambled behind a high stack of two-by-fours for protection. When the strafing stopped, he raised his head to look around and could smell the odor of burning oil. Across the way, almost every building along the flight line seemed to be on fire, and the Japanese pilots continued to strafe hangars, aircraft, and fleeing personnel. The new P-40s were being blown to bits, their burning parts scattering along the ramp in all directions, setting other planes on fire. One P-40 fell apart in two pieces, its prop pointing almost straight up. A P-36 exploded, hurling flaming debris upon a nearby tent, setting it ablaze. A man ran from the tent, climbed into an old Plymouth, and drove only a short distance before being hit by a strafing aircraft. The car burst into flames, then exploded, but the driver jumped out in time, his clothes smoking, and ran into a building unharmed.[13]

Above, all that remained of the lineup of P-40s on the Wheeler flight line.   (Joe K. Harding)

Below, wrecked P-40Bs sit in front of an equally wrecked Hangar 3 at Wheeler Field.

Not as fortunate was PFC Robert R. Shattuck, a switchboard operator assigned to the 15th Pursuit Group's communications section. He and his buddies were eating breakfast when the attack began. They hurriedly left the mess hall and ran down to the tents where they lived, but the first sergeant was there and told them to get out of the area since it was under heavy attack. Some stayed back to help fight fires, and the rest reported to the communications tent. Shattuck, accompanied by Private Nelson, was heading toward his duty station through the tent area when he was hit by shrapnel. One of his legs was torn off, and he died a short time later.[14]

Back at the construction site, two men joined Woodrum behind the lumber pile, sharing his shelter. One was a young, crew-cut lad, about 20 years old, who crawled to the end of the pile with his upper body extending beyond it. Although cautioned to get back before he got hit, he refused, saying, "I can see'em coming from out here." He began to laugh, treating the situation as a joke, but suddenly gasped and rolled halfway over, his body rigid, then quivering, before he flopped back on his belly and died. The rear gunners on the Japanese dive bombers had spotted Woodrum and others hiding among the piles of lumber, so they began to take potshots at them. The men decided to take their chances and make a dash for the barracks, which was only 100 feet or so away. One man reached the crest of the embankment but was mowed down by a line of slugs that stitched their way through the moist dirt, sending him tumbling into a motionless heap at the bottom of the slope. Woodrum and the others, however, managed to make it to safety.[15]

Wheeler personnel inspect what remained of a building site following the 7 December 1941 attack. The new barracks stands on an embankment in background.

The barracks was a scene of confusion and turmoil. There were men dashing around in the supply room helping themselves to equipment and weapons. Many, whose closest friends were suddenly dead, walked around in a daze, exhibiting a wide range of emotions—profound helplessness, rage, berserk and shouting behavior, or a deathly silence. A first sergeant walked by, his hands clenched into fists, tears streaming down his face, as he muttered an endless string of curses. He soon got hold of himself, however, and headed back inside to take charge and start organizing things. Medics picked up the dead and wounded, including the crew-cut lad next to the lumber pile. Along Santos Dumont Avenue, a line of wounded men began to form in front of the dispensary, their arms in slings or heads and faces wrapped in bloody, temporary bandages. Bodies of the dead lay side by side on the lawn, covered with blankets.[16]

Woodrum had grabbed a Springfield 03 from the rifle rack in the supply room. He saw a technical sergeant talking with several men and interrupted him to ask for some ammunition. The sergeant looked Woodrum over for a moment and asked, "You ever fire this piece?" When Woodrum nodded and told him he had just come from two years in the infantry, the sarge directed him to "show these guys how it works. I'll get the ammo." So he turned to face five men—aircraft mechanics who had never trained on rifles—and showed them how the bolt operated, where the safety was located, and how to load. They each went through it a few times before the sergeant returned with a case of ammo and said, "Get

this thing open!" One of the mechanics punched a hole in the tin lid with a screwdriver, then used pliers to peel it open like a can of sardines. It was full of loose ammunition, none in clips. The men filled their pockets and the magazines of the 03s, and every round was a tracer, the bullet red-tipped. They then followed the sarge outside; and he posted the men along the road, leaving one man at each designated spot and instructing him to not let anybody pass "until you identify them as an officer or GI." When only Woodrum was left, they had reached a point opposite a dead-end street in the officers' housing area where a three-strand barbed-wire gate in the fence provided access to Schofield Barracks. The sergeant finally introduced himself as Henderson and ordered Woodrum to stay with him. "You may have showed those guys how to fire an 03 but I don't want any antsy mechanic around me when it [the attack] starts again," he said.[17]

A short while later, three Japanese planes flew in from the south and started strafing the street a half-block away. As he and Henderson blasted away at the aircraft,

Bullet-riddled Army staff car at Wheeler Field.

Woodrum saw a group of small children standing along the street and on the sidewalk watching the action. He ran down the street, gathered the kids together, and herded them through the front door of the nearest house. Dashing back, he saw Henderson get off a couple more shots at two additional planes strafing the street. They then witnessed a Japanese fighter and a P-40 in a dogfight; and when the Japanese plane crashed, leaving smoke billowing upward, a cheer rose from hundreds of GIs around the base. Moments later, a second Japanese plane crashed near the front gate across the road in Wahiawa, triggering another big cheer. Next, a big four-engine bomber flew over, about 1,000 feet above the ground, and Wheeler personnel began firing at it. Woodrum yelled at them to stop, because he had seen one like it on the mainland. It was an American B-17.[18]

Earlier, Sgt George J. Van Gieri was on duty as desk sergeant at the Wheeler Field guardhouse and had just completed posting 80 guards around the base. He was returning to the two-story building that served as a combined guardhouse and fire department when the first bomb struck the field. Van Gieri and others on duty with him tried to call their superiors, but all the phone lines were down. They were concerned that the prisoners incarcerated at the guardhouse for crimes such as burglary and being absent without leave would not be able to escape if the building took a direct hit. Since orders could not be obtained from higher authority, they took it upon themselves to release the prisoners and told them to "come back when it was possible to come back." The freed men immediately joined others in firing back at the Japanese with all weapons available. Van Gieri later received a Purple Heart "for valor and fidelity," as a reward for remaining at his post and continuing to discharge his responsibilities during the severe bombing attack.[19]

When Harry P. Kilpatrick of the 696th Ordnance Company awoke that morning to the hubbub of "people running, yelling, aircraft everywhere, ... it took only seconds to realize this wasn't the Navy giving us one of their Sunday morning buzz jobs." He raced to the weapons shop, only to find it locked; so, he and several others broke off the lock on the door and another lock securing the gun room, then handed out all the guns to whoever came in. "Guess this was the first time in my nearly 11 months in the service that paperwork and signatures were ignored," he said. They set up a .50-caliber water-cooled machine gun just outside the armament shop and fired it at a Japanese plane even before getting water and hooking up the hoses. A few other machine guns were set up elsewhere; but, with the limited ammunition available, they posed little threat to the enemy.[20]

MSgt Joe K. Harding, a photographer assigned to the base photo lab at Wheeler Field, lived on the base with his wife Frances and was still in bed reading the Sunday paper when the attack began. He immediately got up, dashed over to the photo lab to grab his Speed Graphic camera, and with SSgt Morley Bishop carrying a huge sack of film, took off across the street to the burning hangars. He shot dozens of pictures until he ran out of film, then switched to a movie camera and took several rolls of movies. When the enemy aircraft returned, he was out in the middle of the field still taking pictures, so he just turned and started shooting them with his movie camera. The rear gunner on the Japanese plane sprayed the ground around them, but Harding managed to escape with

Wheeler Field personnel manning a 30-caliber machine gun set up behind the main barracks. (Charles L. Hendrix)

only a hole in his coveralls. He had hundreds of feet of movie film, including the gunner shooting at him, and dozens of still pictures; however, except for the photos published here, plus a few others, everything else was left at the lab and apparently "disappeared," although Harding stated that he later saw several of them published with US Navy credit lines.[21]

Chaplain Alvin A. Katt, Wheeler's post chaplain, was lying in bed listening to the mynah birds chattering outside his window, when a series of blasts shook the building. He ran to the window and saw thick smoke billowing up from the hangar line, with flames leaping wildly under the rolling black clouds. Looking up, he saw a plane

with the rising sun emblem painted on its wings. It hung low over his quarters, as if suspended on a string, and its machine-gun bullets sounded like corn popping on a hot fire as they shattered the tile on the roofs of houses across the street. The plane flew so low that its wings seemed to almost touch the buildings. As two officers ran from the barracks toward the hangar line, the Japanese plane swooped down, shooting at them, so they ran into the newly constructed chapel. Incendiary bullets cut through the roof, into the pews and the floor; but miraculously, they did not burst into flame. "God, with whom nothing is impossible, had given His Divine protection to those who sought sanctuary in the chapel," Chaplain Katt said to himself.[22]

In the barracks area and on the hangar line, Chaplain Katt witnessed the devastating results of the exploding bombs. Soldiers leaped out of barracks windows and doors, trying to escape from the rain of bombs and machine-gun bullets. Men eating breakfast in the mess hall were blasted from the building, wounded or dead within a few minutes. A bomb missed the largest

Wheeler Field chapel in 1941. (Douglas Van Valkenburgh)

barracks and set a nearby PX warehouse ablaze. In the tent area, men were strafed and killed. He saw aircraft burning from the incendiary bullets as if they were wax models. All over the field, bullets tore through windows and blasted cement and wooden buildings. Then the enemy planes left as suddenly as they came, leaving raging fires, the dead, and the wounded. As the chaplain headed toward the flight line, where smoke and fire poured from the twisted steel skeletons of the hangars, one of the soldiers told him there was an injured man near the theater. They both ran over to the theater, where Chaplain Katt had been scheduled to hold services and Sunday School that day, and found a soldier on the floor, shot through the leg. They converted a large piece of plywood into a stretcher, placed the wounded man on it, and carried him to the dispensary.[23]

When Chaplain Katt entered the dispensary, he saw the human wreckage of men whose faces were smeared with blood, their bodies torn by shrapnel and bullets. He quickly moved down the line of cots and stretchers, looking for the dying and badly wounded. Kneeling beside the men, he softly repeated the words of the Lord's Prayer over and over. In their last minutes of earthly life, the stricken men lifted their arms and reached for him, seeking spiritual comfort. After he was certain that he had done all he could for those in the Wheeler Field dispensary, he went to the Schofield Barracks hospital and joined other chaplains in tending the wounded who had been taken there. One young man lying on

his bed said grimly, "Those dirty devils, we'll pay 'em back. All I'm waiting for is to get outa here and get at 'em!" Chaplain Katt put his hand on the boy's shoulder, wiped the perspiration from his forehead, and saw there was little likelihood he would ever again be able to fight. Asked to help identify the dead in the morgue, he found men on each side of the room, their personal effects piled up at their feet. "It is amazing," he said later, "how unimportant and useless a man's belongings seem when he is dead." Among the first bodies he examined were two young men from his choir. There was a pilot friend who tried to get to his plane but was cut down by Japanese machine-gun bullets as he ran. Chaplain Katt recalled that he and his friend used to go swimming together, catching the waves as they bodysurfed at the beach.[24]

Chaplain Alvin A. Katt (second from left), following a memorial service he conducted for a pilot who had spun into the Pacific in a P-40 early in 1941. He and the others then boarded the plane to drop leis in the water where the pilot and his P-40 had disappeared. (Col Alvin A. Katt, USAF, Retired)

Bellows Field

Along the beach in Waimanalo, all was serene at Bellows until about dawn when the acting first sergeant ran into the tent area to rouse the sleeping men, yelling that Kaneohe had been "blown to hell." Corporal McKinley thought he was crazy and just turned over in his bed. At 0810, someone called from Hickam Field and asked for a fire truck because they "were in flames." A return call disclosed the fact that they had been attacked, so the Bellows fire chief left for Hickam with the fire truck. Then a lone Japanese fighter plane flew in over the ocean from the east at approximately 0830, firing its machine guns at the tent area, slightly wounding PFC James A. Brown of the medical detachment in his leg. That got everyone's attention! The entire Casual Detachment got up, went over to the armament building, and drew Browning automatic rifles, Springfield rifles, and machine guns. Unable to find belts for the machine guns, they tried aircraft machine gun belts but found they wouldn't work. The only other firepower available was a machine gun on an O-47 belonging to the 86th Observation Squadron and two .30-caliber antiaircraft machine guns which Hawaii National Guard personnel of the 298th Infantry positioned at the end of the runway. Everyone

A lone Japanese fighter plane machine-gunned this tent area at Bellows Field early Sunday morning, 7 December 1941.

dispersed, jumping into ditches, behind buildings, or whatever shelter they could find.[25]

Lt Col Leonard D. Weddington, Bellows Field's commander, was at his home about a mile from the post when his driver rushed over to inform him of the raid. The colonel immediately left for Bellows and was there when nine Japanese fighters (three groups of three planes each in **V** formation) approached from the north about

0900 and attacked for approximately 15 minutes. The raid consisted of gunfire only and started with a diving attack by all nine planes, after which the three-plane formations peeled off and began shooting from various directions. They strafed parked aircraft and also hit a gasoline truck. Pvt Forrest E. Decker of the 428th Signal Maintenance Company, Aviation, was at Bellows visiting friends and witnessed the gas truck's tanker burst into flames immediately. "One man," he said, "whether brave or just stupid, ran to the vehicle, pulled the release lever, got into the cab and drove the tractor away from the tanker." They waited for it to explode, but it never did. It had so many holes in it that it just burned itself out. Bellows' ground defense forces fired back at the Japanese with their Springfield rifles and Browning automatic rifles but inflicted no damage. PFC Raymond F. McBriarty and Pvt William L. Burt of the 86th Observation Squadron grabbed a gun and ammunition from the armament shack, mounted the gun in the rear cockpit of their squadron commander's

This burnt-out fuel truck was a victim of the Japanese strafing attack at Bellows Field. (William E. Simshauser)

parked O-47 aircraft and loaded the gun with ammunition. They were proceeding to put ammunition in the fixed guns when the attack started. They "hit the dust" when the first wave of planes struck, then crawled in the cockpit and expended 450 rounds on the attacking Japanese planes that rushed low over the field. They later received the Silver Star for gallantry in action.[26]

Personnel of the 44th Pursuit Squadron rushed out to disperse, fuel, and arm their twelve P-40 Warhawks, which were lined up on the edge of the runway. Only four of the squadron's officers were at Bellows that morning, and three were pilots. They wanted to get into the air immediately, despite the fact that their aircraft were not completely armed, but Lieutenant Phillips, the armament officer, insisted that all six .50-caliber guns be fully loaded before any aircraft took off. As 2d Lt Hans C. Christiansen started to get into the cockpit of his plane, he was struck in the back by enemy fire and fell at the feet of his mechanic, Cpl Elmer L. Rund, who was standing by the lower right wing. Blood gushed out from a large hole in the life jacket of the fatally wounded pilot. Rund and his crew chief, Joe Ray, then had to quickly duck under the aircraft for protection from the strafing attack by the Japanese planes, which seemed to come at them from all directions.[27]

In the meantime, 2d Lt George A. Whiteman ran up to a P-40 which was still being loaded with ammunition and told the men to get off the wing because he would fly the plane as was. He started the engine and taxied out onto the runway, leaving so quickly that the armorers did not have time to install the gun cowlings back on the wings. Whiteman began his takeoff run and was immediately spotted by two Zeros,

Riddled by machine-gun fire, this was one of 12 P-40s assigned to Wheeler's 44th Pursuit Squadron but deployed to Bellows Field for gunnery training at the time of the attack.

which swooped down on him. He managed to take off and get approximately 50 feet up in the air before the enemy planes opened fire, then tried to turn inside the two Zeros on his tail, but the P-40 was too slow and unmaneuverable. The Japanese struck the engine, wings, and cockpit of his aircraft, which burst into flames. He attempted a belly landing on the beach, but his plane's left wing hit the sand, and a tremendous ball of fire erupted. SSgt Cosmos Manning carried a large fire extinguisher down to the wreckage, and others followed in a hopeless rescue effort. Black smoke rose in a thick column from the crash site, marking the funeral pyre of Lieutenant Whiteman. SSgt Edward J. Covelesky, a P-40 crew chief, had thrown himself down on top of a sand dune to hide in the vegetation when the strafing attack began. He picked himself up and ran down to the beach area, where he saw that the only trace of the P-40 was a few scattered pieces of metal surrounding an ugly black patch of smoldering sand. Fourteen years later, Sedalia AFB in Missouri was renamed Whiteman AFB in honor of Lieutenant Whiteman.[28]

The third pilot at Bellows was 1st Lt Samuel W. Bishop, who taxied into position, turned his plane toward the ocean, and began his takeoff roll directly behind Whiteman. He saw Whiteman's plane go down after a burst of gunfire went right into the cockpit. The only emotion he felt was deep rage as he got airborne, holding the trigger down all the while, as Japanese planes swarmed around him. He retracted his landing gear and hugged the water, trying to gain speed, but the Zeros clung tenaciously to him and shot him down in the ocean about half a mile offshore. Despite a bullet wound in his leg, Bishop managed to get out of his plane and, with his Mae West keeping him afloat, swam to shore.[29]

Sometime between the solo strafing and the attack by nine enemy planes, a crippled B-17C arrived at Bellows. This was one of the twelve Flying Fortresses coming in from Hamilton Field; and its pilot, 1st Lt Robert H. Richards of the 38th Reconnaissance Squadron, had been the last in line to land at Hickam. He never made it there, however, for Japanese Zeros riddled his aircraft from nose to tail, shot away the ailerons, and severely wounded three crew members. Trying to lose his attackers, he sped away at full throttle along the southern coast of Oahu, and roared in over Waimanalo Bay toward Bellows' short fighter strip. As he approached, crew chief Earl Sutton was taxiing his P-40 to a dispersal area and crossed directly in his way, forcing him to pull up and go around again. Sergeant Covelesky recalled that:

No one was aware of the flight of bombers arriving from the states, and to see that approaching monster trailing smoke from its right engines ... was mind boggling. Our asphalt landing strip at Bellows was hardly long enough to accommodate our P-40s, much less a B-17; and when he made an approach from the ocean downwind, we knew we were in for a

breathtaking crash landing. Even though his wheels were down, he flared out and touched down halfway on the strip, knowing he wouldn't be able to stop, retracted the wheels and slid off the runway over a·ditch and into a cane field bordering the air strip.[30]

Fire trucks and an ambulance rushed down to the crash area. The B-17 crew immediately tried to salvage the bombsight so it would not fall into enemy hands should the Japanese invade the island. Pvt Lester A. Ellis of the 86th Observation Squadron was positioned on the runway, armed with a Springfield rifle, and ordered to give a shouted warning whenever the enemy aircraft started their strafing runs. Each time he shouted a warning, everyone ran for cover. After the Japanese planes left, they counted 73 bullet holes in the B-17.[31]

B-17C of the 38th Reconnaissance Squadron, which had the misfortune of arriving in the middle of the Japanese attack and made a belly landing on the short fighter airstrip at Bellows Field.

CHAPTER VII

AFTER THE ATTACK

To You Our Fallen

The barracks now are silent
    Where once your laughter rang,
The steel guitar is broken
    Where around your bunks we sang.
As the stars give way to morning
    In Oahu's cloud-swept sky,
Old Glory's proudly waving there
    Seeped in heroes' crimson dye.
Can you hear us there in heaven
    As the dawn patrol takes flight?
On silvery wings your memory soars
    In holy freedom's fight.
The kona wind blows softly now,
    The palm trees whisper low,
But all America will remember
    Whence came this dastard's blow.
Let the Nipponese remember this,
    As they cringe beneath the sky,
At Hickam's flaming vengeance
    For you, the first to die!

Sgt W. Joe Brimm
Hickam Field

By 1000, the attack was over; and despite rumors to the contrary, the Japanese attempted no landings. In less than two hours, however, they had crippled the Army's air arm on Oahu, leaving wrecked aircraft, hangars, and other buildings, in addition to exacting a heavy toll of nearly 700 casualties.* Only 29 of the Japanese planes failed to return from the attack, and about 50 others were smashed while attempting to land on the pitching decks of carriers tossed around on the rough sea. Of the 50 aircraft, some 20 or more were a total loss. This was a very small price to pay for the extensive damage inflicted on the Americans. Of the 234 aircraft assigned to the Hawaiian Air Force, 146 were in commission before the attack; afterward, only 83 were in commission, and 76 had been totally destroyed. Although caught by surprise, America's military men fought back bravely. Individual acts of heroism were numerous, with five Distinguished

*See Appendix E.

Service Crosses and 65 Silver Stars later awarded to US Army personnel for valor.[1]

The Dependents

Following the attack, Colonel Farthing and Colonel Flood had all women and children evacuated from Hickam and Wheeler Fields. Some had already departed on their own in private automobiles, seeking the comparative safety of Honolulu and other outlying areas. At Hickam, a loud speaker blared, "Get all the women and children off the base." Ira Southern and others helped search the houses and found women and children under beds, outside, or already preparing to leave. They boarded Honolulu Rapid Transit Company buses and trucks provided by the evacuation committee of the Major Disaster Council (an official organization of the City and County of Honolulu formed in June 1941 as a result of increasing concern over the possibility of wartime bombardment). A number of evacuees moved in with friends; the remainder stayed at the University of Hawaii's Hemenway Hall, at public schools designated by the evacuation committee, in private homes of families who had volunteered to house them, and at other places such as plantation clubhouses and the Hongwanji School in Waipahu.[2]

A typical military wife affected by events of the day was Jessie Reed, 29-year-old mother of two small children who had moved to Hickam Field with her husband, Lt Stanley Jennings Reed, only three months before the attack. When the Japanese started bombing and strafing Hickam, she and her children left with neighbors for a friend's home in the mountains some 10 miles away. About 25 people were there, and they all gathered around a radio to listen to the latest news and get instructions on what to do. They

could clearly hear the bombing and see the fires from buildings, planes, and ships. Later, they received word that all evacuees were to go to the University of Hawaii, where students helped care for the children and assisted with various errands. After air raid shelters were built in the housing area at Hickam, they were allowed to return for

Facing page: Lts George S. Welch and Kenneth M. Taylor wearing the Distinguished Service Cross each received for his action during the 7 December 1941 attack.

This page, top: Presentation of Silver Star and Purple Heart decorations on ramp in front of Hangar 3 at Wheeler Field, 3 July 1942. (W. Bruce Harlow)

This page, right: Maj Charles Stewart, 86th Observation Squadron Commander at Bellows, congratulates Pvt William L. Burt and PFC Raymond F. McBriarty, who were awarded the Silver Star for gallantry on 7 December 1941. (John J. Lennon)

a while before being evacuated again, this time by ship to the mainland.[3]

During the evacuation of dependents from Hickam, a group of about 30 wives begged to be allowed to stay and help in the hospital. Several of them had husbands who were killed or wounded during the attack. At first they went to work making dressings and bandages to replace the hospital's depleted stock, since no one knew whether or not the attackers would return. Later, they assisted in the hospital kitchen, releasing military members for other duties. The hospital itself sustained little damage. Besides the large bomb crater on the lawn, there were a few machine-gun bullet holes in the screen of the hospital porches and some bomb fragments on the porch floors. The only casualty from the medical staff was an "aid man" (not further identified) who had been killed by strafing while picking up injured personnel on the flight line. The interior of the hospital, however, was a bloody mess; and clean-up efforts were hampered by the broken water main, which made it necessary to haul water in water carts.[4]

By mid-afternoon, when the excitement of the attack had subsided, people began to get hungry. Sgt Clarence W. Schertz, the hospital mess sergeant, had anticipated this and, with the help of his regular crew and many of the volunteer wives, was soon dishing out food to all comers. Earlier, he had gone to Honolulu with a large truck and returned with a full load of food supplies. Exactly where or how he got all the food, the hospital commander did not know and never asked. The word soon got around that the hospital was feeding the troops, and a steady stream of men showed up and were fed. The little hospital mess, designed to feed about a

hundred people, must have fed well over a thousand that day; and there were none of the usual soldiers' gripes about the quality of the food. Most of the medical personnel stayed in the hospital that night, sleeping on the floors of the offices and dressing rooms. The volunteer wives all slept on mattresses placed on the dining room floor.[5]

The Continuing Search

While the attack was still in progress, personnel at Hickam, Wheeler, and Bellows Fields began preparing available aircraft for search missions to locate the enemy's carriers. Since the Navy was responsible for the search, General Martin called Admiral Bellinger on the field phone which connected their two offices and asked which direction to go to find the carriers; however, the admiral had nothing on this. General Martin subsequently received information that a carrier might be 25 to 40 miles south of Barbers Point. As soon as A-20A aircraft of the 58th Bombardment Squadron had been loaded with bombs, he gave them the mission of finding the carrier. The first flight of four light bombers, headed by Major Holzapfel, took off from Hickam Field at 1127 but found nothing. A second flight of three A-20As became airborne at 1300, led by 1st Lt Perry S. Cole, with TSgt O'Shea as bombardier and Rod House as gunner. They, too, were unsuccessful in their search for the Japanese carriers. Crew members did get a dramatic view of the damage caused by the attack, plus 20 to 30 holes in their aircraft from trigger-happy antiaircraft gunners.[6]

Captain "Blondie" Saunders, who had been named provisional commander of all B-17s, led a three-plane formation of Flying Fortresses which also started off in search of the Japanese carrier force. One aircraft had to abort, however, when its tail wheel started to vibrate and the copilot mistakenly grabbed the lever locking the elevators rather than the tail wheel. This resulted in raising the tail of the B-17, ruining all four propellers. The two remaining B-17D aircraft, piloted by Saunders and Capt Brooke E. Allen, took off at 1140, circled around Diamond Head, and were in the air for about seven hours, arriving back at Hickam around 1800. Allen reported being sent out with information that there were two Japanese carriers to the south, but he found very shortly after takeoff one American carrier to the south. Then, following his personal feeling that the Japanese would have come from the north, he put his compass on "N" and headed straight north. How close he ever came to the carrier task force, he never knew but "returned with minimum fuel and a heart full of disgust that I had been unable to locate them." Saunders recalled that "the military forces on Oahu had seen B-17s around the island for six months but they really let go at us, like we were public enemy number one. I thought we were going to be shot down by our own forces."[7]

Captain Waldron, provisional commander of all B-18s, joined in the search with two aircraft, taking off at 1330 in a northwest direction. His B-18 carried six 100-pound bombs and two .30-caliber machine guns, and 31st Bomb Squadron personnel made up the crew. The bombing capability of this obsolescent aircraft was primitive, so Waldron later considered it fortunate that they did not find the Japanese task force. "I wouldn't have been here if I did," he said. Returning from the search mission, he also faced heavy antiaircraft artillery fire. Although they were operating on radio silence, which was

the routine procedure, he finally got on the radio and said, "This is Gatty, your friend! *Please let me land!*" That went on for some time—45 minutes to an hour—before he finally got clearance to land.[8]

At Wheeler, as soon as available fighter aircraft could be patched together and serviced, they were sent up to patrol the skies. They, too, encountered heavy anti-aircraft artillery fire, especially over Pearl Harbor, then faced a barrage of rifle and machine gun fire when approaching Wheeler to land. One mission flown by an assortment of ten 15th Pursuit Group planes was at dusk escorting B-17s on a search north-northwest of Oahu, in a 200-mile sweep for one and one-half hours. Another was a twilight scramble by Lieutenant Ahola and other 18th Pursuit Group pilots who took off from Wheeler to investigate a bogey (an unknown), with instructions to climb as high as they could and fly toward Diamond Head. The flight commander, 1st Lt Charles H. MacDonald, asked what they were supposed to be going after. When control tower personnel told him it was reported there was a bright light over Diamond Head, he said, "Doesn't anybody know that Venus is bright out there this time of year?" With that, they aborted the mission and returned to Wheeler.[9]

In all, A-20, B-17, B-18, P-40, P-36, and O-47 aircraft flew a total of 48 sorties in a fruitless search for the enemy's carriers. As the cold and weary aircrew members from Hickam climbed stiffly out of their planes that evening, they were anxious to find something to eat. Many had not eaten since the previous night. The enlisted men learned that the base hospital had the only hot food around, so they headed that way. The facility was dimly lit with blankets draped over the windows for blackout purposes. After eating some stew, the men walked back to their units.[10]

Rumors Galore

Maj Rudolph L. Duncan of the US Army Signal Corps commanded the Signal Aircraft Warning Regiment, Hawaii, and a job he had to do quickly after the attack was to check on communications facilities at various bases and installations that might have to be used for landings and takeoffs by the few fighter aircraft left serviceable. At every stop he was confidentially informed about the little Japanese newsboys who, when making their newspaper deliveries very early on Sunday morning, 7 December, told the sentries at each base, "Pretty soon many planes make big attack from sky—better get all ready quick." These alleged words of warning, being entirely the figment of one person's imagination, "followed the natural law of Army gravitation and spread to all bases in Hawaii as fast as only a choice tidbit of like Army confidential information can and does spread." This became a joke of sorts and, until worn out after a few days, the customary greeting in chow lines was "Have you heard about the little Japanese newsboy last Sunday morning who. . . ."[11]

This was just the start of rumors that ran rampant in the hours following the attack. Lieutenant Gray of the 17th Air Base Group recalled that:

Almost everyone had a rumor to tell, some of them initiated by the Japanese themselves aboard their nearby ships.* Broadcasting on a

Hawaiian frequency, their rumors were designed to confuse both the military and civilians. The announcer spoke flawless English to make it appear the program originated in the islands. One admonition at about 10 a.m. on December 7 was to drink no water because the Honolulu water reservoir had been poisoned. Other rumors later in the day were that San Francisco was under bombardment; that the Panama Canal had fallen to Japanese forces; and that Kansas City was the target for enemy planes. A locally concocted rumor had lady-of-the-evening volunteers giving invaluable assistance at Tripler General Hospital. Hardly true; however, some women were asked to leave military areas because they rendered therapy not on the doctor's chart.[12]

A popular but unsubstantiated tale was that some of the Japanese whose bodies were recovered wore class rings from the University of Hawaii and other American colleges. Many believed fifth column work had aided the attackers—that blazed fields marked objectives by day, and gasoline flares by night. A widely circulated story was that arrows had been cut in the cane fields pointing to Pearl Harbor so the Japanese would know where to bomb. This made little sense, considering the size of Pearl Harbor compared to an arrow cut in a cane field, but the rumor persisted. Despite the beliefs to which some people still cling today, all the investigative agencies agreed that there was no fifth column activity of any sort in Hawaii.[13]

Around midafternoon on 7 December, base officials at Hickam asked the hospital

---

*This, too proved to be a rumor. Admiral Nagumo imposed radio silence on his ships when they headed back north toward Japan after the attack.

staff to check out the rumor that the water supply had been poisoned. Not having the facilities for the complicated laboratory analysis required to determine this, Captain Lane sent some soldiers out to catch dogs on which they could test the water. They picked up a couple of half-grown mutts but could not coax them into drinking the water. Finally, with some difficulty, they managed to insert stomach tubes and poured about a gallon of water into each of them, then locked them in a room. After a few hours, finding they had nothing worse than wet feet, Captain Lane proclaimed the water fit to drink. Early the next morning, he received confirmation from the Pearl Harbor surgeon that their analysis of the water found no poison. Later, he heard a rumor that the dogs used for the test at Hickam refused to drink water thereafter and got their moisture by bumming beer from soldiers at the beer garden![14]

The most prevalent rumors involved the expected Japanese invasion. Almost everyone believed the Japanese would be back; consequently, there were reports throughout the day that "a Japanese attack force was about to land, the Japanese had already landed on the opposite side of the island and were hiding in cane fields, a large part of the island population of Japanese ancestry had joined the invaders," etc. The 25th Infantry Division's journal for 7 December 1941 included entries reporting that troop ships were coming in 30 miles southeast of Pearl Harbor escorted by enemy planes, four Japanese transports were off Barbers Point, and many reports that parachute troops wearing blue coveralls with red discs on the left shoulder were landing near Kaneohe Bay, on the North Shore, and at Barbers Point. The latter rumor was so convincing that Headquarters Hawaiian Department issue the following instructions

at 1408 on 8 December 1941: "Effective immediately, uniform for all troops is olive drab, cotton or wool; blue denim will not, repeat, not be worn. All cloth insignia except chevrons will be removed from uniform." These instructions remained in effect until revoked by the Hawaiian Department on 23 December 1941.[15]

Preparations to meet the expected Japanese invasion included the formation of four infantry companies comprised of Wheeler Field personnel, headed by four Army Air Forces officers who had been in the infantry before. They were placed around the field and instructed "to watch for anybody that might come in." Also, a battalion of infantrymen from Schofield Barracks arrived at Wheeler to guard the airfield, at which time Colonel Flood turned his ground personnel over to the army major in command of the battalion. At Hickam, Hawaiian Air Force personnel defended the airfield and bomb dump against the expected Japanese invasion. Outside the military posts, army troops took up defensive positions around the perimeters of the main islands to thwart anticipated attempts to land from the sea. Possible aircraft landing areas were blocked with old trucks, scrap boilers, large tree branches, and other obstacles. If materials were unavailable, furrows were plowed. Trenches soon crisscrossed beautiful parks, pineapple fields ready for harvest, and even school playgrounds far too small for any plane to use. All civilian airports were taken over by the armed forces, and all private planes were grounded.[16]

The Long Night

Since the consolidated barracks at Hickam had been destroyed, many enlisted men slept that night under trees, in the open under blankets, in pup tents, in any unlocked family quarters, or whatever shelter they could find. Members of the Headquarters Squadron, 17th Air Base Group, relocated for the night to an essentially undamaged wooden school building near the water tower. As friends were reunited, they rejoiced, then grieved for those who were killed or seriously injured. After dark, nervous men challenged anyone in sight and shouted at every shadow. Trigger-happy soldiers, sailors, and airmen fired tracer bullets into the sky at the slightest provocation. This tense situation inevitably resulted in tragedy when four of six US Navy fighter aircraft from the carrier *Enterprise* were shot down by "friendly" fire as they headed toward Ford Island, resulting in the death of three pilots.[17]

Throughout the night, everyone was jumpy, convinced that the Japanese would be back to capture the island. PFC Bruno Siko and other members of the 19th Transport Squadron settled in trenches dug in the coral area along the southwest side of the Hickam runway near their aircraft. It was a bright moonlit night, but blackout procedures were in effect, so everything on the ground was dark. Before long, trouble broke out among some of the men who had been drinking a lot of beer, "thought they saw Japs," and started shooting. Cpl Francis L. Mack remembered one individual who went wild with a .30-caliber machine gun and "damn near killed us all." Fortunately, no one was hurt. PFC Christie shared a foxhole with two buddies, Vic Wichansky and Private Gibbs; and the three of them discussed the events of the day and the sad news that their friend Johnny Horan had been killed that morning. Everyone was on edge, so a personal visit by their squadron commander, Maj Charles C.

Cunningham, was most welcome. He walked through the encampment, talking to the men with words of encouragement.[18]

Wheeler Field personnel, armed and waiting for the feared invasion, witnessed the spectacular display of firepower from Pearl Harbor and Hickam Field triggered by the approach of US Navy planes from the *Enterprise*. Thousands of tracer bullets and rounds of antiaircraft fire crisscrossed the sky, which lit up like an orange sheet of flame. Two of the planes approached Wheeler, along the Schofield perimeter, and two .50-caliber machine guns positioned north of the highway began chattering away. One aircraft began to slowly roll over before it nosed down into a pineapple field, skidding through the soft earth, as a second aircraft crashed somewhere farther up the gully. The plane in the gully was almost on its back, its canopy smashed, with the pilot hanging suspended through the opening. As the men from Wheeler arrived at the site, they stopped abruptly upon seeing the insignia on the fuselage which identified the plane as US Navy. Several men eased the pilot from the aircraft and laid him down. Others raced on toward the other plane, which was US Navy also. They carried both pilots to the highway and waited for the ambulance, but both were dead on arrival at the hospital. One of the two gunners was certain he had shot down at least one of the planes. He had been depressed all day after seeing some close friends killed in the barracks during the sneak attack that morning. All day long he wanted to kill Japanese so badly that when the chance came, he took advantage of it. When he learned that the plane he had shot down was American, he fell apart.[19]

It had been raining steadily at Wheeler since noon, and the troops were muddy and miserable that night. Charles Hendrix was shaking from head to foot, the first time he had ever been cold in Hawaii. Then someone yelled "Gas!" and pandemonium erupted until each man found his gas mask and put it on, adding to his discomfort and misery. In the eerie darkness, trucks crept about slowly, their lights dimmed by sheets of carbon paper taped over the headlights. Shots rang out as sentries fired at shadows and sometimes at each other, often not even waiting for a response to their challenge. The sign and countersign at Wheeler Field during the first night of war were "George Washington" and "Valley Forge" (for sentries calm enough to listen).[20]

The long night wore on. Suddenly, someone thought he saw a Japanese and then was *sure* he saw a Japanese, and fired. This kicked off a long, continuous wave of rifle fire as everyone in the Wheeler-Schofield perimeter fired simultaneously. Thousands of rounds of ammunition arched harmlessly into empty fields, serving only to ease some of the tension. Then, on the narrow-gauge railroad tracks running through the field, a locomotive pulling a few cars chugged its way heavily into a siding. As it stopped, armed guards jumped down and said they saw no Japanese on the way from Honolulu, then marched up the street to the 14th Pursuit Wing headquarters. The Hawaiian train crew stayed in the cab, afraid to leave for fear of being mistaken for Japanese, so Private Woodrum and another person took them some coffee. A few minutes later, a loud hissing sound pierced the night and someone shouted at the top of his lungs, "Gas! Gas!" Everyone donned gas masks, looking strange with their bulging eyepieces and dangling throat tubes. A sergeant came back after investigating and ripped off his mask, shouting,

"Take'em off. It's just that damned engine letting off steam." Everyone cursed the train crew.[21]

A little later, a command car came through the gate and parked at the edge of the field. Several men climbed out and began walking toward Woodrum and others in the group, with a man in the center who was obviously the leader. Seeing the glitter of rank on the officer's shoulder, they started to come to attention; but the man held out his hand and said, "At ease, men, at ease." Someone came out of the cook tent with a blue flashlight, and they saw stars on his shoulders. It was General Davidson, the 14th Pursuit Wing commander, who told them "we're going to be all right even though we took a beating." He didn't think the Japanese would return, but said "we would be more ready for them if they did." With him were three pilots who got off the ground—Lieutenants Taylor, Welch, and Rasmussen. They answered all the questions asked, while the general stood back listening, interjecting a remark occasionally, watching as the men began to relax a little. This seemed to be the main reason for the visit. Finally, General Davidson said there were other people to see before the pilots could sleep, and they all walked back to the command car and drove away.[22]

At Bellows, members of the 298th Infantry worked all night putting in gun emplacements and stringing barbed wire on the beach in preparation for an expected Japanese landing at daylight. Others without critical jobs were mustered into guard duty, both on the beaches and within the field. These jobs were taken over by the infantry about three days later, much to the relief of Pvt Decker and others who were alarmed at the number of shots fired for no reason other than nerves and inexperience.

On the first night, for instance, a call was put out that "the Japs were landing on the beach" and everyone was ordered to fix bayonets and head out there. As the first of their group topped the sand dunes, the beach guards opened fire, fortunately for them, over their heads, then informed them that the reported landing was false. Tension and panic caused several near tragedies even in the tent area, so it was not safe to walk around. Consequently, most of the men stayed all night in foxholes dug in the sand.[23]

The Submarine

Several of the 86th Observation Squadron personnel, including 1st Lt Jean K. Lambert, spent the night in the operations shack at Bellows Field listening to the radio. They had been alerted by the Hawaiian Department Headquarters to begin reconnaissance flights after dawn; so between 0600 and 0700 on 8 December, preparations were underway for the first missions. Just about that time, a call from the control tower alerted them to "something strange in the water, out by the reef, off the beach end of the runway." Maj C. B. Stewart, the squadron commander, sent Lambert and 1st Lt James T. Lewis up to see what it was. As soon as they were airborne, Lewis began circling the reef area while Lambert crawled down into the "greenhouse" observation belly of the O-47 to get an unobstructed view. It wasn't light enough to use the aerial camera, so he just scanned the ocean with his naked eyes and quickly saw the Japanese midget submarine. The surf was high, and the big waves rolled the sub to an upright position, allowing Lambert to see the conning tower. It was obvious that the sub was hung up on the reef, and there was no sign of life. Lambert immediately called Major Stewart on the

radio to describe the scene below and told him he would make a sketch or two of the sub, since the light was not strong enough to take pictures. Stewart gave his approval and instructed them to get back after they had seen enough. After circling at low altitude for another 10 to 15 minutes, they returned to Bellows and briefed the major, who then called Department Headquarters to report the situation.[24]

In the meantime, Lt Paul S. Plybon, Executive Officer of "G" Company, 298th Infantry (which had bivouacked for weeks in the ironwood grove at the end of the Bellows runway), took Cpl David Akui with him on beach patrol just before dawn. When it became light enough, he swept the bay with high-powered glasses and saw what he thought was a lobster stake near the entrance to the reef. As they watched, a wave broke on the "stake," revealing the top of the sub's conning tower. About that time, there was a flash of white when a big comber broke in front of them, and they saw that it was a man struggling in the surf. The next wave washed him closer to shore, so they waded out and brought him in. They had "captured" the commander of the sub, Ensign Kazuo Sakamaki, who had been fighting the giant waves for some time and finally lost consciousness. They took him to the operations shack and provided him with a blanket, as he was cold and exhausted. Major Stewart again called Hawaiian Department Headquarters, this time to report that the sub's officer had been apprehended. Within a very short time, 2d Lt Lee E. Metcalfe of the 23d Bomb Squadron at Hickam Field arrived at Bellows, accompanying a military intelligence staff member, to pick up the prisoner.[25]

During interrogation, Sakamaki stated that he was 24 years old, an officer of the

Japanese two-man midget submarine, grounded on the coral reef off Bellows Field.

Japanese Navy, and a graduate of the Imperial Naval Academy. He was the commanding officer and navigator of the midget sub; and his shipmate, Kiyoshi Inagaki,* was the engineer. Sakamaki was greatly distressed over the "disgrace" of being captured and begged to be killed. He said that he wished to commit suicide and had not done so at the time of landing on shore because the possibility had remained of making good his escape and rejoining the Japanese Navy. Now that he had been disgraced, he did not want his name or ship information to be sent back to Japan. Ensign Sakamaki was the first prisoner of war captured by the United States in World War II and became known as POW No. 1.[26]

The midget submarine, Japan's latest "secret weapon," measured approximately 81 feet by 6 feet, carried two 18-inch torpedoes, and was powered by one 600-horsepower electric motor supported by 224 short-lived batteries with no self-recharging capability, which resulted in a very limited operating range. The five involved in the 7 December 1941 attack were hauled from Japan to Hawaii piggyback aboard specially modified "mother" submarines. The plan was to edge as close as possible to the mouth of Pearl Harbor, cut the midgets loose on the eve of "X-Day," have them sneak into the harbor at night, and position themselves so as to travel a circular route around Ford Island and damage any ships missed in the aerial assault against the US Fleet. Meanwhile, the mother subs would lie outside the harbor to attack any ships in flight, then later retrieve their pups at a rendezvous point about seven miles southwest of the island of Lanai. None made it back, however. One was shelled, depth-charged, and sunk outside the harbor

_____
*Seaman Kiyoshi Inagaki drowned in the rough surf, and his body washed up on the beach three days later.

BASIC PERSONNEL RECORD

~~INTERNED ALIEN ENEMY~~

PRISONER OF WAR

SAKAMAKI	Kazuo		ISN-HJ-1-MI	*Kazuo Sakamaki*
Surname	Given Name	Middle Name	Serial Number	Signature

Hostile Unit AT 65 .... Submarine Service (Two man) .... Japanese .... Co. G - 298th I
                                                                Nationality   Arresting Agency

Hostile Rank: Sub Lieutenant .... Hostile Service: Naval .... Capturing Unit

Hostile Serial No. Refused to answer. 0540 8th December 1941, Bellows Field, Hawaii
        Home Address   Time and place of first Capture

Person to be notified in emergency:

Refused to disclose. Notify Navy Department, Tokyo, Japan.
        Name   Address   Relationship

Dependents:

Name	Sex	Age	Address
None			

Home Address: Tokushima Ken, Town of Hayashi, Japan.

Japanese; some Chinese	Naval Officer	Graduate of Japanese Naval Academy
Languages Spoken	Profession	Education

PHYSICAL DESCRIPTION

Age 24. Date of Birth 17 Nov. Sex Male
                        1917
Place of Birth Tokushima, Ken; town of
Hayashi, Japan
Height 63¼" Comp. Yellow Hair Black

Weight 131. Eyes Brown. Build Stocky.

Scars and Marks Three burn scars under each eye.

Basic Personnel Record for Prisoner of War Kazuo Sakamaki (POW No. 1)

by the USS *Ward* an hour before the air attack; a second was sunk outside the harbor after firing its torpedoes at the USS *St. Louis* without result; the third managed to enter Pearl Harbor but was rammed and sunk by the USS *Monaghan*; and a fourth was presumed to have been sunk in the heat of battle.[27]

Sakamaki's midget sub, which had an inoperative gyrocompass, had been depth-bombed by two destroyers, twice struck a reef at the Pearl Harbor entrance, and finally drifted east until it lodged on the coral reef off Bellows Field. About mid-morning on 8 December, some Navy officers arrived at Bellows to look at the submarine, then recommended to their superiors that the sub be freed from the reef by dive

bombing around it. So, a little later, a Navy plane flew over and dropped a few bombs in the vicinity of the submarine, with no visible effect. By then, it was about noon. The 86th Observation Squadron had a huge raft, constructed of heavy lumber with empty 50-gallon drums as flotation gear, which was usually anchored out by the reef for swimming and other activities. That day, however, it was up on the shore for maintenance. Practically everyone in the squadron donned swimming trunks and helped launch the raft, after first affixing a steel cable to it. They pushed it out to the reef, fastened the cable to the submarine's nose area, then attached the other end of the long cable to a huge bulldozer used for construction work at Bellows. The bulldozer then reeled in the cable on the drum

Group portrait, painted on silk by an unknown Japanese artist, of the nine midget submariners killed during the 7 December 1941 attack. Conspicuously absent is Ensign Kazuo Sakamaki, who was captured and became POW No. 1 after his midget sub grounded on the reef at Bellows.

Closeup view of the Japanese midget sub which was dragged to shore by a huge bulldozer at Bellows. Among the articles found in the sub were dried fish, apples, canned goods, American pencils, and one bottle labeled "Wilkens family."

attached to it and just dragged the midget sub right off the reef and up onto the beach. Shortly afterward, a Navy technical intelligence unit from Pearl Harbor arrived with an 18-wheel flatbed trailer and hauled away the sub. It was later refurbished for temporary display in Hawaii before being shipped to the mainland. There it was hauled all across America, where it attracted crowds of astonished people, received sensationalized press coverage, and motivated patriotic citizens and school children to buy War Bonds and Stamps. Ironically, none of Japan's secret weapons inflicted any damage on the "Day of Infamy," but one pathetic little survivor helped raise millions of dollars for America's war effort.[28]

So it was that little Bellows Field in Waimanalo had the honor of capturing not only the first prisoner of war for America but also the first "prize" of war. This, after a long day of tragedy, confusion, loss of life, and despair, provided a glimmer of optimism and hope. It was the first step on the long road back.

APPENDIX A

ARMY AIR FORCES UNITS IN HAWAII ON 7 DECEMBER 1941*

Hickam Field:

Hawaiian Air Force, Hq & Hq Squadron
    7th Air Corps Squadron, Communications
    7th Air Corps Squadron, Weather
    19th Transport Squadron
    58th Bombardment Squadron (Light) = Redesignated 531st Fighter-Bomber Squadron, 14 August 1943
    Hawaiian Air Depot
    Tow Target Detachment
18th Bombardment Wing (Heavy), Hq & Hq Squadron
    5th Bombardment Group (Heavy), Hq & Hq Squadron
        23d Bombardment Squadron (Heavy)
        31st Bombardment Squadron (Heavy)
        72d Bombardment Squadron (Heavy)
        4th Reconnaissance Squadron (Heavy) = Redesignated 394th Bombardment Squadron (Heavy), 22 April 1942
    11th Bombardment Group (Heavy), Hq & Hq Squadron
        26th Bombardment Squadron (Heavy)
        42d Bombardment Squadron (Heavy)
        50th Reconnaissance Squadron (Heavy) = Redesignated 431st Bombardment Squadron (Heavy), 22 April 1942
        98th Bombardment Squadron (Heavy) = Constituted 2 December 1941 but not activated until 16 December 1941
17th Air Base Group, Hq & Hq Squadron
    18th Air Base Squadron
    22d Materiel Squadron
    23d Materiel Squadron
2d Signal Service Battalion
5th Chemical Company, Service, Aviation
12th Signal Platoon (Air Base)
13th Quartermaster Truck Company, Aviation
18th Signal Section, Hq
39th Quartermaster Company (Light Maintenance), Aviation

*List of units assigned compiled from the following sources: "Administrative History of Headquarters Seventh Air Force from 1916 to May 1944," pages 14-18, dated 1 August 1944; list of units serving in Hawaiian Air Force on 7 December 1941, Charles W. Aresta, The Hawaiian Military Insignia Collectors and Study Group, December 1984; Combat Squadrons of the Air Force, World War II, edited by Maurer Maurer, Office of Air Force History, 1982; personal accounts of 7 December 1941 survivors during visits to the 15th Air Base Wing History Office, February 1982 to present.

53d Signal Maintenance Company
324th Signal Company, Air Wing
328th Signal Company, Aviation
407th Signal Company, Aviation
428th Signal Maintenance Company, Aviation
481st Ordnance Company, Aviation
482d Ordnance Company, Aviation
740th Ordnance Company, Aviation
Detachment Finance Department, Hickam Field
Detachment Medical Department, Hickam Field
Quartermaster Detachment Hawaiian Department, Hickam Field = Formerly 259th
    Quartermaster Company (Air Base)
Attached Chaplain, Hickam Field

Wheeler Field:

14th Pursuit Wing, Hq & Hq Squadron
    15th Pursuit Group (Fighter), Hq & Hq Squadron
        45th Pursuit Squadron (Fighter)
        46th Pursuit Squadron (Fighter)
        47th Pursuit Squadron (Fighter)
        72d Pursuit Squadron (Interceptor)
    18th Pursuit Group (Interceptor), Hq & Hq Squadron
        6th Pursuit Squadron (Interceptor)
        19th Pursuit Squadron (Interceptor)
        44th Pursuit Squadron (Interceptor)
        73d Pursuit Squadron (Interceptor)
        78th Pursuit Squadron (Interceptor)
18th Air Base Group, Hq & Hq Squadron
    17th Air Base Squadron
    24th Materiel Squadron
    25th Materiel Squadron
14th Quartermaster Truck Company, Aviation
45th Signal Platoon (Air Base)
307th Signal Company (Air Wing)
674th Ordnance Company, Aviation
696th Ordnance Company, Aviation
741st Ordnance Company, Aviation
Detachment 39th Quartermaster Company (Light Maintenance)
Detachment Finance Department, Wheeler Field
Detachment Medical Department, Wheeler Field
Quartermaster Detachment Hawaiian Department, Wheeler Field = Formerly 258th
    Quartermaster Company (Air Base)
Attached Chaplain, Wheeler Field

Bellows Field:

86th Observation Squadron = Redesignated 43d Reconnaissance Squadron (Long Range, Photographic), 16 June 1945

Detachment Finance Department, Bellows Field

Detachment Medical Department, Bellows Field

Hawaiian Air Force Casual Detachment

Headquarters Detachment, Bellows Field

Quartermaster Detachment Hawaiian Department, Bellows Field

NOTE: The 38th and 88th Reconnaissance Squadrons, although not stationed in Hawaii, had the misfortune of arriving in the middle of the Japanese attack. Sixteen of their B-17s were scheduled to leave Hamilton Field, California, the preceding evening on the first leg of a flight from the United States to the Philippines; three failed to take off, one had to turn back early in the flight, and the twelve remaining aircraft landed at various locations on Oahu.

APPENDIX B

STATUS OF AIRCRAFT ON OAHU, BEFORE AND AFTER THE ATTACK[*]

	On Hand Before Attack	In Commission	Destroyed During Attack	In Commission After Attack
B-17D	12	6	5[+]	4
B-18	33	21	12	11
A-20A	12	5	2	9[@]
P-40C	12	9	5	2
P-40B	87	55	37	25
P-36A	39	20	4	16
P-26A	8	7	5	2
P-26B	6	3	1	2
B-12A	3	1	0	1
A-12A	2	2	0	1
AT-6	4	3	1	2
OA-9	3	3	2	1
OA-8	1	1	0	1
O-47B	7	5	0	5
O-49	2	2	1	1
C-33[#]	2	2	0	0
B-24A[**]	1	1	1	0
TOTALS	234	146	76	83

The aircraft were distributed around the island as follows:

Hickam Field: 12 B-17Ds, 32 B-18s, 12 A-20As, 2 P-26As, 2 A-12As, 2 C-33s, and 1 B-24A.

Wheeler Field: 12 P-40Cs, 87 P-40Bs, 39 P-36As, 6 P-26As, 6 P-26Bs, 3 B-12As, 4 AT-6s, 3 OA-9s, and 1 OA-8.[++]

Bellows Field: 2 O-49s, 7 O-47Bs, and 1 B-18.[@@]

---

[*]All information extracted from "Operational History of the Seventh Air Force, 7 December 1941 to 6 December 1943," on file at Air Force Historical Research Center, Maxwell AFB, AL, unless otherwise noted.

[+]Seventh Air Force and congressional investigation records indicate four B-17s destroyed, but actual maintenance records from Hickam Field as recorded by retired Air Force Lt Col Charles P. Eckhert (deceased), from 1300 hours, 7 December 1941, to 1845 hours, 8 December 1941, show five B-17s damaged beyond repair.

[@]Seventh Air Force and congressional investigation records indicate five A-20As in commission after attack, while Colonel Eckhert's records claim nine were in commission and ready to fly.

[#]C-33s were assigned to the 19th Transport Squadron but were not listed in Seventh Air Force or congressional records. Colonel Eckhert's records clearly identify each aircraft and the damage each sustained. See Appendix C.

[**]See Appendix C for details on the B-24A.

[++]The 47th Pursuit Squadron (Fighter) had deployed to Haleiwa and the 44th Pursuit Squadron (Interceptor) to Bellows for gunnery practice prior to 7 December. Because aircraft may have been flown back and forth between these two fields and Wheeler over the weekend, exact number and types of aircraft physically located at Haleiwa and Bellows cannot be determined at this time. Therefore, both squadrons' aircraft are included with the totals listed for Wheeler Field.

[@@]The B-18 was actually assigned to Hickam Field but spent most of its time at Bellows Field towing the targets used by temporarily assigned fighter units during aerial gunnery practice. In addition, a B-18 assigned to Hickam Field flew out of Wheeler Field. On Sunday morning this aircraft was on the island of Molokai and would return to Wheeler Field during the attack.

APPENDIX C

HICKAM FIELD MAINTENANCE RECORD*

Group Number	Serial Number	Discrepancies as of 1300 7 Dec 41	Status as of 1845 8 Dec 41
		5th Bomb Group (Heavy)	
		B-17D	
92	40-3082		In Commission
52	40-3089		In Commission
1	40-3085	Two oil tanks damaged, one engine bad, two tires destroyed, bullet holes	Repairable
41	40-3092	No engines, no left wheel, no oil tanks	Repairable
90	40-3071	Left and rear tires gone, control wires gone, badly shot up	Destroyed
20	40-3080	Burned up	Destroyed
		B-18	
80	37-1	Hole in left wing and rudder	In commission
81	37-2		In Commission
31	36-339	Located at Hilo, Hawaii, TH	In Commission
62	36-342		In Commission
63	36-329		In Commission
64	36-433	Left wing, vertical fin, and rudder assembly damaged, rudder cables damaged	In Commission
92	?	Not the #92 in 11 Bomb Gp	In Commission
2	36-333	Right wing and elevator damaged	Repairable
83	36-310	Right engine shot, many bullet holes	Repairable
33	36-438	Left wing, ailerons, and elevator bullet holes, left tire bad	Repairable
35	36-337	Right engine prop bad	Repairable
36	36-334	Vertical fin and right tire badly shot up	Repairable
3	37-4		Destroyed
82	37-3	Burned up	Destroyed
32	37-11		Destroyed
37	37-19	Tail wheel, tail surface, right tire and engine badly shot up	Destroyed

*Information extracted from Hickam Field maintenance records as recorded by retired Air Force Lt Col Charles P. Eckhert (deceased), from 1300 hours 7 December 1941 to 1845 hours 8 December 1941.

Group Number	Serial Number	Discrepancies as of 1300 7 Dec 41	Status as of 1845 8 Dec 41

A-20A

Group Number	Serial Number		Status as of 1845 8 Dec 41
5	40-125		In Commission
7	40-127		In Commission
8	40-128		In Commission
9	40-130		In Commission
11	40-133		In Commission
12	40-134		In Commission
13	40-135		In Commission
14	40-136		In Commission
16	40-150		In Commission
10	40-131		Repairable
15	40-137		Destroyed
17	40-151		Destroyed

11th Bombardment Group (Heavy)

B-17D

Group Number	Serial Number	Discrepancies	Status
41	40-3084	Replace #2, #3, and main gas tanks, no tunnel, no nose gun	In Commission
40	40-3060	Change four props	In Commission
60	40-3090	Left wheel fin and stabilizer damaged, fuselage torn above radio compartment	Repairable
61	?		Destroyed
80	40-3077		Destroyed
81	40-3083		Destroyed

B-18

Group Number	Serial Number	Discrepancies	Status
50	36-327		In Commission
52	36-336		In Commission
53	37-20	Need airline patching materiel	In Commission
94	37-5		In Commission
54	36-328	Complete empennage metal work, replace all wheels	Repairable
77	36-436	Need vertical stabilizer, rudder, left wheel, and right aileron	Repairable
78	36-437	Major work required	Repairable
79	37-15	Patching for fin, right wheel, right elevator, oil leak right engine	Repairable
76	36-288	At HAD for complete repair	Repairable
93	37-6	Originally thought to be a complete loss	Repairable

Group Number	Serial Number	Discrepancies as of 1300 7 Dec 41	Status as of 1845 8 Dec 41
4	37-7	Major metal work, right landing gear	Repairable
51	36-335	Burned in HAD	Destroyed
92	36-270	Total loss	Destroyed
95	37-12	Parts being used for #64	Destroyed

Hawaiian Air Force

B-18

1	?	Completely demolished	Destroyed

19th Transport Squadron

C-33/DC-2

1	?	Heavily strafed	Repairable
2	?	Elevator damaged	Repairable

18th Bombardment Wing Heavy

B-18

1	?	Completely demolished	Destroyed

58th Bombardment Squadron (Light)

P-26

47	33-100		In Commission
49	33-186		Repairable

A-12

34	33-227		In Commission
19	33-231		Repairable

Group Number	Serial Number	Discrepancies as of 1300 7 Dec 41	Status as of 1845 8 Dec 41

Transient Aircraft

B-24A

71	40-2371	Burned	Destroyed

NOTE: The B-24A was part of the 44th Bomb Group, assigned to the 1st Photo Group, attached to Ferry Command and had flown to Hawaii from Russia through the Middle East, Singapore, Australia, New Guinea, and Wake Island. It arrived at Hickam Field on 5 December to have guns installed prior to continuing on to the Philippines. Problems were encountered installing the weapons and it was still at Hickam the morning of the attack. The aircraft was assigned to the Philippines to fly reconnaissance missions over Japanese installations in the Marshalls and Carolines.   Information extracted from *Log of the Liberators* by Steve Birdsall, Doubleday & Company, Inc, 1973, pp 44-45; *The Army Air Forces in World War II*, Vol I, Craven and Cate, Washington DC, 1983, pp 189-190; and correspondence 1990-1991 with Dave Aiken of Irving, TX.

APPENDIX D

B-17s ARRIVING DURING THE ATTACK*

88th Reconnaissance Squadron

Model/Serial Number	Pilot	Where Landed	Status as of 1845, 8 Dec 1941
B-17E/41-2429	Capt Richard H. Carmichael	Haleiwa Aux Fld	In Commission
B-17E/41-2430	1st Lt Harold N. Chaffin	Haleiwa Aux Fld	In Commission
B-17E/41-2416	1st Lt Frank P. Bostrom	Kahuku Golf Crs	Repairable
B-17E/41-2432	1st Lt Robert E. Thacker	Hickam Field+	In Commission
B-17E/41-2433	1st Lt Harry N. Brandon	Hickam Field	In Commission
B-17E/41-2434	1st Lt David G. Rawls	Hickam Field	In Commission

88th Reconnaissance Squadron (H) Crew Members

Crew No. 1: Capt Richard H. Carmichael, Capt James W. Twaddell, 2d Lt Donald O. Tower, 2d Lt Kermit E. Meyers, Avn Cdt Theodore I. Pascoe, TSgt Wallace A. Carter, SSgt Jack R. Tribble, SSgt Sam Tower, SSgt Harold D. Boyer.

Crew No. 2: 1st Lt Harold N. Chaffin, 2d Lt Mabry Simmons, 2d Lt Walter H. Johnson, Avn Cdt Hubert S. Mobley, TSgt Russell E. Mackey, SSgt Lucuis W. Weeks, Sgt Irving W. McMichael, PFC Robert K. Barnard.

Crew No. 3: 1st Lt Richard F. Ezzard, 1st Lt E. A. Luke, 2d Lt Vincent J. Roddy, 2d Lt John S. Minahan, Avn Cdt Raymond S. Rollings, TSgt Gola D. McCallister, Sgt Delbert G. Walmer, Pvt Ralph W. Chorn.

---

*Information extracted from Hickam Field maintenance records as recorded by retired Air Force Lt Col Charles P. Eckhert (deceased), from 1300, 7 Dec 41 to 1845, 8 Dec 41; unit history, 38 RS, 12 Jun 1917-May 42; 38 RS deployment orders, Special Order No. 1, 4 Dec 41; 88 RS deployment orders, Annex to Field Order No. 2, 3 Dec 41.

+Several eyewitness accounts, including Brig Gen H. C. Davidson and 2d Lt Henry Wells Lawrence, claim one of the three aircraft listed as landing at Hickam Field initially landed at Wheeler Field. The maintenance records, however, show all three aircraft at Hickam Field immediately after the attack. To further complicate the picture, there was a B-18 which landed from the island of Molokai at Wheeler Field during the attack. It is possible, but highly unlikely, that the eye witness mistook the B-18 for the B-17. A more plausible explanation for the eyewitness accounts would be that one of the B-17s landed at Wheeler and then returned almost immediately to Hickam.

Crew No. 4: 1st Lt Frank W. Potter, 2d Lt Henry F. Smith, 2d Lt Harold W. Edmonds, Avn Cdt Joseph A. Creed, Jr., SSgt Harry B. Shields, SSgt Wayne T. Doyle, Sgt James A. Garson, PFC William M. Edwards.

Crew No. 5: 1st Lt Robert E. Thacker, 2d Lt Donald C. Surles, 2d Lt Roderick M. Stewart, Avn Cdt Albert J. Hobday, SSgt Cal Russell, Sgt Howard K. Beck, Sgt Cyril LaLancet, PFC Edwin Rhodes.

Crew No. 6: 1st Lt Frank P. Bostrom, 2d Lt Wilson L. Cook, 2d Lt Earl Sheggrud, Avn Cdt Rob R. Carruthers, TSgt Herbert B. Collins, SSgt Leslie O. Hansen, PFC Herbert Wheatley Jr., PFC Elwood B. Shouldis, PFC Clyde L. Horn.

Crew No. 7: 1st Lt Harry N. Brandon, 2d Lt Rober L. Ramsey, Avn Cdt Harold E. Snider, TSgt James G. Helton, SSgt David P. Barnard, SSgt Ralph E. Mouser, Sgt Wayne E. Johnson, Pvt Billy B. Sutton.

Crew No. 8: 1st Lt David G. Rawls, 2d Lt John T. Compton, Avn Cdt Robert T. Jones, SSgt Robert J. Dunn, Jr., SSgt Wilson D. Palmer, Sgt Robert K. Palmer, Sgt Sheldon D. Beaton, PFC Aby A. Francisco.

Crew No. 3 aborted in flight and returned to Hamilton Field; Crew No. 4 aborted before takeoff. Six aircraft from the 88th reached Hawaii during the 7 December attack.

38th Reconnaissance Squadron

Model/Serial Number	Pilot	Where Landed	Status as of 1845, 8 Dec 1941
B-17E/41-2413	Maj Truman H. Landon	Hickam Field	In Commission
B-17E/41-2408	1st Lt Karl T. Barthelmess	Hickam Field	In Commission
B-17C/40-2074	Capt Raymond T. Swenson	Hickam Field	Destroyed
B-17C/40-2049	1st Lt Robert H. Richards	Bellows Field	Repairable (Later used for spare parts and not repaired)
B-17C/40-2054	1st Lt Earl J. Cooper	Hickam Field	In Commission
B-17C/40-2063	1st Lt Bruce G. Allen	Hickam Field	In Commission

38th Reconnaissance Squadron (H) Crew Members

<u>Crew No. 1</u>: Maj Truman H. Landon, 1st Lt William B. M. Ellis, 2d Lt George L. Newton, 2d Lt Chester H. Budz, Avn Cdt Erwin F. Cihak, MSgt John B. Meeks, TSgt Jesse L. Schneider, SSgt Albert E. Brawley, and Sgt Benjamin L. Hale.

<u>Crew No. 2</u>: 1st Lt Karl T. Barthelmess, 2d Lt Larry J. Sheehan, 2d Lt Charles E. Bergdoll, Avn Cdt John C. Adams, TSgt Roy H. Coulter, SSgt Nicholas H. Kahlefent, SSgt Lee R. Embree, Sgt Vance H. spears, and Cpl Raymond R. Joslin.

<u>Crew No. 3</u>: Capt Raymond T. Swenson, 1st Lt William R. Schick (flight surgeon assigned to the squadron just before its departure), 2d Lt Ernest L. Reid, 2d Lt Homer R. Taylor, Avn Cdt G. C. Beale, MSgt Leroy B Pouncey, Sgt Earl T. Williams, Cpl Mac L. Lucas, and Pvt Bert Lee, Jr.

<u>Crew No. 4</u>: 1st Lt Bruce G. Allen, 2d Lt Charles N. McArthur, Jr., Avn Cdt Leo M. Eminger, Avn Cdt Walter B. Decker, MSgt Horace K. Hunsberger, Sgt Floyd A. Wright, Jr., PFC Raymond E. Fetty, Pvt Richard E. Morris, and Pvt J. W. Childers.

<u>Crew No. 5</u>: 1st Lt Earl J. Cooper, 2d Lt Richard J. Eberenz, 2d Lt John A. Crockett, Avn Cdt Jim R. Buchanan, TSgt Jesse R. Broyles, Sgt Joseph J. Bruce, Sgt Lee W. Best, Cpl Elmer G. Lippold, and Pvt Don C. McCord, Jr.

<u>Crew No. 6</u>: 1st Lt Harold T. Hastings, 2d Lt Charles E. Norton, Avn Cdt George M. Staples, Avn Cdt James F. Doyle, Sgt Stanley F. Terlep, Cpl Marlin Woodward, Cpl Calvin J. Hammack, PFC Vernon R. Schnuelle, and Pvt William Superak.

<u>Crew No. 7</u>: 1st Lt Robert H. Richards, 2d Lt Leonard S. Humiston, Avn Cdt William F. B. Morris, Avn Cdt George E. Gammans, SSgt Joseph S. Angelini, SSgt Erwin B. Casebolt, SSgt Melvin D. Zajic, SSgt Lawrence B. Velarde, and Pvt Vernon D. Tomlinson.

<u>Crew No. 8</u>: 1st Lt Boris M. Zubko, 2d Lt Alfred H. Oberg, Jr., Avn Cdt Cedric P. Drake, Avn Cdt Milan A. Chiba, TSgt Lew M. Evans, SSgt Robert J. Zimmerman, Sgt Melvin D. Loyd, Cpl Gilbert W. Hewitt, and Pvt Martin M. Newcomer.

Crews 6 and 8 were delayed by engine trouble and did not take off with the original group. Six aircraft from the 38th reached Hawaii during the 7 December attack.

APPENDIX E

ARMY, ARMY AIR FORCES, AND CIVILIAN CASUALTY LIST*

No.	Name and Rank	Serial #	Unit	Status
1.	Adams, Kenneth E., Pvt	17009623	Hq Sq 5th BG	WIA
2.	Akina, August, Civ		Hickam Plumber	KIA
3.	Allen, Edward L., Pvt	7005724	23d Mat Sq	WIA
4.	Allen, Robert G., Pvt	15058940	45th Pur Sq	KIA
5.	Allshouse, Blake C., Pvt	13002334	(Unknown)	WIA
6.	Alois, Ralph, SSgt	6717269	50th Recon Sq	KIA
7.	Ames, George C., Cpl	6150680	72d Pur Sq	WIA
8.	Anderson, Elmer, TSgt	6241317	42d Bomb Sq	WIA
9.	Anderson, Garland C., Pvt	14028405	Hq Sq 18th BW	KIA
10.	Anderson, Loid W., Cpl	6934142	Hq Sq 11th BG	WIA
11.	Anderson, Manfred C., Pvt	16021427	Hq Sq 18th BW	KIA
12.	Anderson, William T., Cpl	6947615	19th Tran Sq	KIA
13.	Angelich, Jerry M., Pvt	19003575	Hq Sq 17th ABG	KIA
14.	Ashker, Samuel E., PFC	6976841	Hq Sq 18th PG	WIA
15.	Aubrey, Herbert, Pvt	6951838	Hq Sq 17th ABG	WIA
16.	Avery, Robert L., PFC	6934108	Hq Sq 11th BG	KIA
17.	Bailey, Earl L., Pvt	36108905	Cst Art	WIA
18.	Baker, Fred F. Jr., PFC	6914477	23d Mat Sq	WIA
19.	Baker, George W., PFC	13001888	22d Mat Sq	KIA
20.	Baker, Leonard A., SSgt	6558082	Hq Sq 15th PG	WIA
21.	Baldwin, Howard, Sgt	6977427	Hq Sq 11th BG	WIA
22.	Baldwin, Robert H., SSgt	6913117	45th Pur Sq	WIA
23.	Bankston, John B. Gordon, Civ		Hawaiian Air Dpt	WIA
24.	Barasha, Walter A., Pvt	13007256	58th Bomb Sq	WIA
25.	Barbour, Leonard A., Pvt	13023349	Fld Art	WIA
26.	Barker, Bruce B. S., 1st Lt	0-428793	42d Bomb Sq	WIA
27.	Barksdale, James M., SSgt	6887682	73d Pur Sq	KIA
28.	Barnes, Leonard M. Jr., Pvt	6950778	Hq Sq 5th BG	WIA
29.	Bartlett, Charles W., PFC	6934647	42d Bomb Sq	WIA
30.	Basa, Frank R., PFC	7023005	22d Mat Sq	WIA
31.	Bauer, John F., SSgt	6078351	Hq Sq 5th BG	WIA

*Civilians listed include only those killed or wounded on Army Air Forces installations. Casualty List compiled from the following sources: Ltr, Hq Hawaiian Air Force, to Commanding General Hawaiian Department, "Report of casulties [sic]," 16 Dec 41; list, Fort Shafter, "Hawaiian Islands Casualties (Army)," n.d.; list of casualties, by Mr. Raymond D. Emory, Honolulu, HI, 1988; ltr, Hq Hawaiian Department, to Adjutant General, Washington, DC, "Battle Casualties," 1 Mar 42; memo, Office Chief of Staff US Army, to Chief Legislative and Liaison Division, "Casualties of Pearl Harbor on 7 Dec 41," 20 Oct 47; Killed in Action List, 11th Bomb Group (H) Association, 1 Dec 90; ltr, National Personnel Records Center, [verification of 11th BG (H) KIA list, 6 Aug 90], 31 Aug 90; ltr, National Personnel Records Center, 26 Feb 91 and 12 Jul 91; History of 15th Pursuit Group (F), 1 Dec 40 to 31 Dec 41; Arizona Memorial casualty list, 20 Jul 90; various publications regarding 7 Dec 41 attack (see bibliography for complete listing).

No.	Name and Rank	Serial #	Unit	Status
32.	Bays, Donald E., Pvt	6948505	Tow Trgt Det	KIA
33.	Beale, G. C., Avn Cdt	18036583	38th Recon Sq	WIA
34.	Beasley, Herschel N., TSgt	6251816	19th Tran Sq	WIA
35.	Beasley, Leland V., Pvt	7003158	42d Bomb Sq	KIA
36.	Beatty, Howard J., Pvt	6980240	QM Det HAD	WIA
37.	Beitler, Henry C. Jr., PFC	6936109	42d Bomb Sq	WIA
38.	Bellue, Thomas E., PFC	7000795	72d Pur Sq	WIA
39.	Benedict, William L., Civ		Fire Chief	WIA
40.	Bennett, Gordon R. Jr., Pvt	16012883	Hq Sq 18th BW	KIA
41.	Bennett, Howard A., SSgt	6979441	Hq Sq 15th PG	WIA
42.	Berard, Edmond H., PFC	16021386	18th AB Sq	WIA
43.	Big Thunder, Elmer, Pvt	6919179	19th Tran Sq	WIA
44.	Bills, Mathew T., Pvt	12014696	QM Det HAD	KIA
45.	Bise, Delmas F., PFC	6996842	26th Bomb Sq	WIA
46.	Bishop, Samuel W., 1st Lt	0-396359	44th Pur Sq	WIA
47.	Blackmon, Leonard, Sgt	6289781	Hq Sq 18th BW	WIA
48.	Blackwell, Henry C., Cpl	20920836	Cst Art	KIA
49.	Blakley, William T., Pvt	18046224	19th Tran Sq	KIA
50.	Bloom, Robert E., Cpl	7022832	Hq Sq 11th BG	WIA
51.	Bloxham, Robert W., Pvt	19010611	19th Pur Sq	WIA
52.	Boersema, Joel J., Pvt	6913095	Hq Sq 5th BG	WIA
53.	Bois, Jack L., Pvt	16012899	18th AB Sq	WIA
54.	Bolan, George P., SSgt	6930952	Hq Sq 5th BG	KIA
55.	Bonaventura, Joseph A., PFC	15019584	(Unknown)	WIA
56.	Bonina, Vincent J., PFC	13004082	Tow Trgt Det	WIA
57.	Bonnie, Felix, SSgt	R-1005587	26th Bomb Sq	KIA
58.	Borgelt, Harold W., Cpl	6276330	7th AC Sq	KIA
59.	Boswell, Frank G., Pvt	6834448	Hq Sq 18th BW	KIA
60.	Bowen, Frank W., SSgt	6657666	26th Bomb Sq	WIA
61.	Bowsher, Paul T. Jr., Pvt	6991972	42d Bomb Sq	WIA
62.	Boyd, Herman, Pvt	19058806	Hq Sq 17th ABG	WIA
63.	Boyer, Paul R., Pvt	7022177	Cst Art	WIA
64.	Boyle, Arthur F., Pvt	6152392	22d Mat Sq	KIA
65.	Bradshaw, Thomas E., Pvt	6580885	50th Recon Sq	WIA
66.	Brandt, Billy O., SSgt	6883472	22d Mat Sq	KIA
67.	Brewer, Roy G., PFC	6998320	Hq Sq 17th ABG	WIA
68.	Brissenden, Harris, PFC	6799709	26th Bomb Sq	WIA
69.	Brooks, Charles S. Jr., PFC	6993821	22d Mat Sq	WIA
70	Brooks, B. J., Pvt	7021066	Hq Sq 17th ABG	KIA
71.	Broughton, Alfred W., Pvt	16003053	23d Bomb Sq	WIA
72.	Brower, Rennie V. Jr., Pvt	6934751	22d Mat Sq	KIA
73.	Brown, Clyde C., Cpl	20920839	Cst Art	KIA
74.	Brown, Douglas L., Pvt		Hq Sq 11th BG	WIA
75.	Brown, James A., PFC	6951101	Med Det	WIA
76.	Brown, Robert L., Pvt	6983675	Unknown	WIA

No.	Name and Rank	Serial #	Unit	Status
77.	Brown, Robert S., Pvt	11020247	Hq Sq 11th BG	KIA
78.	Brownlee, William J., Pvt	6299891	22d Mat Sq	KIA
79.	Brubaker, Brooks J., Pvt	7021066	22d Mat Sq	KIA
80.	Brummwell, Malcolm J., 1st Lt	0-341888	Hq Sq 17th ABG	KIA
81.	Bryant, Claude L., Cpl	6999009	Cst Art	KIA
82.	Bryant, William M., Sgt	7002366	Hq Sq 18th BW	WIA
83.	Bubb, Eugene R., Pvt	7026660	Cst Art	KIA
84.	Bunn, Raymond A., PFC	16010118	39th QM Co	WIA
85.	Burger, Alfred, Pvt	19053458	Cst Art	WIA
86.	Burlison, Weldon C., Pvt	6377063	22d Mat Sq	KIA
87.	Burns, Edward J., 1st Sgt	6144931	72d Pur Sq	KIA
88.	Burns, James R. Jr., Pvt	13006867	(Unknown)	WIA
89.	Bush, Joseph, Pvt	6023658	18th AB Sq	KIA
90.	Bush, Francis R., (Unk)	15019135	23d Bomb Sq	WIA
91.	Bushey, George O., Pvt	16012754	Hq Sq 17th ABG	WIA
92.	Buss, Robert P., Cpl	16003452	45th Pur Sq	KIA
93.	Butler, George B., Cpl	6968733	Fld Art	WIA
94.	Byers, Roy W., Pvt	6998810	Hq Sq 11th BG	WIA
95.	Byrd, Bert E. Jr., PFC	6667932	Hq Sq 11th BG	WIA
96.	Byrd, Louis J., Pvt	6915390	QM Det HAD	WIA
97.	Byrd, Robert T., Pvt	14046406	Hq Sq 5th BG	WIA
98.	Byrd, Theodore F. Jr., PFC	14019881	Hq Sq 18th PG	KIA
99.	Calderon, Carmel R., PFC	6955786	Hq Sq 11th BG	WIA
100.	Cameron, Charles B., SSgt	6904645	22d Mat Sq	WIA
101.	Campbell, Edward J., Pvt	12006221	Cst Art	WIA
102.	Campiglia, Francis E., Pvt	11020150	23d Mat Sq	KIA
103.	Carazo, Ramon A., Pvt	13026714	(Unknown)	WIA
104.	Carey, Lawrence D., Pvt	11027098	18th AB Sq	WIA
105.	Carlson, Lawrence R., Pvt	16017324	4th Recon Sq	KIA
106.	Carr, James W., TSgt	6381552	72d Pur Sq	WIA
107.	Carreira, John, Civ		Hon Fire Dept	KIA
108.	Carroll, James G., 2d Lt	0-417185	(Unknown)	WIA
109.	Cashen, Malachy J., Pvt	16008039	72d Pur Sq	KIA
110.	Cashman, Edward J., TSgt	R-4311524	Hq Sq 11th BG	KIA
111.	Cassel, Charles G., 1st Lt	0-302301	Army	WIA
112.	Cawley, Dennis, Pvt	6955831	23d Mat Sq	WIA
113.	Cebert, Dean W., Pvt	16017559	72d Pur Sq	KIA
114.	Chabalowski, Richard X., Pvt	16001809	Tow Trgt Det	WIA
115.	Chagnon, Joseph J., Sgt	6908124	QM Det HAD	KIA
116.	Chambers, Eugene L., PFC	13010833	Hq Sq 15th PG	KIA
117.	Chaplick, Frank G., PFC	6148215	18th AB Sq	WIA
118.	Chapman, Donal V., Cpl	6914156	Hq Sq 11th BG	KIA
119.	Charron, Evariste E., PFC	R-1075852	31st Bomb Sq	WIA
120.	Childress, Herbert J. W., S/Sgt	20920356	Cst Art	WIA
121.	Christiansen, Hans C., 2d Lt	0-406482	44th Pur Sq	KIA

No.	Name and Rank	Serial #	Unit	Status
122.	Church, Leroy R., Pvt	16007873	22d Mat Sq	KIA
123.	Clague, Charles S., Pvt	16017442	Hq Sq 11th BG	WIA
124.	Clark, Monroe M., SSgt	6254875	Hq Sq 11th BG	KIA
125.	Clendenning, Charles P., Pvt	16021440	23d Bomb Sq	WIA
126.	Clendenning, Lee I., PFC	16021445	23d Bomb Sq	KIA
127.	Coale, Lee R., Pvt	6934632	Hq Sq 5th BG	WIA
128.	Collins, Raymond J., Cpl	6980929	Hq Sq 18th PG	WIA
129.	Collins, Walter L., Pvt	6397839	6th Pur Sq	WIA
130.	Conant, Clarence A., Pvt	7003044	26th Bomb Sq	KIA
131.	Conner, Fred R., Pvt	16017249	26th Bomb Sq	WIA
132.	Cooper, Frank B., Pvt	7021035	Hq Sq 18th BW	KIA
133.	Cooper, Howard F., 1st Lt	0-353462	Hq Sq 17th ABG	WIA
134.	Correa, George, Civ		Hon Fire Dept	WIA
135.	Corter, James P., Pvt	12028663	Fld Art	WIA
136.	Cossack, Michael T., Sgt	6987369	78th Pur Sq	WIA
137.	Coster, Richard L., Pvt	16017463	23d Bomb Sq	KIA
138.	Couhig, John H., Pvt	6427420	18th AB Sq	KIA
139.	Cox, Eugene C., Sgt	6928554	Hq Sq 11th BG	WIA
140.	Coyne, William Jr., PFC	6934771	42d Bomb Sq	KIA
141.	Craig, Charles W., Pvt	16017241	26th Bomb Sq	WIA
142.	Creech, William C., PFC	7023159	72d Pur Sq	KIA
143.	Cremer, Eilert H., Sgt	6608654	22d Mat Sq	WIA
144.	Crocker, Erwin E., Pvt	6143857	Hq Sq 17th ABG	WIA
145.	Crouse, Robert G., Cpl	6844093	23d Mat Sq	WIA
146.	Crum, Lincoln M., PFC	6919774	23d Mat Sq	WIA
147.	Cruthirds, John E., PFC	6298043	Hq Sq 18th BW	KIA
148.	Currence, Clarence F. Jr., Cpl	6667759	19th Tran Sq	WIA
149.	Dabney, Fred A., Sgt	6994288	72d Pur Sq	WIA
150.	Dacon, Charles R., Pvt	11015145	(Unknown)	WIA
151.	Dains, John L., 2d Lt	0-424923	47th Pur Sq	KIA
152.	Dallas, Frank R., Pvt	19020842	(Unknown)	WIA
153.	Damsky, Robert P., Pvt	11020220	Hq Sq 11th BG	WIA
154.	Dasenbrock, Louis H., Pvt	16040328	50th Recon Sq	KIA
155.	DaTorre, Oreste, Pvt	12006276	(Unknown)	KIA
156.	Davenport, James M., Sgt	6292373	72d Pur Sq	WIA
157.	David, Arthur E., PFC	6132614	72d Bomb Sq	WIA
158.	Davis, Allen D., Pvt	16003027	Hq Sq 11th BG	WIA
159.	Davis, Spencer L., Pvt	6967237	Hq Sq 11th BG	WIA
160.	Davis, Sydney A., Pvt	16007702	23d Mat Sq	WIA
161.	Deeter, Charles R., Pvt	6669195	Hq Sq 17th ABG	WIA
162.	Defenbaugh, Russell C., Pvt	16017271	19th Tran Sq	KIA
163.	Denson, Eugene B., PFC	7002423	42d Bomb Sq	KIA
164.	DePolis, Frank J., SSgt	6946517	26th Bomb Sq	KIA
165.	Deraney, George, PFC	6148095	Hq Sq 18th PG	WIA
166.	Derthick, James H., Sgt	6668189	Hq Sq 18th PG	KIA

No.	Name and Rank	Serial #	Unit	Status
167.	Devera, Joseph, PFC	20011832	298th Inf	WIA
168.	Dickerson, Richard A., Cpl	6296796	Hq Sq 5th BG	KIA
169.	Dietterick, Robert P., Pvt	13004007	23d Mat Sq	WIA
170.	Dinagin, James E., Sgt	11011326	50th Recon Sq	WIA
171.	Dodd, Harry O., PFC	16002286	Hq Sq 15th PG	WIA
172.	Donart, Mathias E., Sgt	6568848	42d Bomb Sq	WIA
173.	Dorondo, John F., TSgt	6949822	Hq Sq 18th BW	WIA
174.	Downs, Jack A., Pvt	18059915	Hq Sq 17th ABG	KIA
175.	Dragon, Charles R., Pvt	11015145	22d Mat Sq	WIA
176.	Drechsler, Carl, Pvt	6934744	22d Mat Sq	WIA
177.	Drisner, Joseph R., Pvt	15059459	Hq Sq 11th BG	WIA
178.	Dubois, Ivan C., Maj	0-227384	(Unknown)	WIA
179.	Dudley, George G., SSgt	6296835	Hq Sq 18th BW	WIA
180.	Duff, Robert C. Jr., Pvt	6998717	Hq Sq 18th BW	KIA
181.	Duquette, Donat G., Pvt	6149887	Cst Art	KIA
182.	Durbin, Noel E., PFC	16017279	Hq Sq 15th PG	WIA
183.	Duvall, William T., Pvt	6952778	23d Mat Sq	WIA
184.	Dwyre, George T., Sgt	6917063	Hq Sq 17th ABG	WIA
185.	Dye, Cecil W., Cpl	6925026	Hq Sq 17th ABG	WIA
186.	Dyer, Daniel A. Jr., TSgt	6293492	7th AC Sq	KIA
187.	Edwards, Lyle O., Pvt	16012846	Hq Sq 18th BW	KIA
188.	Ehrke, Jack O., Sgt	6584308	19th Tran Sq	WIA
189.	Eichelberger, Paul R., Pvt	13030353	Hq Sq 17th ABG	KIA
190.	Eldred, Philip Ward, Civ		Hawiian Air Dep	KIA
191.	Ellick, James B., Cpl	6997158	Tow Trgt Det	WIA
192.	Ellick, John L., Cpl		(Unknown)	WIA
193.	Elliott, Byron G., Pvt	17011087	23d Bomb Sq	KIA
194.	Elyard, Harold C., SSgt	6839725	18th AB Sq	KIA
195.	Enchelmeyer, Stanton H., Pvt	6152290	50th Recon Sq	WIA
196.	English, James T., Cpl	16040972	72d Pur Sq	WIA
197.	Esley, Benjamin F. Jr., Pvt	13023635	Cst Art	WIA
198.	Evans, Vernon W., PFC	7002345	42d Bomb Sq	WIA
199.	Even, Jerome A., Pvt	16003121	26th Bomb Sq	WIA
200.	Everett, James, SSgt	6296829	72d Pur Sq	KIA
201.	Ewers, James F., Pvt	16040940	Hq Sq 15th PG	WIA
202.	Exum, Grady E., PFC	6921577	22d Mat Sq	WIA
203.	Fadon, Paul J., Sgt	6564392	INF	KIA
204.	Fairbanks, Vernon W. J., Pvt	20920723	Cst Art	WIA
205.	Fairchild, Willard E., Pvt	16003011	18th AB Sq	KIA
206.	Falkenburg, Irwin A., SSgt	6719395	6th Pur Sq	WIA
207.	Favreau, Arthur A., PFC	6154534	Cst Art	KIA
208.	Fay, Charles A., SSgt	6148050	72d Pur Sq	WIA
209.	Feldman, Jack H., Pvt	13027061	22d Mat Sq	KIA
210.	Fellman, Paul V., SSgt	6630437	18th AB Sq	KIA
211.	Ferris, Homer E., TSgt	R-339200	18th AB Sq	KIA

No.	Name and Rank	Serial #	Unit	Status
212.	Fessler, Robert G., Pvt	16007607	19th Tran Sq	WIA
213.	Fiander, Stuart H., Pvt	6151801	18th AB Sq	KIA
214.	Field, Arnold E., Pvt	16007828	Hq Sq 17th ABG	KIA
215.	Finney, Patrick L., Cpl	6268780	26th Bomb Sq	KIA
216.	Fitzsimons, Robert G., Pvt	16003456	72d Pur Sq	WIA
217.	Fleming, Robert G., Pvt	16003290	(Unknown)	WIA
218.	Fox, Jack W., PFC	6570562	31st Bomb Sq	KIA
219.	Frazier, Edwin, PFC	6871586	22d Mat Sq	WIA
220.	Free, Paul B., SSgt	6946529	72d Pur Sq	KIA
221.	French, Walter R., Pvt	18008040	Fld Art	KIA
222.	Fuller, Carl W., PFC	6925285	26th Bomb Sq	WIA
223.	Fuller, Kenneth A., Pvt	16017234	42d Bomb Sq	WIA
224.	Gabik, George J., PFC	16007559	19th Tran Sq	WIA
225.	Gagne, Leo E. A., Pvt	11020246	22d Mat Sq	KIA
226.	Gaines, Jesse D., Pvt	7003670	18th AB Sq	WIA
227.	Gallagher, Russell E., Pvt	6953547	Hq Sq 18th BW	KIA
228.	Gangrusky, Richard I., SSgt	6913556	23d Mat Sq	WIA
229.	Gannam, George K., SSgt	6926173	17th AB Sq	KIA
230.	Garrett, Robert R., Cpl	6803095	42d Bomb Sq	KIA
231.	Garrety, Richard S., Pvt	6940928	23d Mat Sq	WIA
232.	Gautier, Bill P., Pvt	7023696	22d Mat Sq	WIA
233.	Gese, Walter J., Pvt	6587391	22d Mat Sq	WIA
234.	Gilman, John A., Civ		Hon Fire Dept	WIA
235.	Gleason, James J., PFC	6947032	18th AB Sq	KIA
236.	Godley, Sidney, Pvt	14012588	QM Det HAD	WIA
237.	Goff, George W., Pvt	15069219	Hq Sq 17th ABG	WIA
238.	Good, Joseph E., SSgt	6948037	72d Pur Sq	KIA
239.	Gooding, Robert H., Pvt	6561586	Hq Sq 11th BG	KIA
240.	Gossard, James E. Jr., PFC	7002430	Hq Sq 18th BW	KIA
241.	Goudy, Allen E. W., Pvt	17025242	22d Mat Sq	KIA
242.	Gradle, Kenneth A., Cpl	6912391	Tran B-24	WIA
243.	Graf, Harold F., Cpl	6954302	7th AC Sq	WIA
244.	Green, Virgil A., Pvt	16007810	31st Bomb Sq	WIA
245.	Greene, Johon Sherman 1st Lt	0-283511	Hq Sq 18th BW	KIA
246.	Greenmore, Kenneth W., PFC	16021375	45th Pur Sq	WIA
247.	Gross, Carl R., PFC	6669177	Det Fin Dpt	WIA
248.	Gudinas, Edward J., Sgt	6664374	22d Mat Sq	WIA
249.	Gummelt, Edward L., Cpl	6296871	23d Mat Sq	WIA
250.	Gummerson, Elwood R., SSgt	6844737	26th Bomb Sq	KIA
251.	Gurkin, Archie R., Pvt	7005835	11th QMC	WIA
252.	Guthrie, James E., SSgt	6948331	72d Pur Sq	KIA
253.	Guttmann, Joseph H., Pvt	6979230	19th Tran Sq	KIA
254.	Halbert, Rowland F., Avn Cdt		(Unknown)	WIA
255.	Hall, Elbert H., Sgt	6387356	39th QM Co	WIA
256.	Hall, John B. Jr., Pvt	13034728	Hq Sq 14th PW	WIA

No.	Name and Rank	Serial #	Unit	Status
257.	Hall, Melvin L., MSgt	6458333	50th Recon Sq	WIA
258.	Hall, Rogers W., PFC	14004268	19th Pur Sq	WIA
259.	Hamm, Cleason S., Pvt	6880866	22d Mat Sq	WIA
260.	Hammond, Walter A., PFC	6986727	Hq Sq 5th BG	WIA
261.	Hamrick, Robert D., Pvt	16017439	72d Bomb Sq	WIA
262.	Harden, Wayne L., Pvt	19030016	11th QMC	WIA
263.	Harrell, Turner G., SSgt	7023675	22d Mat Sq	WIA
264.	Harrison, John L., Pvt	19052509	5th Chem Co Srv	WIA
265.	Hartford, Carlton H., Pvt	11015352	QM Det HAD	KIA
266.	Hasenfuss, William E. Jr., PFC	6977347	22d Mat Sq	KIA
267.	Hasty, Ardrey V., Pvt	14037508	QM Det HAD	KIA
268.	Haughey, John T., PFC	6982631	50th Recon Sq	KIA
269.	Hawkins, Harold H., Pvt	14037911	Hq Sq 11th BG	WIA
270.	Hays, Alfred, Pvt	16017464	Hq Sq 5th BG	KIA
271.	Heffelfinger, Gerald R., Sgt	6890694	13th QM Trk Co	WIA
272.	Hefley, Elton C., Avn Cdt	18040582	Hq Sq 17th ABG	WIA
273.	Helms, Frank B., 1st Sgt	6653968	23d Bomb Sq	WIA
274.	Henson, Raymond H., Pvt	18063000	Hq Sq 17th ABG	WIA
275.	Herbert, Joseph C., SSgt	6844109	Hq Sq 18th PG	KIA
276.	Hill, Charles W. Jr., Pvt	11027412	18th AB Sq	WIA
277.	Hill, Harry O., Cpl	6946549	Hq Sq 18th BW	WIA
278.	Hislop, William, PFC	6396064	23d Bomb Sq	KIA
279.	Hobbie, Theodore V., SSgt	6573738	Tran B-24	WIA
280.	Hodder, Charles W., Pvt	6900833	(Unknown)	WIA
281.	Holbert, Rowland F., 1st Lt	0-433047	(Unknown)	WIA
282.	Holley, Lester W., PFC	6954251	47th Pur Sq	WIA
283.	Holloway, John P., Pvt	16007867	42d Bomb Sq	WIA
284.	Hood, Earl A., Pvt	7083304	Hq Sq 18th BW	KIA
285.	Hooper, Melvin F., SSgt	6142712	23d Mat Sq	WIA
286.	Hopkins, Jack P., 2d Lt	0-417839	31st Bomb Sq	WIA
287.	Horan, John J., Pvt	7071018	19th Tran Sq	KIA
288.	Horan, Vincent M., Cpl	6148539	78th Pur Sq	KIA
289.	Horner, James A., PFC	6950776	Hq Sq 11th BG	KIA
290.	Howard, George F., PFC	6936803	Hq Sq 11th BG	KIA
291.	Howe, Sidney C., SSgt	R-153039	19th Tran Sq	WIA
292.	Howell, Elbert E., Cpl	6923855	22d Mat Sq	WIA
293.	Howland, Lawrence B., PFC	6980306	50th Recon Sq	WIA
294.	Hoyt, Clarence E., PFC	7070685	50th Recon Sq	KIA
295.	Hrusecky, Charles L., Pvt	6980546	42d Bomb Sq	KIA
296.	Hudson, William H., Cpl	6887491	42d Bomb Sq	WIA
297.	Hughes, Earl F., Pvt	6291170	17th AB Sq	WIA
298.	Hughes, Edward R., Pvt	15012648	72d Bomb Sq	KIA
299.	Hull, Robert L., Pvt	15012450	72d Pur Sq	KIA
300.	Humphrey, Henry J., SSgt	6570614	50th Recon Sq	KIA
301.	Humphries, Farris M., Pvt	6839291	23d Mat Sq	WIA

No.	Name and Rank	Serial #	Unit	Status
302.	Hunt, Herman D., Pvt	6960535	804th Engrs	WIA
303.	Hunter, Duncan, Sgt	6979365	19th Pur Sq	WIA
304.	Hymson, Lawrence, Pvt	6980991	18th AB Sq	WIA
305.	Infantolino, Alfred A., SSgt	6145811	19th Pur Sq	WIA
306.	Irons, William E., PFC	6830499	26th Bomb Sq	WIA
307.	Isaac, Chesley A., Pvt	16017282	18th AB Sq	WIA
308.	Jacobson, Dave, MSgt	R-1551856	Hq Sq HAF	KIA
309.	Jedrysik, Joseph, Pvt	11023613	Hq Sq 17th ABG	KIA
310.	Jencuis, Joseph N., Pvt	11016568	42d Bomb Sq	KIA
311.	Jenkins, George O., PFC	6668596	23d Mat Sq	WIA
312.	Johnson, Carl A., Pvt	6981067	19th Tran Sq	KIA
313.	Johnson, Clyde D., Pvt	6988789	22d Mat Sq	WIA
314.	Johnson, James R., Pvt	16017373	22d Mat Sq	KIA
315.	Johnson, Olaf A., PFC	16007617	19th Tran Sq	KIA
316.	Johnson, Robert H., Pvt	16012646	22d Mat Sq	KIA
317.	Jones, James F., PFC	14039397	42d Bomb Sq	WIA
318.	Jorda, Louis, Pvt	34004214	23d Mat Sq	WIA
319.	Jordan, Bert J., Pvt	16017391	Hq Sq 18th BW	WIA
320.	Joyce, Don R., Pvt	17010329	22d Mat Sq	WIA
321.	Joyner, Theodore K., Pvt	7002425	Hq Sq 18th BW	KIA
322.	Kaminski, Walter L., Pvt	13004062	22d Mat Sq	WIA
323.	Kalilikane, Moses, Civ		Hon Fire Dept	WIA
324.	Kawa, Russell J., PFC	6145929	72d Pur Sq	WIA
325.	Kealoha, Frederick Lt., Civ		Hon Fire Dept	WIA
326.	Kechner, Vincent J., Pvt	6979463	26th Bomb Sq	KIA
327.	Keith, Bert, Pvt	18052447	Cst Art	WIA
328.	Kelley, Ralph, SSgt	6842632	18th AB Sq	WIA
329.	Kelley, Robert R., PFC	6996638	42d Bomb Sq	KIA
330.	Kelly, Henry T., Cpl	7020458	72d Pur Sq	WIA
331.	Kempen, Wallace A., Pvt	16007866	22d Mat Sq	WIA
332.	Kennington, Robert E., Pvt	14027756	35th Inf	WIA
333.	Kern, Donald A., PFC	6991939	58th Bomb Sq	WIA
334.	Kimble, Thomas P. Jr., Pvt	14028203	72d Pur Sq	WIA
335.	Kimmey, Robert Doyle, SSgt	6265447	19th Tran Sq	KIA
336.	Kinder, Andrew J., Pvt	18000244	Hq Sq 17th ABG	KIA
337.	King, Cecil E., PFC	6936624	Hq Sq 11th BG	WIA
338.	King, Howard E., PFC	7026071	13th QM Trk Co	WIA
339.	King, Marion E. Jr., Pvt	6936734	22d Mat Sq	KIA
340.	King, Phelps W., Pvt	16012767	18th AB Sq	WIA
341.	King, Sherwood D., Pvt	11015087	26th Bomb Sq	WIA
342.	Kissel, George, Sgt	6979839	6th Pur Sq	WIA
343.	Klahn, Lester W., Cpl	16008121	72d Pur Sq	WIA
344.	Klein, Otto C., Pvt	13037387	18th AB Sq	KIA
345.	Klubertanz, Roderick O., Pvt	16007806	22d Mat Sq	KIA
346.	Knox, Alfred J., PFC	6152460	(Unknown)	WIA

No.	Name and Rank	Serial #	Unit	Status
347.	Kobylinski, Pierre A., Pvt	7013627	18th AB Sq	WIA
348.	Koch, Ewald A., PFC	6669097	31st Bomb Sq	WIA
349.	Kohl, John J., PFC	6987358	72d Bomb Sq	KIA
350.	Kouche, Joseph F., Cpl	6947396	Cst Art	WIA
351.	Krison, John, Pvt	16007631	Hq Sq 11th BG	WIA
352.	Kujawa, Conrad, Sgt	6668643	Cst Art	KIA
353.	Kuropatwa, Charles C., PFC	6946502	18th AB Sq	WIA
354.	Kyes, William B., 2d Lt	0-425090	(Unknown)	WIA
355.	La Blanc, John D., PFC	6919769	23d Mat Sq	WIA
356.	Lango, Frank J., Pvt	18018359	31st Bomb Sq	KIA
357.	Lantis, Melvin J., Pvt	16012725	23d Bomb Sq	WIA
358.	Lapie, Walter H., Pvt	16002988	Hq Sq 11th BG	WIA
359.	Larson, Richard A., Sgt	6913677	Hq Sq 11th BG	WIA
360.	Lawing, James E., Pvt	14009207	13th QM Trk Co	WIA
361.	Lee, Bert Jr., Pvt	19051486	38th Recon Sq	WIA
362.	Lenburg, Harold, Pvt	16003268	50th Recon Sq	WIA
363.	Leonardo, Arthuro N., Pvt	6739584	(Unknown)	KIA
364.	Lepper, Edmond B., Sgt	6562432	Hq Sq 18th BW	KIA
365.	Leslie, George G., Pvt	13037089	72d Pur Sq	KIA
366.	Levine, Sherman, PFC	16003162	7th AC Sq	KIA
367.	Lewis, Ivan C., PFC	7021090	42d Bomb Sq	WIA
368.	Lewis, James I., PFC	6931732	19th Tran Sq	KIA
369.	Lewis, Theodore J., Cpl	6897750	Fld Art	KIA
370.	Libby, Keith E., Pvt	11013386	Hq Sq 18th PG	WIA
371.	Libolt, Lester H., Cpl	6936136	50th Recon Sq	KIA
372.	Liddick, Walter A., Sgt	6946538	Hq Sq 18th PG	WIA
373.	Livingston, Richard E., Pvt	6987527	Hq Sq 5th BG	KIA
374.	Longest, Owen E., Sgt	6298925	50th Recon Sq	WIA
375.	Loos, John P., Pvt	6983703	23d Mat Sq	WIA
376.	Lord, Harry W. Jr., Pvt	11013292	18th AB Sq	KIA
377.	Lott, Lewis J., Cpl	6289417	Cst Art	WIA
378.	Lovelace, William D., Pvt	14037516	QM Det HAD	WIA
379.	Luckey, Leonard G., Pvt	16012742	72d Bomb Sq	WIA
380.	Luczyk, Theodore C., Cpl	6948081	42d Bomb Sq	WIA
381.	Ludwig, Charles A., Pvt	16003255	86th Obs Sq	WIA
382.	Lukosus, Felix J., Sgt	6917061	Hq Sq 18th BW	WIA
383.	Lundgren, WIlliam F., Pvt	6916953	22d Mat Sq	WIA
384.	Lusk, Howard N., Pvt	6557378	23d Bomb Sq	KIA
385.	Lynach, Edmond F., Cpl	7021251	27th Inf	WIA
386.	Lyon, Warren, Pvt	6579593	18th AB Sq	WIA
387.	Lyons, Lawrence P. Jr., Pvt	11020276	Hq Sq 11th BG	KIA
388.	Macois, Henry, Pvt	16041444	(Unknown)	WIA
389.	Macy, Thomas S., Civ		Hon Fire Dept	KIA
390.	Malatak, Joseph, Pvt	13025035	18th AB Sq	KIA
391.	Manley, William H., PFC	14032737	Hq Sq 18th PG	KIA

No.	Name and Rank	Serial #	Unit	Status
392.	Mann, John H., SSgt	6906443	22d Mat Sq	KIA
393.	Mann, Pell R., Cpl	6971931	22d Mat Sq	WIA
394.	Markley, Robert H., 2d Lt	0-424975	26th Bomb Sq	KIA
395.	Martin, Furman C. Jr., PFC	6970418	Hq Sq 18th BW	WIA
396.	Martin, George M. Jr., Sgt	6934682	Hq Sq 5th BG	KIA
397.	Martin, Herbert B., 1st Sgt	6333078	23d Mat Sq	KIA
398.	Martin, Robert H., Sgt	6949387	7th AC Sq	WIA
399.	Martin, Wallace R., 1st Sgt	6378440	Hq Sq 11th BG	KIA
400.	Maser, Karl O., PFC	11015139	Hq Sq 18th PG	WIA
401.	Mason, Merion L., Pvt	13000505	Hq Sq 11th BG	WIA
402.	Matouka, Michael, PFC	13027089	QM Det HAD	WIA
403.	Mattox, Harell K., PFC	6297644	50th Recon Sq	KIA
404.	Mattox, James A., Pvt	15063344	35th Inf	WIA
405.	Mayo, Raymond, Cpl	6266644	72d Bomb Sq	WIA
406.	McAbee, William E., PFC	6934856	19th Tran Sq	KIA
407.	McAdams, James W., TSgt	6251313	Hq Sq 18th PG	WIA
408.	McCabe, Patrick J., Civ		Hon Fire Dept	WIA
409.	McCall, Albert C. Jr., PFC	7020297	42d Bomb Sq	WIA
410.	McClellan, Robert W., Pvt	20433822	18th AB Sq	WIA
411.	McClintock, James J., PFC	6950013	22d Mat Sq	KIA
412.	McClung, Richard G., Pvt	16012892	22d Mat Sq	WIA
413.	McCuiston, Carlos F., 1st Sgt	6373104	19th Tran Sq	WIA
414.	McDonnell, Herbert F., Pvt	34076710	35th Inf	WIA
415.	McGuire, Jack P., PFC	14047242	QM Det HAD	WIA
416.	McInnis, William G., PFC	16012734	23d Mat Sq	WIA
417.	McKray, Russell O., 1st Lt	0-283518	23d Bomb Sq	WIA
418.	McLaughlin, Herbert E., Pvt	16021346	Hq Sq 17th ABG	KIA
419.	McLeod, Bernice P., Pvt	7005848	Hq Sq 11th BG	WIA
420.	McLeod, Stanley A., Sgt	6849363	19th Tran Sq	KIA
421.	McRoberts, James H., Pvt	16017310	50th Recon Sq	WIA
422.	Meadows, Durward A., PFC	6955891	Hq Sq 18th BW	KIA
423.	Meagher, Donald F., Cpl	6587289	4th Recon Sq	KIA
424.	Medlen, Joseph A., Cpl	6291014	Cst Art	KIA
425.	Meehan, John J., TSgt	6949374	4th Recon Sq	WIA
426.	Merithew, William W., PFC	6977647	Hq Sq 11th BG	KIA
427.	Messam, Horace A., PFC	6667770	22d Mat Sq	KIA
428.	Meyers, Victor L., Pvt	6939609	22d Mat Sq	KIA
429.	Migita, Torao, Pvt	30101619	INF	KIA
430.	Miller, Orvil T., Cpl	6578192	90th Fld Art	WIA
431.	Minnich, James S., Sgt	6893377	22d Mat Sq	WIA
432.	Mintz, Darrell K., SSgt	6819562	Hq Sq 11th BG	WIA
433.	Mitchell, Donald K., PFC	6149254	18th AB Sq	WIA
434.	Mitchell, Edwin N., Cpl	6275082	22d Mat Sq	KIA
435.	Mitchell, John G., Cpl	16012572	Hq Sq 15th PG	KIA
436.	Mitchell, Paul, Pvt	6292158	18th AB Sq	WIA

No.	Name and Rank	Serial #	Unit	Status
437.	Moniz, Alfred, PFC	20011222	(Unknown)	WIA
438.	Montgomery, Frederick D., PFC	7026827	6th Pur Sq	WIA
439.	Moore, Joseph T., 2d Lt	0-428407	Hq Sq 5th BG	WIA
440.	Moorhead, Lionel J., PFC	6934656	23d Bomb Sq	KIA
441.	Moran, George A., Pvt	11020207	Hq Sq 11th BG	KIA
442.	Morgan, Leith C., PFC	6999212	42d Bomb Sq	WIA
443.	Morris, Emmett E., Cpl	6887300	Hq Sq 17th ABG	KIA
444.	Morrisson, Clarence C., PFC	7025453	4th Recon Sq	WIA
445.	Moser, Joseph G., Pvt	6974050	23d Mat Sq	KIA
446.	Moslener, Louis G., 2d Lt	0-409917	Tran B-24	KIA
447.	Mougin, Kenneth L., Pvt	11008152	22d Mat Sq	WIA
448.	Moyer, James I., Cpl	7025139	Hq Sq 15th PG	WIA
449.	Naauao, Solomon H. Jr., Civ		Hon Fire Dept	WIA
450.	Napier, Eugene E., PFC	6980075	Hq Sq 17th ABG	WIA
451.	Narehood, Charles W., PFC	7021105	42d Bomb Sq	WIA
452.	Narramore, Roth J., Sgt	6936636	Hq Sq 11th BG	WIA
453.	Nau, Ralph E., Pvt	13002055	(Unknown)	WIA
454.	Neal, William W., Sgt	R-1536577	72d Bomb Sq	WIA
455.	Needham, LaVerne J., Cpl	6569747	Hq Sq 18th BW	KIA
456.	Neitzel, Gordon N., Sgt		AAF	KIA
457.	Nelles, Joseph F., PFC	6920307	Hq Sq 17th ABG	KIA
458.	Newman, Harry, PFC	6905738	4th Recon Sq	WIA
459.	Niedzwiecki, Robert R., Pvt	16012747	Hq Sq 15th PG	WIA
460.	Nolan, Robert F., PFC	6936156	(Unknown)	WIA
461.	Northam, Floyd A., Pvt	18041885	18th AB Sq	WIA
462.	Northway, William M., Pvt	11011279	31st Bomb Sq	KIA
463.	Nuttall, Roland L., SSgt	6559665	Hq Sq 15th PG	WIA
464.	O'Brien, Michael L., PFC	12018370	Hq Sq 18th PG	WIA
465.	O'Brien, William H. Jr., Cpl	11007591	19th Pur Sq	WIA
466.	O'Donovan, James E., Pvt	12011872	741st Ord Co	WIA
467.	Odete, Ben, PFC	6560560	31st Bomb Sq	WIA
468.	Offutt, William H., Cpl	6917189	50th Recon Sq	KIA
469.	Olsen, Marvin, PFC	6291167	Hq Sq 11th BG	WIA
470.	Orr, Willard C., PFC	6149312	Hq Sq 17th ABG	KIA
471.	Osborne, William A., Pvt	19053031	19th Tran Sq	WIA
472.	Ovecka, Edward M., Pvt	6946508	22d Mat Sq	WIA
473.	Panek, Joseph J., PFC	6148686	Hq Sq 11th BG	WIA
474.	Pang, Henry T.L., Civ		Hon Fire Dept	KIA
475.	Paschall, Ralph G., Pvt	13027979	23d Bomb Sq	WIA
476.	Penny, Russell M., Pvt	6981089	18th AB Sq	KIA
477.	Penven, Louis, Pvt	6978557	31st Bomb Sq	WIA
478.	Perry, Hal H. Jr., Pvt	7002551	42d Bomb Sq	KIA
479.	Peterson, Donald H., Pvt	19044364	22d Mat Sq	WIA
480.	Peterson, William H., Pvt	19020929	22d Mat Sq	WIA
481.	Philipsky, Thomas F., PFC	6915458	22d Mat Sq	KIA

No.	Name and Rank	Serial #	Unit	Status
482.	Phillips, Edgar L., Pvt	6980163	42d Bomb Sq	WIA
483.	Phipps, Claude E., PFC	7082694	Fld Art	WIA
484.	Pickard, Wallace F., 2d Lt	0-428377	4th Recon Sq	WIA
485.	Pickerel, Robert L., Pvt	6291444	Hq Sq 17th ABG	WIA
486.	Pietzsch, Jay E., 2d Lt	0-426961	26th Bomb Sq	KIA
487.	Pirga, Michael J., SSgt	6098440	4th Recon Sq	WIA
488.	Plant, Donald D., Pvt	16007493	46th Pur Sq	KIA
489.	Plaster, Gilbert A., Pvt	6955823	23d Mat Sq	WIA
490.	Pope, Roy T., PFC	6976316	22d Mat Sq	WIA
491.	Porga, Nichael J., SSgt	6098440	(Unknown)	WIA
492.	Porterfield, Charles P., PFC	6936174	42d Bomb Sq	WIA
493.	Posey, Frank St. E., TSgt	6369072	23d Mat Sq	KIA
494.	Pouncey, LeRoy B., MSgt	R-792748	38th Recon Sq	WIA
495.	Powell, Raymond E., TSgt	6783478	23d Mat Sq	KIA
496.	Powloski, Daniel J., Pvt	6673769	Tran B-24	KIA
497.	Praniewicz, Michael M., PFC	6948014	22d Mat Sq	WIA
498.	Price, George, Pvt	6955774	72d Bomb Sq	KIA
499.	Price, John A., SSgt	6971149	72d Pur Sq	KIA
500.	Price, Robert F., Pvt	37047354	86th Obs Sq	WIA
501.	Price, Walter J., Sgt	6954205	Hq Sq 15th PG	WIA
502.	Pryor, James W., PFC	6914063	22d Mat Sq	WIA
503.	Pulley, Issac H. Jr., PFC	7020156	50th Recon Sq	WIA
504.	Rader, James A., Pvt	6981885	23d Bomb Sq	WIA
505.	Rae, Allen G., Pvt	12027324	18th AB Sq	KIA
506.	Raines, Raymond, Pvt	6937867	22d Mat Sq	WIA
507.	Rainey, Harry C., Sgt	6949495	22d Mat Sq	WIA
508.	Ramm, Richard K., Sgt	6150132	Hq Sq HAF	WIA
509.	Randall, Hermon T., TSgt	6924702	Hq Sq 11th BG	WIA
510.	Randolph, Edward, Pvt	6947932	(Unknown)	WIA
511.	Rasmussen, Warren D., Sgt	20920790	Cst Art	KIA
512.	Ratliff, Bill J., PFC	6274750	Fld Art	WIA
513.	Ray, Eugene R., PFC	6958584	Hq Sq 11th BG	WIA
514.	Ray, Robert W., TSgt	6544986	42d Bomb Sq	WIA
515.	Reber, Paul D., Sgt	6946984	22d Mat Sq	WIA
516.	Redburn, Ralph A., Cpt	0-258373	Hq Sq 17th ABG	WIA
517.	Reddick, Robert C., Cpl	6295721	Hq Sq 11th BG	WIA
518.	Reed, Marston C., Avn Cdt	38051997	72d Bomb Sq	WIA
519.	Reilly, James H., Avn Cdt	1107026	Hq Sq 5th BG	WIA
520.	Reiter, Matthew P., Pvt	13013159	Cst Art	WIA
521.	Restivo, Anthony B., SSgt	6889085	6th Pur Sq	WIA
522.	Reuss, Herman C., TSgt	6795518	Hq Sq 11th BG	KIA
523.	Reynolds, Burkett A., Pvt	6991434	18th AB Sq	WIA
524.	Rhodes, William T., PFC	6152352	23d Mat Sq	KIA
525.	Richards, John N., Pvt	6999151	Hq Sq 15th PG	WIA
526.	Richardson, Milroy L., Pvt	17001408	6th Pur Sq	WIA

No.	Name and Rank	Serial #	Unit	Status
527.	Richey, Robert M., 1st Lt	0-305011	Hq Sq 11th BG	KIA
528.	Riddle, Donald T., Pvt	35124782	(Unknown)	WIA
529.	Robbins, Anson E., Pvt	11009597	25th Mat Sq	KIA
530.	Roberts, Edwin, Pvt	7006560	50th Recon Sq	WIA
531.	Roberts, Thomas E., Cpl	6580141	Hq Sq 11th BG	WIA
532.	Robertson, Paul D., Pvt	14037062	QM Det HAD	WIA
533.	Robinson, John E., Sgt	6527154	25th Fld Art	WIA
534.	Rockman, Walter H., Pvt	6939634	Hq Sq 11th BG	WIA
535.	Rodriguez, Earl B., Pvt	11008147	6th Pur Sq	WIA
536.	Rodrigues, Ruperto B., PFC	6296828	Hq Sq 11th BG	WIA
537.	Rogness, Halvor E., Pvt	37047377	Hq Sq 17th ABG	KIA
538.	Rose, Elmer P., Maj	0-17044	Hq Sq 18th BW	WIA
539.	Roseman, Herbert J., Pvt	12027334	Hq Sq 17th ABG	WIA
540.	Rosenberry, Glen R., Pvt	6987821	Hq Sq 18th BW	WIA
541.	Ross, Newba, Pvt	14039386	Hq Sq 5th BG	WIA
542.	Roy, Leo A., Pvt	11011304	23d Bomb Sq	WIA
543.	Ryan, Thomas W., Pvt	11007940	Hq Sq 18th PG	WIA
544.	Sackett, Malcolm D., SSgt	6977798	31st Bomb Sq	WIA
545.	Sallick, George, SSgt	6851526	19th Pur Sq	WIA
546.	Salloum, Naif J., Pvt	16012822	72d Pur Sq	WIA
547.	Sampson, Roger F., PFC	11007674	6th Pur Sq	WIA
548.	Samulevich, Alphonse J., PFC	6148928	23d Mat Sq	WIA
549.	Sanchez, Servando, Pvt	18035190	Hq Sq 17th ABG	WIA
550.	Sanders, Henry C., 1st Sgt	6718423	72d Bomb Sq	WIA
551.	Sbraccia, Bernard D., Pvt	11020149	23d Mat Sq	WIA
552.	Scalzo, Louis J., PFC	11010866	(Unknown)	WIA
553.	Scheidt, Paul J., SSgt	6668704	6th Pur Sq	WIA
554.	Schick, William R., 1st Lt	0-412256	38th Recon Sq	KIA
555.	Schleifer, Louis, PFC	6981087	4th Recon Sq	KIA
556.	Schmersahl, George R., Sgt	6979080	Hq Sq 18th PG	KIA
557.	Schott, Robert L., PFC	15059273	Hq Sq 15th PG	KIA
558.	Schwartzkopf, Victor O., SSgt	6826441	18th AB Sq	WIA
559.	Seals, Joseph P., SSgt	R-565457	(Unknown)	WIA
560.	Sesody, Anthony L., PFC	6913920	22d Mat Sq	WIA
561.	Shattuck, Robert R., PFC	16007831	Hq Sq 15th PG	KIA
562.	Sherman, Robert O., Sgt	6980227	Hq Sq 18th PG	KIA
563.	Shields, William F., Pvt	15020006	22d Mat Sq	KIA
564.	Shoff, Raymond C., PFC	7021031	9th Sig Srv	WIA
565.	Sidak, Julius D., Sgt	6565769	50th Recon Sq	WIA
566.	Sidoti, Vincent P., Cpl	6978060	63d Fld Art	WIA
567.	Silverwatch, Walter, PFC	6147909	Hq Sq 18th PG	WIA
568.	Sloboda, John, Sgt	6977547	Hq Sq 18th PG	WIA
569.	Smith, Edwin G., Sgt	6947462	45th Pur Sq	WIA
570.	Smith, George J., PFC	6150664	18th AB Sq	KIA
571.	Smith, Harry E., Pvt	16003275	Hq Sq 11th BG	KIA

No.	Name and Rank	Serial #	Unit	Status
572.	Smith, Norman A., Cpl	6148224	50th Recon Sq	WIA
573.	Smith, Ralph S., PFC	6948901	22d Mat Sq	KIA
574.	Smith, Walter H., Pvt	7002560	Hq Sq 18th BW	WIA
575.	Smith, Walter S. III, 2d Lt	0-398524	Tran B-24	WIA
576.	Snyder, George S., Pvt	7020830	31st Bomb Sq	WIA
577.	South, Elmer W., Pvt	6990788	18th AB Sq	KIA
578.	Spallone, Nicholas J. Jr., Pvt	13030340	Hq Sq 17th ABG	WIA
579.	Sparks, John B., PFC	6955782	22d Mat Sq	KIA
580.	Spickler, Howard M., Pvt	17003472	(Unknown)	WIA
581.	St Germain, Maurice J., Pvt	6137168	23d Mat Sq	KIA
582.	Stacey, Morris, Sgt	6661840	78th Pur Sq	KIA
583.	Stallings, Kenneth L., Cpl	36051619	(Unknown)	WIA
584.	Stanfield, James C., PFC	700654	(Unknown)	WIA
585.	Stanley, Joe B., Sgt	6634439	22d Mat Sq	WIA
586.	Stanley, Richard C., Sgt	6987675	6th Pur Sq	WIA
587.	Stanley, Robert W., PFC	6981992	22d Mat Sq	WIA
588.	Stanley, William A., PFC	6975259	22d Mat Sq	WIA
589.	Staples, Merton I., Pvt	0149201	22d Mat Sq	KIA
590.	Staton, Paul L., Pvt	6987468	Hq Sq 18th BW	KIA
591.	Steff, Jonah A., Cpl	12006466	72d Pur Sq	WIA
592.	Stephanik, Walter E., Cpl	13011049	42d Bomb Sq	WIA
593.	Stephenson, David B.		17th AB Sq	WIA
594.	Sterling, Gordon H. Jr., 2d Lt	0-411852	46th Pur Sq	KIA
595.	Stinson, Clarence E., SSgt	6799585	Hq Sq 11th BG	WIA
596.	Stockwell, Carey K., Pvt	15056470	42d Bomb Sq	KIA
597.	Stoner, Charles E., Pvt	20919976	(Unknown)	WIA
598.	Strickland, James E. Jr., Pvt	7003254	23d Mat Sq	KIA
599.	Strong, Kenneth E., PFC	16021420	Hq Sq 15th PG	WIA
600.	Strunk, Leslie G., Pvt	13004060	(Unknown)	WIA
601.	Suffern, Richard H., Cpl	12006334	45th Pur Sq	WIA
602.	Sullivan, Edward F., Pvt	6978109	Cst Art	KIA
603.	Suppes, David Jr., TSgt	6253796	Hq Sq 17th ABG	WIA
604.	Surrells, Leo H., Pvt	16028525	Hq Sq 17th ABG	KIA
605.	Sylvester, William G., 1st Lt	0-363247	Cst Art	KIA
606.	Szematowicz, Jerome J., PFC	6911554	22d Mat Sq	KIA
607.	Tafoya, Antonio S., Cpl	6296794	26th Bomb Sq	KIA
608.	Taylor, Homer R., 2d Lt	0-409908	38th Recon Sq	WIA
609.	Taylor, Kenneth M., 1st Lt	0-409061	47th Pur Sq	WIA
610.	Tennison, Anderson G., PFC	6955659	Hq Sq 18th BW	KIA
611.	Tholke, Henry E., PFC	6948604	23d Mat Sq	WIA
612.	Thomure, Jasper E., Pvt		Inf	KIA
613.	Thon, Hans S., Pvt	16021398	19th Pur Sq	WIA
614.	Thornhill, William R., PFC	7002255	Hq Sq 11th BG	WIA
615.	Tibbets, Hermann K. Jr., Pvt	11029005	18th AB Sq	KIA
616.	Tiffany, Horace J., Pvt	16003540	6th Pur Sq	WIA

No.	Name and Rank	Serial #	Unit	Status
617.	Tillett, George, Pvt	7021673	72d Pur Sq	WIA
618.	Timmerman, William F., Pvt	7070825	22d Mat Sq	KIA
619.	Tischbirek, Edwin A., PFC	18000639	804th Engr	WIA
620.	Tobias, Donald R., Pvt	13002000	22d Mat Sq	WIA
621.	Tolen, James M., SSgt	6664930	QM Det HAD	WIA
622.	Tomkins, Paul N., Pvt	6949535	Hq Sq 11th BG	WIA
623.	Tomlinson, Vernon D., Sgt	19030242	38th Recon Sq	WIA
624.	Topalian, James M., Cpl	6922392	7th AC Sq	KIA
625.	Travaline, Anthony T., PFC	7021419	72d Bomb Sq	WIA
626.	Travis, Robert, Pvt	6979013	QM Det HAD	WIA
627.	Tuckerman, George W., Pvt	6997660	18th AB Sq	KIA
628.	Tuley, Paul W., Sgt	6572980	42d Bomb Sq	WIA
629.	Turnbull, Robert L., Sgt	13009092	22d Mat Sq	WIA
630.	Tussio, Domenico A., PFC	6148540	22d Mat Sq	WIA
631.	Tyleshevski, John, Pvt	7022222	72d Bomb Sq	WIA
632.	Tyra, Garrett C., PFC	6296347	Hq Sq 11th BG	WIA
633.	Uhlenburg, Charles L., PFC	6949904	22d Mat Sq	WIA
634.	Van Wirt, Clarence A., Sgt	6708799	Hq Sq 11th BG	WIA
635.	Vanderelli, Martin, Pvt	7022224	18th AB Sq	KIA
636.	Velarde, Lawrence B., SSgt	6555988	38th Recon Sq	WIA
637.	Ventress, Clifford C., Cpl	16040907	6th Pur Sq	WIA
638.	Vernick, Edward F., PFC	6578335	Hq Sq 11th BG	KIA
639.	Vidoloff, Russell P., Pvt	15015473	Hq Sq 15th PG	KIA
640.	Viers, Joseph L., Cpl	R-1440483	50th Recon Sq	WIA
641.	Vinci, Benjamin, Pvt	32110948	(Unknown)	WIA
642.	Wagaman, Lester, PFC	6993849	Hq Sq 11th BG	WIA
643.	Waite, Charles E. Jr., Pvt	6986825	Hq Sq 14th PW	WIA
644.	Walczynski, Andrew A., SSgt	6802945	6th Pur Sq	KIA
645.	Walker, Ernest M. Jr., Pvt	13009151	22d Mat Sq	KIA
646.	Walker, Lumus E., Pvt	16040974	Hq Sq 15th PG	KIA
647.	Wallace, Frank L., Pvt	6845163	6th Pur Sq	WIA
648.	Ward, Howard C., PFC	6936137	Hq Sq 17th ABG	WIA
649.	Wardigo, Walter H., Pvt	6997635	18th AB Sq	KIA
650.	Wargo, Peter, Jr., Pvt	13026891	86th Obs Sq	WIA
651.	Waugh, Robert S., Pvt	12008663	Hq Sq HAF	WIA
652.	Weber, Allan J., Pvt	6915455	Hq Sq 5th BG	WIA
653.	Webster, John J., 1st Lt	0-396499	Hq Sq 15th PG	WIA
654.	Wegrzyn, Felix S., Pvt	11019658	31st Bomb Sq	KIA
655.	Wells, Charles W., Pvt	6153100	Hq Sq 18th BW	WIA
656.	Wenzel, Theodore A., Pvt	11030694	407th Sig Co	WIA
657.	West, Kenneth H., Pvt	16007613	50th Recon Sq	WIA
658.	Westbrook, Robert H. Jr., Pvt	7000318	26th Bomb Sq	KIA
659.	Westhaver, Clayton M., Sgt	6151526	46th Pur Sq	WIA
660.	White, Edward M., Pvt	16012623	73d Pur Sq	WIA
661.	White, Lewis B., Pvt	6974778	22d Mat Sq	WIA

No.	Name and Rank	Serial #	Unit	Status
662.	Whiteman, George A., 2d Lt	0-399683	44th Pur Sq	KIA
663.	Wiedling, Louis J., Pvt	19058880	(Unknown)	WIA
664.	Wiener, Hugo I., Pvt	6983904	(Unknown)	WIA
665.	Williams, Jack A., PFC	6934696	42d Bomb Sq	WIA
666.	Wilson, Joe F., Sgt	6295303	4th Recon Sq	WIA
667.	Wilson, Lowell R., Cpl	6993928	19th Pur Sq	WIA
668.	Wilson, Martin C., Pvt	18052270	86th Obs Sq	WIA
669.	Wilson, Sam H., Cpl	6582979	Hq Sq 11th BG	WIA
670.	Wimbiscus, Donald E., Cpl	6976628	Hq Sq 11th BG	WIA
671.	Wingrove, Marvin V., PFC	6955738	Det Fin Dpt	WIA
672.	Wolfe, Vaughn E., Pvt	6851532	18th AB Sq	WIA
673.	Wood, Earl A., Pvt	7083304	Hq Sq 18th BW	KIA
674.	Woods, Justin W., 2d Lt	0-428890	19th Tran Sq	WIA
675.	Woodworth, Lawton J., Pvt	12025014	18th AB Sq	KIA
676.	Workman, William G., 1st Lt		31st Bomb Sq	WIA
677.	Wright, Joe O., SSgt	6252026	(Unknown)	WIA
678.	Wright, Thomas M., Pvt	15069262	18th AB Sq	KIA
679.	Xerri, Benjamin J., PFC	6975721	19th Tran Sq	WIA
680.	Yarbrough, Thomas A., Cpl	6970441	26th Bomb Sq	WIA
681.	Young, Ralph W. Jr., Pvt	6151797	18th AB Sq	WIA
682.	Young, Virgil J., Pvt	18052212	18th AB Sq	KIA
683.	Zaczkiewicz, Marion H., PFC	7024628	Hq Sq 11th BG	KIA
684.	Zangari, Anthony A., Pvt	6996067	23d Mat Sq	WIA
685.	Zappala, Joseph S., Pvt	11020151	23d Mat Sq	KIA
686.	Zeiss, Charles L., SSgt	6984022	6th Pur Sq	WIA
687.	Zeock, Andrew N. Jr., PFC	6948809	22d Mat Sq	WIA
688.	Ziskind, Samuel J., Pvt	12000726	(Unknown)	KIA
689.	Zuckoff, Walter D., Pvt	7071280	19th Tran Sq	KIA
690.	Zuercher, Charles P., Cpl	16017205	45th Pur Sq	WIA
691.	Zuschlag, Walter J., Sgt	6975453	23d Mat Sq	KIA

APPENDIX F

HAWAIIAN AIR FORCE MILITARY CASUALTY LIST[*]

Name and Rank	Serial #	Status

HICKAM FIELD

Hq & Hq Sq Hawaiian Air Force

Name and Rank	Serial #	Status
Jacobson, Dave, MSgt	R-1551856	KIA
Ramm, Richard K., Sgt	6150132	WIA
Waugh, Robert S., Pvt	12008663	WIA

7th Air Corps Sq (Weather)

Name and Rank	Serial #	Status
Borgelt, Harold W., Cpl	6276330	KIA
Dyer, Daniel A. Jr., TSgt	6293492	KIA
Levine, Sherman, PFC	16003162	KIA
Topalian, James M., Cpl	6922392	KIA
Graf, Harold F., Cpl	6954302	WIA
Martin, Robert H., Sgt	6949387	WIA

19th Transport Squadron

Name and Rank	Serial #	Status
Anderson, William T., Cpl	6947615	KIA
Blakley, William T., Pvt	18046224	KIA
Defenbaugh, Russell C., Pvt	16017271	KIA
Guttmann, Joseph H., Pvt	6979230	KIA
Horan, John J., Pvt	7071018	KIA
Johnson, Carl A., Pvt	6981067	KIA
Johnson, Olaf A., PFC	16007617	KIA
Kimmey, Robert Doyle, SSgt	6265447	KIA
Lewis, James I., PFC	6931732	KIA
McAbee, William E., PFC	6934856	KIA
McLeod, Stanley A., Sgt	6849363	KIA
Zuckoff, Walter D., Pvt	7071280	KIA

[*]See Appendix E for list of sources.

Name and Rank	Serial #	Status

19th Transport Squadron (Continued)

Name and Rank	Serial #	Status
Beasley, Herschel N., TSgt	6251816	WIA
Big Thunder, Elmer, Pvt	6919179	WIA
Currence, Clarence F. Jr., Cpl	6667759	WIA
Ehrke, Jack O., Sgt	6584308	WIA
Fessler, Robert G., Pvt	16007607	WIA
Gabik, George J., PFC	16007559	WIA
Howe, Sidney C., SSgt	R-153039	WIA
McCuiston, Carlos F., 1st Sgt	6373104	WIA
Osborne, William A., Pvt	19053031	WIA
Woods, Justin W., 2d Lt	0-428890	WIA
Xerri, Benjamin J., PFC	6975721	WIA

58th Bombardment Sq (Light)

Name and Rank	Serial #	Status
Barasha, Walter A., Pvt	13007256	WIA
Kern, Donald W., PFC	6991939	WIA

Tow Target Detachment

Name and Rank	Serial #	Status
Bays, Donald E., Pvt	6948505	KIA
Bonina, Vincent J., PFC	13004082	WIA
Chabalowski, Richard X., Pvt	16001809	WIA
Ellick, James B., Cpl	6997158	WIA

Hq & Hq Sq 18th Bomb Wing

Name and Rank	Serial #	Status
Anderson, Garland C., Pvt	14028405	KIA
Anderson, Manfred C., Pvt	16021427	KIA
Bennett, Gordon R. Jr., Pvt	16012883	KIA
Boswell, Frank G., Pvt	6834448	KIA
Cooper, Frank B., Pvt	7021035	KIA
Cruthirds, John E., PFC	6298043	KIA
Duff, Robert C. Jr., Pvt	6998717	KIA
Edwards, Lyle O., Pvt	16012846	KIA
Gallagher, Russell E., Pvt	6953547	KIA
Gossard, James E. Jr., PFC	7002430	KIA
Greene, Johon Sherman, 1st lt	0-283511	KIA
Hood, Earl A., Pvt	7083304	KIA
Joyner, Theodore K., Pvt	7002425	KIA

Name and Rank	Serial #	Status

Hq & Hq Sq 18th Bomb Wing (Continued)

Name and Rank	Serial #	Status
Lepper, Edmond B., Sgt	6562432	KIA
Meadows, Durward A., PFC	6955891	KIA
Needham, LaVerne J., Cpl	6569747	KIA
Staton, Paul L., Pvt	6987468	KIA
Tennison, Anderson G., PFC	6955659	KIA
Wood, Earl A., Pvt	7083304	KIA
Blackmon, Leonard, Sgt	6289781	WIA
Bryant, William, Sgt	7002366	WIA
Dorondo, John F., TSgt	6949822	WIA
Dudley, George G., SSgt	6296835	WIA
Hill, Harry O., Cpl	6946549	WIA
Jordan, Bert J., Pvt	16017391	WIA
Lukosus, Felix J., Sgt	6917061	WIA
Martin, Furman C. Jr., PFC	6970418	WIA
Rose, Elmer P., Major	0-17044	WIA
Rosenberry, Glen R., Pvt	6987821	WIA
Smith, Walter H., Pvt	7002560	WIA
Wells, Charles W., Pvt	6153100	WIA

Hq & Hq Sq 5th Bomb Group

Name and Rank	Serial #	Status
Bolan, George P., SSgt	6930952	KIA
Dickerson, Richard A., Cpl	6296796	KIA
Hays, Alfred, Pvt	16017464	KIA
Livingston, Richard E., Pvt	6987527	KIA
Martin, George M. Jr., Sgt	6934682	KIA
Adams, Kenneth E., Pvt	17009623	WIA
Barnes, Leonard M. Jr., Pvt	6950778	WIA
Bauer, John F., SSgt	6078351	WIA
Boersema, Joel J., Pvt	6913095	WIA
Byrd, Robert T., Pvt	14046406	WIA
Coale, Lee R., Pvt	6934632	WIA
Hammond, Walter A., PFC	6986727	WIA
Moore, Joseph T., 2d Lt	0-428407	WIA
Reilly, James H., Avn Cdt	1107026	WIA
Ross, Newba, Pvt	14039386	WIA
Weber, Allan J., Pvt	6915455	WIA

Name and Rank	Serial #	Status

23d Bomb Squadron

Name and Rank	Serial #	Status
Clendenning, Lee I., PFC	16021445	KIA
Coster, Richard L., Pvt	16017463	KIA
Elliott, Byron G., Pvt	17011087	KIA
Hislop, William, PFC	6396064	KIA
Lusk, Howard N., Pvt	6557378	KIA
Moorhead, Lionel J., PFC	6934656	KIA
Broughton, Alfred W., Pvt	16003053	WIA
Bush, Francis R., (Unk)	15019135	WIA
Clendenning, Charles P., Pvt	16021140	WIA
Helms, Frank B., 1st Sgt	6653968	WIA
Lantis, Melvin J., Pvt	16012725	WIA
McKray, Russel O., 1st Lt	0-283518	WIA
Paschall, Ralph G., Pvt	13027979	WIA
Rader, James A., Pvt	6981885	WIA
Roy, Leo A., Pvt	11011304	WIA

31st Bomb Squadron

Name and Rank	Serial #	Status
Fox, Jack W., PFC	6570562	KIA
Lango, Frank J., Pvt	18018359	KIA
Northway, William M., Pvt	11011279	KIA
Wegrzyn, Felix S., Pvt	11019658	KIA
Charron, Evariste E., PFC	R-1075852	WIA
Green, Virgil A., Pvt	16007810	WIA
Hopkins, Jack P., 2d Lt	0-417839	WIA
Koch, Ewald A., PFC	6669097	WIA
Odete, Ben, PFC	6560560	WIA
Penven, Louis, Pvt	6978557	WIA
Sackett, Malcolm D., SSgt	6977798	WIA
Snyder, George S., Pvt	7020830	WIA
Workman, William G., 1st Lt		WIA

72d Bomb Squadron

Name and Rank	Serial #	Status
Hughes, Edward R., Pvt	15012648	KIA
Kohl, John J., PFC	6987358	KIA
Price, George, Pvt	6955774	KIA
David, Arthur E., Pvt	6132614	WIA

Name and Rank	Serial #	Status

72d Bomb Squadron (Continued)

Name and Rank	Serial #	Status
Hamrick, Robert D., Pvt	16017439	WIA
Luckey, Leonard G., Pvt	16012742	WIA
Mayo, Raymond, Cpl	6266644	WIA
Neal, William, W., Sgt	R-1536577	WIA
Reed, Marston C., Avn Cdt	38051997	WIA
Sanders, Henry C., 1st Sgt	6718423	WIA
Travaline, Anthony T., Pvt	7021419	WIA
Tyleshevski, John, Pvt	7022222	WIA

4th Reconnaisance Squadron

Name and Rank	Serial #	Status
Carlson, Lawrence R., Pvt	16017324	KIA
Meagher, Donald F., Cpl	6587284	KIA
Schleifer, Louis, PFC	6981087	KIA
Meehan, John J., TSgt	6949374	WIA
Morrisson, Clarence C., PFC	7025453	WIA
Newman, Harry, PFC	6905738	WIA
Pickard, Wallace F., 2d Lt	0-428377	WIA
Pirga, Michael J., SSgt	6098440	WIA
Wilson, Joe F., Sgt	6295303	WIA

Hq & Hq Sq 11th Bomb Group

Name and Rank	Serial #	Status
Avery, Robert L., PFC	6934108	KIA
Brown, Robert S., Pvt	11020247	KIA
Cashman, Edward J., TSgt	R-4311524	KIA
Chapman, Donal V., Cpl	6914156	KIA
Clark, Monroe M., SSgt	6254875	KIA
Gooding, Robert H., Pvt	6561586	KIA
Horner, James A., PFC	6950776	KIA
Howard, George F., PFC	6936803	KIA
Lyons, Lawrence P. Jr., Pvt	11020276	KIA
Martin, Wallace R., 1st Sgt	6378440	KIA
Merithew, William W., PFC	6977647	KIA
Moran, George A., Pvt	11020207	KIA
Reuss, Herman C., TSgt	6795518	KIA
Richey, Robert M., 1st Lt	0-305011	KIA
Smith, Harry E., Pvt	16003275	KIA
Vernick, Edward F., PFC	6578335	KIA
Zaczkiewicz, Marion H., PFC	7024628	KIA

Name and Rank	Serial #	Status

Hq & Hq Sq 11th Bomb Group (Continued)

Name and Rank	Serial #	Status
Anderson, Loid W., Cpl	6934142	WIA
Baldwin, Howard, Sgt	6077427	WIA
Brown, Douglas L., Pvt		WIA
Bloom, Robert E., Cpl	7022832	WIA
Byers, Roy W., Pvt	6998810	WIA
Byrd, Bert E. Jr., PFC	6667932	WIA
Calderon, Carmel R., PFC	6955786	WIA
Clague, Charles S., Pvt	16017442	WIA
Cox, Eugene C., Sgt	6928554	WIA
Damsky, Robert P., Pvt	11020220	WIA
Davis, Allen D., Pvt	16003027	WIA
Davis, Spencer L., Pvt	6967237	WIA
Drisner, Joseph R., Pvt	15059459	WIA
Hawkins, Harold H., Pvt	1403791	WIA
King, Cecil E., PFC	6936624	WIA
Krison, John, Pvt	16007631	WIA
Lapie, Walter H., Pvt	16002988	WIA
Larson, Richard A., Sgt	6913677	WIA
Mason, Merion L., Pvt	13000505	WIA
McLeod, Bernice P., Pvt	7005848	WIA
Mintz, Darrell K., SSgt	6819562	WIA
Narramore, Roth J., Sgt	6936636	WIA
Olsen, Marvin, PFC	6291167	WIA
Panek, Joseph J., PFC	6148686	WIA
Randall, Hermon T., TSgt	6958584	WIA
Ray, Eugene R., PFC	6958584	WIA
Reddick, Robert C., Cpl	6295721	WIA
Roberts, Thomas E., Cpl	6580141	WIA
Rockman, Walter H., Pvt	6939634	WIA
Rodrigues, Ruperto B., PFC	6296828	WIA
Stinson, Clarence E., SSgt	6799585	WIA
Thornhill, William R., PFC	7002255	WIA
Tomkins, Paul N., Pvt	6949535	WIA
Tyra, Garrett, C., PFC	6296347	WIA
Van Wirt, Clarence A., Sgt	6708799	WIA
Wagaman, Lester, PFC	6993849	WIA
Wilson, Sam H., Cpl	6582979	WIA
Wimbiscus, Donald E., Cpl	6976628	WIA

Name and Rank	Serial #	Status

26th Bomb Squadron

Name and Rank	Serial #	Status
Bonnie, Felix, SSgt	R-1005587	KIA
Conant, Clarence A., Pvt	7003044	KIA
DePolis, Frank J., SSgt	6946517	KIA
Finney, Patrick L., Cpl	6268780	KIA
Gummerson, Elwood R., SSgt	6844737	KIA
Kechner, Vincent J., Pvt	6979463	KIA
Markley, Robert H., 2d Lt	0-424975	KIA
Pietzsch, Jay E., 2d Lt	0-426961	KIA
Tafoya, Antonio S., Cpl	6296794	KIA
Westbrook, Robert H. Jr., Pvt	7000318	KIA
Bise, Delmas F., PFC	6996842	WIA
Bowen, Frank W., SSgt	6657666	WIA
Brissenden, Harris, PFC	6799708	WIA
Conner, Fred R., Pvt	16017249	WIA
Craig, Charles W., Pvt	16017241	WIA
Even, Jerome A., Pvt	16003121	WIA
Fuller, Carl W., PFC	6925285	WIA
Irons, William E., PFC	6830499	WIA
King, Sherwood D., Pvt	11015087	WIA
Yarbrough, Thomas A., Cpl	6970441	WIA

42d Bomb Squadron

Name and Rank	Serial #	Status
Beasley, Leland V., Pvt	7003158	KIA
Coyne, William Jr., PFC	6934771	KIA
Denson, Eugene B., PFC	7002423	KIA
Garrett, Robert R., Cpl	6803095	KIA
Hrusecky, Charles L., Pvt	6980546	KIA
Jencuis, Joseph N., Pvt	11016568	KIA
Kelley, Robert R., PFC	6996638	KIA
Perry, Hal H. Jr., Pvt	7002551	KIA
Stockwell, Carey K., Pvt	15056470	KIA
Anderson, Elmer, TSgt	6241317	WIA
Barker, Bruce B. S., 1st Lt	0-428793	WIA
Bartlett, Charles W., PFC	6934647	WIA
Beitler, Henry C., PFC	6936109	WIA
Bowsher, Paul T. Jr., Pvt	6991972	WIA
Donart, Kathias E., Sgt	6568848	WIA
Evans, Vernon W., PFC	7002345	WIA
Fuller, Kenneth A., Pvt	16017234	WIA

Name and Rank	Serial #	Status

42d Bomb Squadron (Continued)

Name and Rank	Serial #	Status
Holloway, John P., Pvt	16007867	WIA
Hudson, William H., Cpl	6887491	WIA
Jones, James F., PFC	1403939	WIA
Lewis, Ivan C., PFC	7021090	WIA
Luczyk, Theodore C., Cpl	6948081	WIA
McCall, Albert C. Jr., PFC	7020297	WIA
Morgan, Leith C., PFC	6999212	WIA
Narehood, Charles W., PFC	7021105	WIA
Phillips, Edgar L., Pvt	6980163	WIA
Porterfield, Charles P., PFC	6936174	WIA
Ray, Robert W., TSgt	6544986	WIA
Stephanik, Walter E., Cpl	13011049	WIA
Tuley, Paul W., Sgt	6572980	WIA
Williams, Jack A., PFC	6934696	WIA

50th Reconnaissance Squadron

Name and Rank	Serial #	Status
Alois, Ralph, SSgt	6717269	KIA
Dasenbrock, Louis H., Pvt	16040328	KIA
Haughey, John T., PFC	6982631	KIA
Hoyt, Clarence E., PFC	7070685	KIA
Humphrey, Henry J., SSgt	6570614	KIA
Libolt, Lester H., Cpl	6936136	KIA
Mattox, Harell K., PFC	6297644	KIA
Offutt, William H., Cpl	6917189	KIA
Bradshaw, Thomas E., Pvt	6580885	WIA
Dinagin, James E., Sgt	11011326	WIA
Enchelmeyer, Stanton H., Pvt	6152290	WIA
Hall, Melvin L., MSgt	6458333	WIA
Howland, Lawrence B., PFC	6980306	WIA
Lenburg, Harold, Pvt	16003268	WIA
Longest, Owen E., Sgt	6298925	WIA
McRoberts, James H., Pvt	16017310	WIA
Pulley, Issac H. Jr., PFC	7020156	WIA
Roberts, Edwin, Pvt	7006560	WIA
Sidak, Julius O., Sgt	6565769	WIA
Smith, Norman A., Cpl	6148224	WIA
Viers, Joseph L., Cpl	R-1440483	WIA
West, Kenneth H., Pvt	16007613	WIA

Name and Rank	Serial #	Status

Hq & Hq Sq 17th Air Base Group

Name and Rank	Serial #	Status
Angelich, Jerry M., Pvt	19003575	KIA
Brooks, B. J. Jr., Pvt	7021066	KIA
Brummwell, Malcolm J., 1st Lt	0-341888	KIA
Downs, Jack A., Pvt	18059915	KIA
Eichelberger, Paul R., Pvt	13030353	KIA
Field, Arnold E., Pvt	16007828	KIA
Jedrysik, Joseph, Pvt	11023613	KIA
Kinder, Andrew J., Pvt	18000244	KIA
McLaughlin, Herbert E., Pvt	16021346	KIA
Morris, Emmett E., Cpl	6887300	KIA
Nelles, Joseph F., PFC	6920307	KIA
Orr, Willard C., PFC	6149312	KIA
Rogness, Halvor E., Pvt	37047377	KIA
Surrells, Leo H., Pvt	16028525	KIA
Aubrey, Herbert, Pvt	6951838	WIA
Boyd, Herman, Pvt	19058806	WIA
Brewer, Roy G., PFC	6998320	WIA
Bushey, George O., Pvt	16012754	WIA
Cooper, Howard F., 1st Lt	0-353462	WIA
Crocker, Erwin E., Pvt	6143857	WIA
Deeter, Charles R., Pvt	6669195	WIA
Dwyre, George T., Sgt	6917063	WIA
Dye, Cecil W., Cpl	6925026	WIA
Goff, George W., Pvt	15069291	WIA
Hefley, Elton C., Avn Cdt	18040582	WIA
Henson, Raymond H., Pvt	18063000	WIA
Napier, Eugene E., PFC	6980075	WIA
Pickerel, Robert L., Pvt	6291444	WIA
Redburn, Ralph A., Cpt	0-258373	WIA
Roseman, Herbert J., Pvt	12027334	WIA
Sanchez, Servando, Pvt	18035190	WIA
Spallone, Nicholas J. Jr., Pvt	13030340	WIA
Suppes, David Jr., TSgt	6253796	WIA
Ward, Howard C., PFC	6936137	WIA

18th Air Base Squadron

Name and Rank	Serial #	Status
Bush, Joseph, Pvt	6023658	KIA
Couhig, John H., Pvt	6427420	KIA
Elyard, Harold C., SSgt	6839725	KIA
Fairchild, Willard E., Pvt	16003011	KIA

Name and Rank	Serial #	Status

18th Air Base Squadron (Continued)

Name and Rank	Serial #	Status
Fellman, Paul V., SSgt	6630437	KIA
Ferris, Homer E., TSgt	R-339200	KIA
Fiander, Stuart H., Pvt	6151801	KIA
Gleason, James J., PFC	6947032	KIA
Klein, Otto C., Pvt	13037387	KIA
Lord, Harry W. Jr., Pvt	11013292	KIA
Malatak, Joseph, Pvt	13025035	KIA
Penny, Russell M., Pvt	6981089	KIA
Rae, Allen G., Pvt	12027324	KIA
Smith, George J., PFC	6150664	KIA
South, Elmer W., Pvt	6990788	KIA
Tibbets, Hermann K. Jr., Pvt	11029005	KIA
Tuckerman, George W., Pvt	6997660	KIA
Vanderelli, Martin, Pvt	7022224	KIA
Wardigo, Walter H., Pvt	6997635	KIA
Woodworth, Lawton J., Pvt	12025014	KIA
Wright, Thomas M., Pvt	15069262	KIA
Young, Virgil J., Pvt	18052212	KIA
Berard, Edmond H., PFC	16021386	WIA
Bois, Jack L., Pvt	16012899	WIA
Carey, Lawrence D., Pvt	11027098	WIA
Chaplick, Frank G., PFC	6148215	WIA
Gaines, Jesse D., Pvt	7003670	WIA
Hill, Charles W. Jr., Pvt	11027412	WIA
Hymson, Lawrence, Pvt	6980991	WIA
Issac, Chesley A., Pvt	16017282	WIA
Kelly, Ralph, SSgt	6842632	WIA
King, Phelps W., Pvt	16012767	WIA
Kobylinski, Pierre A., Pvt	7013627	WIA
Kuropatwa, Charles C., PFC	6946502	WIA
Lyon, Warren, Pvt	6579593	WIA
McClellan, Robert W., Pvt	20433822	WIA
Mitchell, Donald K., PFC	6149254	WIA
Mitchell, Paul, Pvt	6292158	WIA
Northam, Floyd A., Pvt	18041885	WIA
Reynolds, Burkett A., Pvt	6991434	WIA
Schwartzkopf, Victor O., SSgt	6826441	WIA
Wolfe, Vaughn E., Pvt	6851532	WIA
Young, Ralph W. Jr., Pvt	6151797	WIA

Name and Rank	Serial #	Status

22d Materiel Squadron

Name and Rank	Serial #	Status
Baker, George W., PFC	13001888	KIA
Boyle, Arthur F., Pvt	6152392	KIA
Brandt, Billy O., SSgt	6883472	KIA
Brower, Rennie V. Jr., Pvt	6934751	KIA
Brownlee, William J., Pvt	6299891	KIA
Brubaker, Brooks J., Pvt	7021066	KIA
Burlison, Weldon C., Pvt	6377063	KIA
Church, Leroy R., Pvt	16007873	KIA
Feldman, Jack H., Pvt	13027061	KIA
Gagne, Leo E. A., Pvt	11020246	KIA
Goudy, Allen E. W., Pvt	17025242	KIA
Hasenfuss, William E. Jr., PFC	6977347	KIA
Johnson, James R., Pvt	16017373	KIA
Johnson, Robert H., Pvt	16012646	KIA
King, Marion E. Jr., Pvt	6936734	KIA
Klubertanz, Roderick O., Pvt	16007806	KIA
Mann, John H., SSgt	6906443	KIA
McClintock, James J., PFC	6950013	KIA
Messam, Horace A., PFC	6667770	KIA
Meyers, Victor L., Pvt	6939609	KIA
Mitchell, Edwin N., Cpl	6275082	KIA
Philipsky, Thomas F., PFC	6915458	KIA
Shields, William F., Pvt	15020006	KIA
Smith, Ralph S., PFC	6948901	KIA
Sparks, John B., PFC	6955782	KIA
Staples, Merton I., Pvt	20149201	KIA
Szematowicz, Jerome J., PFC	6911554	KIA
Timmerman, William F., Pvt	7070825	KIA
Walker, Ernest M. Jr., Pvt	13009151	KIA
Basa, Frank R., PFC	7023005	WIA
Brooks, Charles S. Jr., PFC	6993821	WIA
Cameron, Charles B., SSgt	6904645	WIA
Cremer, Eilert H., Sgt	6608654	WIA
Dragon, Charles R., Pvt	11015145	WIA
Drechsler, Carl, Pvt	6934744	WIA
Exum, Grady E., PFC	6921577	WIA
Frazier, Edwin, PFC	6871586	WIA
Gautier, Bill P., Pvt	7023696	WIA
Gese, Walter J., Pvt	6587391	WIA
Gudinas, Edward J., Sgt	6664374	WIA
Hamm, Cleason S., Pvt	6880866	WIA
Harrell, Turner G., SSgt	7023675	WIA

Name and Rank	Serial #	Status

22d Materiel Squadron (Continued)

Name and Rank	Serial #	Status
Howell, Elbert E., Cpl	6923855	WIA
Johnson, Clyde D., Pvt	6988789	WIA
Joyce, Don R., Pvt	17010329	WIA
Kaminski, Walter L., Pvt	13004062	WIA
Kempen, Wallace A., Pvt	16007866	WIA
Lundgren, William F., Pvt	6916953	WIA
Mann, Pell R., Cpl	6971931	WIA
McClung, Richard G., Pvt	16012892	WIA
Minnich, James S., Sgt	6893377	WIA
Mougin, Kenneth L., Pvt	11008152	WIA
Ovecka, Edward M., Pvt	6946508	WIA
Peterson, Donald H., Pvt	19044364	WIA
Peterson, William H., Pvt	19020929	WIA
Pope, Roy T., PFC	6976316	WIA
Praniewicz, Michael M., PFC	948014	WIA
Pryor, James W., PFC	6914063	WIA
Raines, Raymond, Pvt	6937867	WIA
Rainey, Harry C., Sgt	6949495	WIA
Reber, Paul D., Cpl	6946984	WIA
Sesody, Anthony L., PFC	6913920	WIA
Stanley, Joe B., Sgt	6634439	WIA
Stanley, Robert W., PFC	6981992	WIA
Stanley, William A., PFC	6975359	WIA
Tobias, Donald E., Pvt	13002000	WIA
Turnbull, Robert L., Sgt	13009092	WIA
Tussio, Domenico A., PFC	6148540	WIA
Uhlenburg, Charles L., PFC	6949904	WIA
White, Lewis B., Pvt	6974778	WIA
Zeock, Andrew N. Jr., PFC	6948809	WIA

23d Materiel Squadron

Name and Rank	Serial #	Status
Campiglia, Francis E., Pvt	11020150	KIA
Martin, Herbert B., 1st Sgt	6333078	KIA
Moser, Joseph G., Pvt	6974050	KIA
Posey, Frank St. E., TSgt	6369072	KIA
Powell, Raymond E., TSgt	6783478	KIA
Rhodes, William T., PFC	6152352	KIA
St Germain, Maurice J., Pvt	6137168	KIA
Strickland, James E. Jr., Pvt	7003254	KIA
Zappala, Joseph S., Pvt	11020151	KIA
Zuschlag, Walter J., Sgt	6975453	KIA

Name and Rank	Serial #	Status

23d Materiel Squadron (Continued)

Name and Rank	Serial #	Status
Allen, Edward L., Pvt	7005724	WIA
Baker, Fred F. Jr., PFC	6914477	WIA
Cawley, Dennis, Pvt	6955831	WIA
Crouse, Robert G., Cpl	6844093	WIA
Crum, Lincoln M., PFC	6919744	WIA
Davis, Sydney A., Pvt	16007702	WIA
Dietterick, Robert P., Pvt	13004007	WIA
Duvall, William T., Pvt	6952778	WIA
Gangrusky, Richard I., SSgt	6913556	WIA
Garrety, Richard S., PFC	6940928	WIA
Gummelt, Edward L., Cpl	6296871	WIA
Hooper, Melvin F., SSgt	6142712	WIA
Humphries, Farris M., Pvt	6839291	WIA
Jenkins, George O., PFC	6668596	WIA
Jorda, Louis, Pvt	34004214	WIA
La Blanc, John D., PFC	6919769	WIA
Loos, John P., Pvt	6983703	WIA
McInnis, William G., PFC	16012734	WIA
Plaster, Gilbert A., Pvt	6955823	WIA
Samulevich, Alphonse, PFC	6148928	WIA
Sbraccia, Bernard D., Pvt	11020149	WIA
Tholke, Henry E., PFC	6948604	WIA
Zangari, Anthony A., Pvt	6996067	WIA

5th Chemical Company Service, Aviation

Name and Rank	Serial #	Status
Harrison, John L., Pvt	19052509	WIA

13th Quartermaster Truck Co, Aviation

Name and Rank	Serial #	Status
Heffelfinger, Gerald R., Sgt	6890694	WIA
King, Howard E., PFC	7026071	WIA
Lawing, James E., Pvt	14009207	WIA

39th Quartermaster Co (Light Maintenance), Aviation

Name and Rank	Serial #	Status
Bunn, Raymond A., PFC	16010118	WIA
Hall, Elbert H., Sgt	6387356	WIA

Name and Rank	Serial #	Status

407th Signal Company (Aviation)

Wenzel, Theodore A., Pvt	11030694	WIA

Detachment Finance Department Hickam Fld

Gross, Carl R., PFC	6669177	WIA
Wingrove, Marvin, PFC	6955738	WIA

Quartermaster Detachment Hawaiian Dept Hickam Fld

Bills, Mathew T., Pvt	12014696	KIA
Chagnon, Joseph J., Sgt	6908124	KIA
Hartford, Carlton H., Pvt	11015352	KIA
Hasty, Ardrey V., Pvt	14037508	KIA
Beatty, Howard J., Pvt	6980240	WIA
Byrd, Louis J., Pvt	6915390	WIA
Godley, Sidney, Pvt	14012588	WIA
Lovelace, William D., Pvt	14037516	WIA
Matouka, Michael, PFC	13027089	WIA
McGuire, Jack P., PFC	14047242	WIA
Robertson, Paul D., Pvt	14037062	WIA
Tolen, James M., SSgt	6664930	WIA
Travis, Robert, Pvt	6979013	WIA

38th Reconnaisance Squadron (Transient)

Schick, William R., 1st Lt	0-412256	KIA
Beale, G. C., Avn Cdt	18036583	WIA
Lee, Bert Jr., Pvt	19051486	WIA
Pouncey, LeRoy B., MSgt	R-792748	WIA
Taylor, Homer., 2d Lt	0-409908	WIA
Tomlinson, Vernon D., Sgt	19030242	WIA
Velarde, Lawrence B., SSgt	6555988	WIA

B-24 Crew (Transient)

Moslener, Louis G., 2d Lt	0-409917	KIA
Powloski, Daniel J., Pvt	6673769	KIA

Name and Rank	Serial #	Status

B-24 Crew (Transient) (Continued)

Name and Rank	Serial #	Status
Gradle, Kenneth A., Cpl	6912391	WIA
Hobbie, Theodore V., SSgt	6573738	WIA
Smith, Walter S. III, 2d Lt	0-398524	WIA

WHEELER FIELD

Hq & Hq Sq 14th Pursuit Wing

Name and Rank	Serial #	Status
Hall, John B., Pvt	13034728	WIA
Waite, Charles A. Jr., Cpl	6986825	WIA

Hq & Hq Sq 15th Pursuit Group

Name and Rank	Serial #	Status
Chambers, Eugene L., PFC	13010833	KIA
Mitchell, John G., Cpl	16012572	KIA
Schott, Robert L., PFC	15059273	KIA
Shattuck, Robert R., PFC	16007831	KIA
Vidoloff, Russell P., PFC	15015473	KIA
Walker, Lumus E., Pvt	16040974	KIA
Baker, Leonard A., SSgt	6558082	WIA
Bennett, Howard A., SSgt	6979441	WIA
Dodd, Harry O., PFC	16002286	WIA
Durbin, Noel E., PFC	16017279	WIA
Ewers, James F., Pvt	16040940	WIA
Moyer, James I., Cpl	7025139	WIA
Niedzwiecki, Robert R., Pvt	16012747	WIA
Nuttall, Rolland L., SSgt	6559665	WIA
Price, Walter J., Sgt	6954205	WIA
Richards, John N., Pvt	6999151	WIA
Strong, Kenneth E., PFC	16021420	WIA
Webster, John J., 1st Lt	0-396499	WIA

45th Pursuit Squadron

Name and Rank	Serial #	Status
Allen, Robert G., Pvt	15058940	KIA
Buss, Robert P., Cpl	16003452	KIA
Baldwin, Robert H., SSgt	6913117	WIA

Name and Rank	Serial #	Status

45th Pursuit Squadron (Continued)

Greenmore, Kenneth W., PFC	16021375	WIA
Smith, Edwin G., Sgt	6947462	WIA
Suffern, Richard H., CplPvt	12006334	WIA
Zuercher, Charles P., Cpl	16017205	WIA

46th Pursuit Squadron

Plant, Donald D., Pvt	16007493	KIA
Sterling, Gordon H. Jr., 2d Lt	0-411852	KIA
Westhaver, Clayton M., Sgt	6151526	WIA

47th Pursuit Squadron

Dains, John L., 2d Lt	0-424923	KIA
Holley, Lester W., PFC	6954251	WIA
Taylor, Kenneth M., 1st Lt	0-409061	WIA

72d Pursuit Squadron

Burns, Edward J., 1st Sgt	6144931	KIA
Cashen, Malachy J., Pvt	16008039	KIA
Cebert, Dean W., Pvt	16017559	KIA
Creech, William C., PFC	7023159	KIA
Everett, James, SSgt	6296829	KIA
Free, Paul B.,	6946529	KIA
Good, Joseph E., SSgt	6948037	KIA
Guthrie, James E., SSgt	6948331	KIA
Hull, Robert L., Pvt	15012450	KIA
Leslie, George G., Pvt	13037089	KIA
Price, John A., SSgt	6971149	KIA
Ames, George C., Cpl	61500680	WIA
Bellue, Thomas E., PFC	7000795	WIA
Carr, James W., TSgt	6381552	WIA
Dabney, Fred A., Sgt	6994288	WIA
Davenport, James M., Sgt	6292373	WIA
English, James T., Cpl	16040972	WIA
Fay, Charles A., SSgt	6148050	WIA

Name and Rank	Serial #	Status

72d Pursuit Squadron (Continued)

Name and Rank	Serial #	Status
Fitzimmons, Robert G., Pvt	16003456	WIA
Kawa, Russell J., PFC	6145929	WIA
Kelly, Henry T., Cpl	7020458	WIA
Kimble, Thomas P. Jr., Pvt	14028203	WIA
Klahn, Lester W., Cpl	16008121	WIA
Salloum, Naif J., Pvt	16012822	WIA
Steff, Jonah A., Cpl	12006466	WIA
Tillett, George, Pvt	7021673	WIA

Hq & Hq Sq 18th Pursuit Group

Name and Rank	Serial #	Status
Byrd, Theodore F. Jr., PFC	14019881	KIA
Derthick, James H., Sgt	6668189	KIA
Herbert, Joseph C., SSgt	6844109	KIA
Manley, William H., PFC	14032737	KIA
Schmersahl, George R., Sgt	6979080	KIA
Sherman, Robert O., Sgt	6980227	KIA
Ashker, Samuel E., PFC	6976841	WIA
Collins, Raymond J., Cpl	6980929	WIA
Deraney, George, PFC	6148095	WIA
Libby, Keith E., Pvt	11013386	WIA
Liddick, Walter A., Sgt	6946538	WIA
Maser, Karl O., PFC	11015139	WIA
McAdams, James W., TSgt	6251313	WIA
O'Brien, Michael L., PFC	12018370	WIA
Ryan, Thomas W., Pvt	11007940	WIA
Silverwatch, Walter, PFC	6147909	WIA
Sloboda, John, Sgt	6977547	WIA

6th Pursuit Squadron

Name and Rank	Serial #	Status
Walczynski, Andrew A., SSgt	6802945	KIA
Collins, Walter L., Pvt	6397839	WIA
Falkenburg, Irwin A., SSgt	6719395	WIA
Kissel, George, Sgt	6979839	WIA
Montgromery, Frederick D., PFC	7026827	WIA
Restivo, Anthony B., SSgt	6889085	WIA
Richardson, Milroy L., Pvt	17001408	WIA
Rodriguez, Earl B., Pvt	11008147	WIA

<u>Name and Rank</u>	<u>Serial #</u>	<u>Status</u>

6th Pursuit Squadron (Continued)

Sampson, Roger F., PFC	11007674	WIA
Scheidt, Paul J., SSgt	6668704	WIA
Stanley, Richard C., Sgt	6987675	WIA
Tiffany, Horace J., Pvt	16003540	WIA
Ventress, Clifford C., Cpl	16040907	WIA
Wallace, Frank L., Pvt	6845163	WIA
Zeiss, Charles L., SSgt	6984022	WIA

19th Pursuit Squadron

Bloxham, Robert W., Pvt	19010611	WIA
Hall, Rogers W., PFC	14004268	WIA
Hunter, Duncan, Sgt	6979365	WIA
Infantolino, Alfred A., SSgt	6145811	WIA
O'Brien, William H. Jr., Cpl	11007591	WIA
Sallick, George, SSgt	6851526	WIA
Thon, Hans S., Pvt	16021398	WIA
Wilson, Lowell R., Cpl	6993928	WIA

44th Pursuit Squadron

Christiansen, Hans C., 2d Lt (KIA at Bellows Field)	0-406482	KIA
Whiteman, George A., 2d Lt (KIA at Bellows Field)	0-399683	KIA
Bishop, Samuel W., 1st Lt (WIA at Bellows Field)	0-396359	WIA

73d Pursuit Squadron

Barksdale, James M. SSgt	6887682	KIA
White, Edward M., Pvt	16012623	WIA

78th Pursuit Squadron

Horan, Vincent M., Cpl	6148539	KIA
Stacey, Morris, Sgt	6661840	KIA
Cossack, Michael T.,	6987369	WIA

Name and Rank	Serial #	Status

17th Air Base Squadron

Gannam, George K., SSgt (KIA at Hickam Field)	6926173	KIA
Hughes, Earl F.	6291170	WIA
Stephenson, David B.		WIA

25th Materiel Squadron

Robbins, Anson E., Pvt	11009597	KIA

741st Ordnance Company, Aviation

O'Donovan, James E., Pvt	12011872	WIA

BELLOWS FIELD*

86th Observation Squadron

Ludwig, Charles A., Pvt	16003255	WIA
Price, Robert F., Pvt (Wounded at Hickam Field)	18036583	WIA
Wargo, Peter, Jr., Pvt (Wounded at Hickam Field)	13026891	WIA
Wilson, Martin C., Pvt	18052270	WIA

Medical Detachment

Brown, James A., PFC	6951110	WIA

---

*The 16 December 1941 Casualty Report lists one wounded and four missing. The 86th Observation Squadron history written after the war states there were no casualties at Bellows Field, but one man was killed and two wounded at Hickam Field. Two personnel from the 86th were in fact wounded at Hickam Field, as verified in the 1946 casualty list, which stated that two of the four named in the 1941 report as missing were in fact alive and well. In addition, a report written by Lt Col Clyde K. Rich, Executive Officer, Bellows Field, to Col E. W. Raley, HQ Hawaiian Air Force, dated 20 Dec 1941, states two enlisted men from the 86th were wounded at Bellows during the second attack. The National Personnel Records Center confirmed four Bellows personnel as wounded. No records have been found identifying any Bellows Field personnel who were killed at Bellows during the attack, but several personal accounts discuss a Sgt Brown from the Medical Department being wounded.

NOTES

Chapter I - Hawaiian Air Force: Before the Attack

1. *Hearings Before the Joint Committee on the Investigation of the Pearl Harbor Attack, Congress of the United States, Seventy-Ninth Congress* (Washington, DC, 1946), Part 22, p 36 [hereafter cited as Congressional Report].

2. Congressional Report, Part 15, pp 1625-1626; Administrative History, Hq Seventh Air Force, 1916-May 1944.

3. Congressional Report, Part 27, pp 156-158; rpt, HQ Wheeler Field/S-2 to Hawaiian Air Force/G-2, "Narrative Report of Enemy Activities, Wheeler Field, 7 December 1941," 10 Dec 41.

4. Congressional Report, Part 22, pp 201-203; Prange, Gordon W., *At Dawn We Slept*, Penguin Books, 1981, pp 89-91 [hereafter cited as Prange, At Dawn].

5. See note above.

6. W.F. Craven and J.L. Cate, ed, *The Army Air Forces in World War II - Volume One, Plans and Early Operations*, (Washington, DC, 1983), pp 170-171 [hereafter cited as Craven and Cate].

7. J. McCarthy, "Introducing—A Typical Hickam Soldier!!", *Honolulu Advertiser* or *Star-Bulletin* [ca. Jan 41]; John Milton Neuhauser, *Growing Up Gentle* (Phillips, Wisconsin, 1988), p 101.

8. See note above; photos, papers, and recollections of military members formerly stationed in Hawaii (filed in 15 ABW History Office); Scrapbooks donated to 15 ABW History Office; Russell J. Tener, "A First Person Account of the Japanese Attack on Pearl Harbor," 31 Jul 82, p 7 [hereafter cited as Tener]; ltr, John W. Wilson, To Whom It May Concern, [request for *Hickam: The First Fifty Years* book], [ca. Dec 90].

9. Congressional Report, Part 22, pp 349-351.

10. Congressional Report, Part 22, p 309.

11. Appendix B lists all the aircraft available at the time of the attack; Congressional Report, Part 22, pp 309-311; Reardin, Jim, *Cracking The Zero Mystery*, 1990, pp 15-25; Gunston, Bill, *The Encyclopedia of the World's Combat Aircraft*, 1976, p 161.

12. Congressional Report, Part 22, pp 119-121, 202-206.

13. Lambert, John W., *The Pineapple Air Force: Pearl Harbor to Tokyo*, (Phalanx Pub., 1990), p 7 [hereafter cited as Lambert, Pineapple Air Force]; Congressional Report, Part 22, pp 111, 202-204, 211-212, 225-228.

14. Lambert, Pineapple Air Force, p 7; Congressional Report, Part 22, pp 211-212.

15. Lambert, Pineapple Air Force, p 7; Congressional Report, Part 3, pp 1070-1073, Part 22, pp 114-115, 119-121.

16. Congressional Report, Part 22, pp 114-115, 119-121, 226-227.

17. Congressional Report, Part 18, p 3187, Part 24, pp 2010-2011.

18. Congressional Report, Part 22, pp 221-224.

19. Congressional Report, Part 28, pp 986-982.

Chapter II - Assignment Paradise: Bomber Command

1. Douglas Boswell, ed, *All About Hawaii* (Honolulu, 1960), pp 13-14; Craven and Cate, p 173.

2. Ltr, Brig Gen E. T. Conley, War Dept Acting Adj Gen, to Mrs. Horace M. Hickam, [designation of Hickam Field], 20 May 35; GO 4, War Dept, 21 May 35; "Hickam Field Largest U.S. Air Corps Station," *Honolulu Advertiser* or *Star-Bulletin* [ca. 1940]; *The*

Hickam Bomber, Hickam Field, 1942 [hereafter cited as *The Hickam Bomber*].

3. Hewlett, "Luke Field Passes On," *Honolulu Star-Bulletin*, 4 Nov 39; Maurer Maurer, *Aviation in the U.S. Army, 1919-1939*, Office of AF History, 1987, p 371.

4. "Largest Air Corps Mecca Under Flag," *Honolulu Advertiser* or *Star-Bulletin*, 19 Jun 38.

5. *Ibid.*; "Hickam Field Development As Biggest Aerodrome Told," *Honolulu Star-Bulletin*, 11 Dec 36.

6. Basic History of Army Air Base, APO 953, 1 Jun 44.

7. Administrative History of Headquarters Seventh Air Force, from 1916 to May 1944 [hereafter cited as 7AF Admin Hist]; Preliminary History of VII Air Force Service Command, 25 Dec 41 to 15 Oct 42; F. Hewlett, "Luke Field Passes On," *Honolulu Star-Bulletin*, 4 Nov 39.

8. Hewlett, "Luke Field Passes On," *Honolulu Star-Bulletin*, 4 Nov 39.

9. 7AF Admin Hist.

10. "Hickam Men Live in Tents Until Barracks Finished," *Honolulu Advertiser* or *Star-Bulletin*, [ca. 1939]; H. Albright, "Tent Village Springs Up On Hangar Line at Army's Largest Air Base," *Honolulu Advertiser*, 19 Feb 38; Erwin N. Thompson, *Pacific Ocean Engineers, History of the US Army Corps of Engineers in the Pacific, 1905-1980*, p 82.

11. M. McCoskrie, "Hickam Hotel Under Management of Uncle Sam," *The Honolulu Advertiser*, 25 May 41, p 3.

12. H. Albright, "'Come and Get It' Means Big Rush At Hickam Where 1,600 Feed Daily," *Honolulu Advertiser* or *Star-Bulletin*, [ca. 1940]; A. Kreiner, "Hickam's Mess Hall Big as a Balloon Hangar," *Honolulu Advertiser* or *Star-Bulletin*, [ca. 1940].

13. Denver D. Gray, "I Remember Pearl Harbor: A Nebraska Army Air Force Officer in the Pacific Theatre During World War II," *Nebraska History*, V62 (Winter 1981), p 449 [hereafter cited as Gray].

14. "Largest Air Corps Mecca Under Flag," *Honolulu Advertiser* or *Star-Bulletin*, 19 Jun 38.

15. *Ibid.*; M. Mathews, "Crash Boat Rescue Fleet Pride of Hickam," *Honolulu Advertiser* or *Star-Bulletin*, [ca. 1940].

16. *The Hickam Bomber*.

17. M. Mathews, "Airforce [sic] Schools Turn Out Technical Experts," *Honolulu Advertiser* or *Star-Bulletin*, 18 Jan 41; J. McCarthy, "Hickam Trade School Has Big Attendance," *Honolulu Advertiser* or *Star-Bulletin*, [ca. 1941]; *Hickam Highlights*, Vol V, No. 2, 11 Jul 41, p 17; US Army Air Corps diploma for Aircraft Mechanics course, PFC Herbert J. Kelly, 5 Jun 40.

18. See note 16 above; J. McCarthy, "Hickam Trade School Has Big Attendance," *Honolulu Advertiser* or *Star-Bulletin*, [ca. 1941].

19. See note 16 above; "Hawaiian Air Depot," *Origins of Air Force in Hawaii, 1889-1957*, pp 238-253.

20. See note 16 above.

21. Capt Kenneth L. Bayley, USAF (Ret), "Life at Hickam, 1940," Mar 88, pp 2-3.

22. *Ibid.*; G. Papanic, *Who Else Was Guilty at "Pearl"?* (New York, 1982), pp 13-14 [hereafter cited as Papanic]; A. C. Fryman, "Sampling of Items from the 1941 Menu of Black Cat Cafe, Honolulu, Hawaii."

23. Papanic, pp 13-14; R. Jacobs, "Afterthoughts: Cheeseburgers in Paradise," *Honolulu*, Dec 87, p 162; Tener, p 9.

24. See notes 16 and 22 above; intvw, L. R. Arakaki, Historian, with Maj Gen Russell L. Waldron, USAF (Ret), 7 Feb 86, p 8.

25. See notes 16 and 21 above.

26. See note above.

27. *Hickam News*, Vol I, No. 1, 15 Mar 40, p 11.

28. Forrest A. Brandt, Addendum to "Some World War II Recollections," 8 Dec 81.

29. 7AF Admin Hist, p 7; Craven and Cate, pp 172-173.

30. Craven and Cate, pp 174-179.

31. Ltr w/1 Incl, Research Studies Institute, Air University, "Commanding Officers of Hickam AFB," 25 Apr 58; Congressional Report, pp 432-433;intvw, Dr. Ronald E. Marcello, North Texas State University, with Maj Gen Russell Waldron, 7 Dec 80, p 8 [hereafter cited as Waldron].

32. I. W. Southern, "Roosevelts [sic] Day of Infamy, My Day of Hell: Pearl Harbor - December 7th. 1941," n.d., p 3 [hereafter cited as Southern]; Tener, pp 10-11.

33. Gray, pp 448-449; Waldron, pp 12-13.

Chapter III - Assignment Paradise: Fighter Command

1. 7AF Admin Hist, pp 2-3; Lt W. C. Addleman, "History of the US Army in Hawaii, 1849 to 1939," pp 34-35.

2. See note above; Preliminary History of VII Air Force Service Command (25 Dec 41 - 15 Oct 42), p 27.

3. Historical Review - Engineer Library, US Army Corps of Engineers, Vols 1, 2 & 3, Covering Operations During World War II, Pacific Ocean Area, pp 61-62.

4. Wheeler Field/Wheeler AFB Chronology, pp 3 and 5.

5. 7AF Admin Hist, p 6; Preliminary History of VII AF Service Command (25 Dec 41 - 15 Oct 42), pp 28-30.

6. See Appendix A.

7. Craven and Cate, p 172; John W. Lambert, *The Long Campaign: The History of the 15th Fighter Group in World War II*

(Manhattan, Kansas, 1982), p 12 [hereafter cited as Lambert, Long Campaign]; M. Mathews, "30 Army Pursuit Planes Make Dramatic, Unannounced Arrival," *Honolulu Advertiser* or *Star-Bulletin*, 22 Feb 41.

8. Craven and Cate, p 172; Lambert, Pineapple Air Force, p 5; Lambert, Long Campaign, p 12.

9. Lambert, Pineapple Air Force, pp 6-7.

10. Memoirs of Edward J. White, ASN 6151708, 16 Oct 86.

11. *Ibid.*

12. *Ibid.*

13. Lani Nedbalek, *Wahiawa: From Dream to Community*, (Mililani, Hawaii, 1984), pp 73, 78-79.

14. "GALADAY," a historical brochure commemorating the dedication of Wheeler Field Airdrome and Post Office, 7 Aug 41; Prange, at Dawn, p 178.

15. GO 68, Hq Hawaiian Department, 27 Oct 41; Lambert, Pineapple Air Force, p 9.

16. Congressional Reports: Part 28, pp 1488-1489; Part 29, pp 2116-2117.

17. Lambert, Pineapple Air Force, p 12.

18. Lt W. C. Addleman, "History of the US Army in Hawaii, 1849 to 1939," p 17; GO 8, War Dept, 19 Aug 33; History of Bellows Field from Time of Inception to 31 Mar 44 [hereafter cited as Bellows History], p 1.

19. *Ibid.*, p 2.

20. *Ibid.*, pp 2-3; War Dept QMC Form No. 117, "Airplane Runway," 11 Jan 33; Congressional Report, Part 28, p 1573.

21. Bellows History, pp 3-4.

22. *Ibid.*, p 2.

23. *Ibid.*, p 3; Statement by Woodrow W. (Chuck) Fry, former corporal assigned to

86th Observation Squadron, 16 Jun 90 [hereafter cited as Fry].

24. Bellows History, pp 3 and 5; TSgt Donald C. Cameron, "A History of the Eighty Sixth Combat Mapping Squadron AAF" [hereafter cited as 86th Sq History]; Maurer Maurer, *Combat Squadrons of the Air Force, World War II*, (Washington, 1982), p 638; Fry; Statement by Edward J. Covelesky, former staff sergeant assigned to 44th Pursuit Sq [hereafter cited as Covelesky].

25. 86th Sq History; Fry; Covelesky; Bellows History, p 6.

26. 86th Sq History.

27. *Ibid.*, pp 6 and 8.

28. Fry; Ltr from J. R. (Roger) Langley, former staff sergeant assigned to 86th Observation Sq, to Ronald J. Nash, 24 Mar 83; Stanley Thomas, "Bellows Field," *Memorial Military Museum Newsletter*, Jan 84, p 3 [hereafter cited as Thomas].

29. Bellows History, p 7.

30. *Ibid.*, p 7; Ltr from Mrs. James D. (Catherine) McFall, Jr. to Ronald J. Nash, 6 Apr 83.

31. Bellows History, p 7; 86th Sq History; Ted Darcy, *Army Aviation in Hawaii*, 1913-1941, Apr 1991, p 130.

32. 86th Sq History.

33. Congressional Report, Part 23, p 744.

34. Ltr, 44 Ftr Sq to Comdg Ofcr, 18 Ftr Gp, "Organization History from Date of Activation to 31 December 1943," 20 Dec 44, p 1; Covelesky; Congressional Report, Part 28, pp 1572-1573.

35. Bellows History, pp 10-11; Thomas.

36. Statement by Howard Taylor, former Provost Sergeant assigned to Hq Sq Hawaiian Air Force; Bellows History, pp 10-11.

Chapter IV - 7 December 1941: A Day That Will Live in Infamy

1. Prange, At Dawn, pp 490-492 and chart on pg 375; *Senshi Sosho: Hawai Sakusen*, (BKS Vol 10), pp 596-616 [hereafter cited as Senshi Sosho].

2. See note above; Bill Gunston, *The Encyclopedia of the World's Combat Aircraft* (London, 1976), p 167.

3. See note above.

4. See note 2; Jim Reardon, *Cracking the Zero Mystery* (Harrisburg, PA; 1990).

5. Prange, At Dawn, pp 490-492; Senshi Sosho pp 596-616.

6. Report, Brig Gen H. C. Davidson, Commanding Officer, Hawaiian Interceptor Comd, to Commanding General, Hawaiian Air Force, "Report of Enemy Activity over Oahu, 7 December 1941," 18 Dec 1941 [hereafter cited as Davidson Report]; Congressional Report, Part 22, pp 193-196.

7. Interview, authors with Herbert E. Garcia, Curator, Tropic Lightning Museum, July 1990.

8. Prange, At Dawn, pp 524-525; memorandum, Lt Col Clyde K. Rich to Col Raley, 20 Dec 1941.

9. Congressional Report, Part 1, pp 49-50.

10. Prange, At Dawn, pp 490-492, and chart on pg 375; Congressional Report, Part 1, pp 49-50; memorandum, Lt Col Clyde K. Rich to Col Raley, 20 Dec 1941; Davidson Report; Senshi Sosho, pp 596-616.

11. See note above.

12. See note 10.

13. Congressional Report, Part 10, pp 5076-5080; Part 18, p 3187.

14. Congressional Report, Part 10, pp 538-541, 560-576.

15. Congressional Report, Part 18, pp 3014-3015; Part 25, item 123.

16. Congressional Report, Part 10, pp 5038-5041, 5059-5080; Part 18, pp 3014-3015; Part 27, pp 517-536,566-571.

17. See note above.

18. See note above; Congressional Report, Part 32, pp 341-351.

19. See notes 17 and 18.

20. Congressional Report, Part 3, pp 1120-1121; Craven and Cate, pg 193.

21. Prange, At Dawn, pp 481-482; Congressional Report, Part 18, p 3015; Part 27, pp 430-431.

22. Congressional Report, Part 28, pp 1571-1573; Part 27, pp 430-431; correspondence with Mr. David Aiken, Irving, Texas.

23. See Appendices C and D.

24. Lambert, Pineapple Air Force, p 20; Congressional Report, Part 22, pp 125-126; Appendices C and D.

25. See Appendix C.

26. Information about the attack that morning is as numerous as there are participants. The following is a list of the most pertinent data that seems to correspond with the preponderance of information: Lambert, p 202 Appendix 3, and pp 17-23 of the text, which is made up of primarily firsthand accounts of the action that morning by the participants. Craven and Cate, pp 198-201; information taken from official reports, Congressional testimony, and several firsthand accounts. Congressional Report, Part 12, pp 323-324; Part 22, pp 249-257; Part 24, p 1834. Figures and times given in the Congressional Record are open for debate; however, the descriptive testimony, especially by Welch and Taylor, agrees basically with later interviews given by the participants. *Air Force Aerial Victory Credits: WWI, WWII, Korea, and Vietnam*, USAF Historical Research Center (1988) p 473. This official publication confirms ten of the eleven victories mentioned in text.

Chapter V - Hell in Paradise: Bomber Command

1. Prange, At Dawn, p 25.

2. Congressional Report, Part 1, pp 49-50.

3. Congressional Report, Part 27, pp 434-440; Gordon W. Prange, *Dec. 7, 1941* (Warner Books, 1988), p 185 [hereafter cited as Prange, Dec 7].

4. Interview, Dr. James C. Hasdorff with Lt Gen Gordon A. Blake, 14-15 Dec 83, pp 31-32 [hereafter cited as Blake].

5. Prange, Dec 7, p 192; Blake, pp 32-33.

6. Congressional Report, Part 27, p 641; handwritten notes of Maj Charles P. Eckhert, 8-10 Dec 41, p 1 [hereafter cited as Eckhert].

7. "Diary of events, morale, strength of employee personnel, and behavior of Depotpersonnel during the period 7 to 15 Dec 41," HQ HAD, 15 Dec 41; "Bankston Receives Purple Heart," *HAD News*, 20 Mar 44, p 9.

8. Eckhert, pp 1-2; Blake, pp 33-34.

9. News Release 75115, [CMSgt Chase retires from military service], 15 ABW Chief of Information, 13 Jun 75; Southern, pp 4-5.

10. Southern, pp 5-7.

11. Harold S. Kaye, "Hickam Field, 7 December 1941—The First US Army Air Corps Flying Fortress (B-17D) Combat Mission in World War II," *Aerospace Historian*, Dec 86, p 220 [hereafter cited as Kaye]; Walter Lord, *Day of Infamy* (Bantam Books, Inc., 1957), pp 109-110, 152 [hereafter cited as Lord]; Michael Slackman, *Target: Pearl Harbor* (Honolulu, 1990), p 129 [hereafter cited as Slackman]; "Remember!", *Hickam Highlights* Souvenir Issue, Vol 3, Nr 1, 7 Dec 45, pp 6-7 [hereafter cited as Remember!].

12. Prange, Dec 7, pp 188, 193, 293; Slackman, p 130; Southern, p 9.

13. William Melnyk, "Events on December 7, 1941," [ca. Sep 1990], p 1 [hereafter cited as Melnyk].

14. Tener, pp 12-13.

15. Melnyk, p 1; Blake Clark, *Remember Pearl Harbor!* (New York, 1942), p 40.

16. Melnyk, p 2; Gray, p 451.

17. Gray, pp 451-452,480; Lord, pp 76, 151-152; Prange, At Dawn, pp 534-535.

18. Gray, pp 455-456.

19. Gabriel W. Christie, "Pearl Harbor - The Day of Infamy," [ca. Jan 88], p 1 [hereafter cited as Christie].

20. George J. Gabik, "Dec. 7th Memories," pp 1-2 [hereafter cited as Gabik]; Christie, p 1; Marion W. Hudson, "Dec. 7th Memories"; Carlos F. McCuiston, "December 7th Memories," p 1 [hereafter cited as McCuiston].

21. Christie, p 2.

22. McCuiston, pp 2-3; History of 19th Troop Carrier Sq, 1941-1945, pp 3-4 [hereafter cited as 19 TCS History]; Gabik, p 2.

23. Slackman, p 132; intvw, L. R. Arakaki, 15 ABW Historian, with Mr. Raymond L. Perry, former PFC assigned to 29th Car Company at Fort Shafter, 11 Mar 91.

24. Interview with Maj Frank H. Lane, Hospital Commander, Hickam Field, 7 Dec 41 [n.d.], pp 1-2 [hereafter cited as Lane].

25. *Ibid.*, pp 2-3.

26. *Ibid.*; *The Hickam Bomber*, Hickam Field, 1942; "Hickam's Hospital J-Day," *Hickam Highlights*, 1 Jan 42, p 3; Lord, pp 55-56.

27. Lane, pp 3-5; *The Hickam Bomber*, Hickam Field, 1942; "Hickam's Hospital J-Day," *Hickam Highlights*, 1 Jan 42, p 3.

28. Lane, pp 4-5; "Hickam's Hospital J-Day," *Hickam Highlights*, 1 Jan 42, p 3; *The*

Hickam Bomber, Hickam Field, 1942; "Obituary: Annie Gayton Fox," *San Francisco Examiner*, 25 Jan 87, p B-7.

29. Lane, p 4.

30. Waldron, pp 13-15.

31. *Ibid.*, pp 15-18.

32. 19 TCS History, p 3; Samuel D. Rodibaugh, "Dec. 7th Memories," p 1; Arthur C. Townsend, [Dec. 7 memories], w/GO 23 (extract copy), Hq VII AF Base Comd, 27 Jun 42.

33. "General L. G. Saunders, Commanding Officer 23rd Bomb Squad," *Pearl Harbor - Gram*, Apr 78, pp 1 and 15 [hereafter cited as PH-Gram].

34. "December 7th Memories of Lee E. Metcalfe," n.d., pp 1-2.

35. Prange, Dec 7, pp 185-186; Jessie Reed Seyle, "Pearl Harbor, Dec. 1941, as I Remember It," pp 1-2 [hereafter cited as Seyle]; Lord, pp 108-109; Kaye, p 220.

36. Remember!, pp 4-5.

37. Lambert, p 108; P. Lovinger, "Hickam Fire Chief on Pearl Harbor Day Pays Visit," *Honolulu Star-Bulletin*, 27 Nov 60.

38. J. Y. Bowman, "The City Burned on Dec. 7th," *1976 Fire Prevention Week* booklet by Hawaii Fire Fighters Association; "Heroes in Fire Helmets," *The National Firefighters Journal*, Nov/Dec 1980, p 44; J. E. Bowen, "December 7, 1941—The Day the Honolulu Fire Department Went to War," *The Hawaiian Journal of History*, Vol 13, 1976, pp 126-128 [hereafter cited as Bowen].

39. See note above.

40. Bowen, pp 129-130; Slackman, p 131.

41. Ltr, Maj Rod House, USAF (Ret), [58 Bomb Sq], 18 Apr 90 [hereafter cited as House]; Prange, Dec 7, pp 183, 188, 243-244, 294,329; Operational History of the Seventh Air Force, 7 Dec 41-6 Dec 43, p 5 [hereafter cited as 7AF Op Hist]; Kaye, pp 218 and 224.

Chapter VI - Hell in Paradise: Fighter
Command

1. Congressional Report, Part 1, pp 50-
51; Part 28, p 1486.

2. *Ibid.*, Part 28, p 1487.

3. Letter, Brig Gen H. C. Davidson to
CG, Hawaiian AF, "Report of Enemy
Activity over Oahu, 7 Dec 41," 18 Dec 41.

4. Wilfred D. Burke, "Remembering
Pearl Harbor," *Saga*, Dec 1981, pp 14-16
[hereafter cited as Burke].

5. History of the 15th Pursuit Group
(F), 17 Jan 42, p 24; Prange, Dec 7, p 197;
Burke, p 16; Memoirs of Edward J. White, 16
Oct 86, p 5.

6. Burke, p 16; Congressional Report,
Part 22, pp 116-118 and 257-259; ltr, Wesley
Warnock, to 15 ABW, "Wheeler Airdrome's
65th Anniversary Book," 12 Oct 86;
"Squadron History of the Sky-Riders" by
1st Sgt Clarence W. Kindl; Prange, Dec 7, p
199; Lambert, pp 16-17.

7. Burke, pp 16-17; Lambert, p 17.

8. Burke, pp 17 and 52.

9. Burke, pp 52-53; Henry C. Woodrum,
"Cloak of Darkness," *Aerospace Historian*,
Dec 1988, p 282 [hereafter cited as
Woodrum]; Prange, Dec 7, p 195.

10. Burke, pp 53-54.

11. Intvw, L. R. Arakaki, 15 ABW
Historian, with Col T. Ahola, USAF (Ret),
15 Apr 91; Lambert, p 16; W. Hoover, "This
pilot was caught on the ground," *The Sunday
Star-Bulletin & Advertiser*, 7 Dec 86, p A-18.

12. Woodrum, p 282.

13. *Ibid.*, pp 282-283.

14. History of the 15th Pursuit Group
(F), 17 Jan 42, p 24.

15. Woodrum, pp 283-284.

16. *Ibid.*, pp 284-285.

17. *Ibid.*, pp 284-285.

18. *Ibid.*, pp 285-286.

19. Statement by George J. Van Gieri,
30 Sep 86; "Servicemen remember Pearl
Harbor 46 years later," *The Village Times*, 10
Dec 87, pp 3 and 6.

20. Ltr, CMSgt Harry P. Kilpatrick,
USAF (Ret), to Capt Kevin Krejcarek, 15
ABW Public Affairs Officer, [info on
Wheeler Field], 19 Nov 86.

21. Ltr, CWO Joe K. Harding, USAF
(Ret), to L. Arakaki, [7 Dec 41 experience],
circa Jan 1987.

22. Christopher Cross, *Soldiers of God*
(New York, date unknown), p 28.

23. *Ibid.*, p 29.

24. *Ibid.*, pp 29-32.

25. Bellows History, p 11; Congressional
Report: Part 1, p 51, and Part 23, p 744; ltr,
Lt Col C. K. Rich, Bellows Executive Ofcr,
to G-2, Hawaiian AF, "Report of Enemy
Operations 7 Dec 41," 12 Dec 41.

26. See note above; Congressional
Report: Part 22, p 294, and Part 23, p 742;
memo to Col Raley from Lt Col Clyde K.
Rich, [report of 7 Dec 41 attack], 20 Dec 41,
pp 1-3 [hereafter cited as Rich]; History of
the 86th Combat Mapping Squadron AAF by
TSgt Donald C. Cameron; Forrest E. Decker,
CWO, USA (Ret), "His Experience on 7 Dec
41," p 2 [hereafter cited as Decker].

27. Thomas, pp 2-3; ltr, Elmer L. Rund
to Betsy Camacho, [7 Dec 41 attack on
Bellows Field], 7 Sep 90, p 2 [hereafter cited
as Rund].

28. Brief History of Sedalia AFB, 1942-
1954; Rund, p 3; Covelesky, p 3.

29. Lambert, Pineapple Air Force, p 18.

30. Bellows History, p 13; Rich, p 2;
Martin Caidin, *Flying Forts* (Meredith Press,
1968), pp 177-182; unit history, 38 RS, 12
Jun 17 - May 42; 38 RS deployment orders,
Special Order No. 1, 4 Dec 41; Rund, p 1;
Covelesky, p 2.

31. Ltr, Lester A. Ellis to Betsy Camacho, 29 May 90, pp 1-2.

Chapter VII - After the Attack

1. Congressional Report, Part 1, pp 52-59; Craven and Cate, p 200.

2. Congressional Report: Part 1, p 58; Part 27, p 435; Part 28, p 1486; Southern, p 9; Gwenfread Allen, *Hawaii's War Years* (University of Hawaii Press, 1950), pp 29 and 32 [hereafter cited as Gwenfread Allen].

3. Seyle, pp 1-3.

4. Lane, pp 4-6, 7-8; "Hickam's Hospital J-Day," *Hickam Highlights*, 1 Jan 42, p 3.

5. Lane, p 8.

6. Congressional Report, Part 22, p 194; 7AF Op Hist, p 5; House, p 2.

7. PH-Gram, p 15; Kaye, pp 224-225; 7AF Op Hist, p 5; Oral History #566, "Historical Documentation of Maj Gen Brooke E. Allen," Dec 65, pp 6-7.

8. Waldron, pp 19-22; 7AF Op Hist, p 5.

9. Lambert, Pineapple Air Force, pp 23-24; intvw, L. R. Arakaki, 15 ABW Historian, with Col T. Ahola, USAF (Ret), 15 Apr 91; W. Hoover, "This pilot was caught on the ground," *The Sunday Star-Bulletin & Advertiser*, 7 Dec 86, p A-19.

10. Craven and Cate, p 200; Kaye, p 227.

11. Report by Col Rudolph L. Duncan, US Army Signal Corps (Ret), "If I'd Only Had the Right Information from Washington," p 5.

12. Gray, p 456.

13. Prange, Dec 7, p 336; 1st Sgt Charles Leyshock, "Monroe Soldier Tells of Attack on Hawaii," p 4; Gwenfread Allen, p 131.

14. Lane, p 7.

15. Lane, p 6; 25 Inf Div Journal, 7 Dec 41, pp 4-11; Memo No. 24, Hq Hawaiian Dept, 23 Dec 41, par 1.

16. Prange, Dec 7, p 347; Gwenfread Allen, p 89.

17. Prange, Dec 7, pp 353, 359-360; Gray, p 455.

18. Statement by Bruno Siko, "Dec. 7th Memories"; statement by Francis L. Mack, "Dec. 7th Memories"; Christie, p 3.

19. Woodrum, p 290.

20. Recollections of Charles L. Hendrix, 12 Dec 41; Burke, p 55.

21. Woodrum, p 289.

22. *Ibid*.

23. Ltr, Paul C. Plybon, Sr., to Betsy Camacho, [Dec 7 and 8 experience], 6 Sep 90 [hereafter cited as Plybon]; Decker, pp 2-3; Thomas, p 5.

24. Ltr, Col Jean K. Lambert, USAF (Ret), to Betsy Camacho, [midget sub], 20 Jun 90.

25. *Ibid*., p 3; Plybon, p 2; Metcalfe, p 3.

26. Congressional Report, Part 37, p 1148; Kazuo Sakamaki, *I Attacked Pearl Harbor* (New York, 1949), p 108.

27. "2-Man Midget Submarine," *Wings 72*, Grand Rapids, Michigan.

28. *Ibid*.; Lambert, Pineapple Air Force, pp 5-6.

BIBLIOGRAPHY

Books

Allen, Gwenfread. *Hawaii's War Years: 1941-1945*. Honolulu: University of Hawaii Press, 1950.

Army Times Publishing Company Editors. *Pearl Harbor and Hawaii: A Military History*. New York: Bonanza Books.

Clark, Blake. *Remember Pearl Harbor!* New York: Modern Age Books, 1942.

Gunston, Bill. *The Encyclopedia of the World's Combat Aircraft*. London: Salamander Books Ltd, 1976.

Hoehling, A. A. *The Week Before Pearl Harbor*. New York: W. W. Norton & Company, Inc., 1963.

Jablonski, Edward. *Flying Fortress*. Garden City, New York: Doubleday and Company, c1965.

Lambert, John W. *The Long Campaign: The History of the 15th Fighter Group in World War II*. Manhattan, Kansas: Sunflower University Press, 1982.

Lambert, John W. *The Pineapple Air Force: Pearl Harbor to Tokyo*. St. Paul: Phalanx Publishing Co., Ltd., 1990.

Lloyd, Alwyn and Moore, Terry D. *B-17 Flying Fortress*. London: Aero Publishers Inc, c1981.

Lord, Walter. *Day of Infamy*. New York: Bantam Books, 1958.

Prange, Gordon W., in collaboration with Donald M. Goldstein and Katherine V. Dillon. *At Dawn We Slept*. New York: Penguin Books, 1982.

Prange, Gordon W., with Donald M. Goldstein and Katherine V. Dillon. *Dec. 7, 1941*. New York: Warner Books, 1989.

Rearden, Jim. *Cracking The Zero Mystery*. Harrisburg, PA: Stackpole Books, 1990.

Sakamaki, Kazuo. *I Attacked Pearl Harbor*. New York: Association Press, 1949.

Stillwell, Paul, ed, *Air Raid: Pearl Harbor!* Annapolis, Maryland: Naval Institute Press, 1981.
Theobald, RAdm Robert A., USN, Retired. *The Final Secret of Pearl Harbor*. New York: The Devin-Adair Company, 1954.

Toland, John. *Infamy*. New York: Berkley Books, 1983.

Published Sources

Gray, Lt Col Denver D., USAF (Retired). "I Remember Pearl Harbor: A Nebraska Army Air Force Officer in the Pacific Theatre During World War II." *Nebraska History*, Winter 1981, pp 437-480.

Hearings Before the Joint Committee on the Investigation of the Pearl Harbor Attack, Congress of the United States, Seventy-Ninth Congress. Washington, DC, 1946.

The Hickam Bomber: A Pictorial Review of the Hawaiian Bomber Command. Hickam Field, T. H., 1942.

INDEX

www.ingramcontent.com/pod-product-compliance
Lightning Source LLC
Chambersburg PA
CBHW050411110426
42812CB00006BA/1863